The Agony of an American Wilderness

The Agony of an American Wilderness

Loggers, Environmentalists, and the Struggle for Control of a Forgotten Forest

Samuel A. MacDonald

ROWMAN & LITTLEFIELD PUBLISHERS, INC.
Lanham • Boulder • New York • Toronto • Oxford

ROWMAN & LITTLEFIELD PUBLISHERS, INC.

Published in the United States of America
by Rowman & Littlefield Publishers, Inc.
A wholly owned subsidiary of The Rowman & Littlefield Publishing Group, Inc.
4501 Forbes Boulevard, Suite 200, Lanham, Maryland 20706
www.rowmanlittlefield.com

PO Box 317
Oxford
OX2 9RU, UK

British Library Cataloguing in Publication Information Available

Library of Congress Cataloging-in-Publication Data

MacDonald, Samuel A., 1972–
    The agony of an American wilderness : loggers, environmentalists, and the struggle for control of a forgotten forest / Samuel A. MacDonald.
        p.   cm.
    Includes bibliographical references and index.
    ISBN 0-7425-4157-6 (cloth : alk. paper)—ISBN 0-7425-4158-4 (pbk : alk. paper)
    1. Logging—Environmental aspects—Pennsylvania—Allegheny National Forest.
    2. Forest conservation—United States.   3. Wilderness areas—United States.
    4. Environmental protection—United States.   5. Conservation of natural resources—
    United States.   6. Allegheny National Forest (Pa.)   I. Title.
    SD538.2.P4M33 2005
    333.75′16′097486—dc22   2004028127

Printed in the United States of America

♾ ™ The paper used in this publication meets the minimum requirements of American National Standard for Information Sciences—Permanence of Paper for Printed Library Materials, ANSI/NISO Z39.48-1992.

To Bill and Dolly MacDonald, my parents,
for their undying faith, good humor,
love, and support

Contents

Acknowledgments

I owe an enormous debt of gratitude to the Phillips Foundation for providing the journalism fellowship that made this book possible. Special thanks go to Chairman Thomas L. Phillips and trustees Becky Norton Dunlop, Thomas A. Fuentes, Donald P. Hodel (emeritus), Robert D. Novak, and Alfred S. Regnery for selecting this project and supporting it so generously. Foundation Secretary John W. Farley and Assistant Secretary D. Jeffrey Hollingsworth deserve special mention for their patient and reliable counsel. Chuck Freund showed true grit as my mentor, enduring countless drafts, e-mails, and phone calls while providing guidance that kept me reasonably sane throughout the writing process.

John A. Baden, Pete Geddes, and the rest of the excellent folks at the Foundation for Research on Economics and the Environment in Bozeman, Montana, provided crucial support in helping me understand the struggle for the Allegheny National Forest in a larger context. They also introduced me to Jack Ward Thomas, Randal O'Toole, and other experts who helped me grasp the complexities of federal forest management.

I would also like to thank the people of the Allegheny region for enduring my incessant inquiries. People on both sides of the logging issue provided access to a wealth of critical information and insights. These include, but are certainly not limited to: Dale Anderson, Blair and Dave Anundson, Bill Belitskus, Liz and Rick Boni, Andy Buehler, Larry Buehler, Doug Carlson, Dick Cooney, Kevin Elliott, Jack Hedlund, Bob Imhof, Kirk Johnson, Ken Kane, Dave Kiehl, Fritz Kilhoffer, Chad Klawhun, Jim Kleissler, Ed Kocjancic, Chip Lawrie, Rachel Martin, Mike Miles, Steve Miller, Chuck Novosel, Don Payne, Tim Spilka, Susan Stout, Sue Swanson, and Ryan Talbott.

Special thanks also to Rosa, Bobby, Ernie, and Mary Jo Aiello; the Kane Hardwood Division of Collins Pine; the Charles G. Koch Charitable Foundation; Jared Kuleck; John Paul MacDonald; Dan Peterson; all the people at

Docksiders; everyone at the Buckhorn, Cougar Bob's, the Hallton Hilton, the Westside and numerous Elks clubs throughout the region; and of course my family, especially my wife, Michelle. I never would have completed this book without their support.

Any lapses, interpretive or otherwise, are of course my own.

Introduction: Welcome to Pennsyltucky—A Strange New Front in the Great American Timber War

"Loggers: The Next Endangered Species," reads a sign prominently displayed outside a shop. Another store sells t-shirts saying, "Hug a logger. You'll never go back to trees." Sounds like Northern California?

Nope. This is Northwestern Pennsylvania, where the timber beast has been roaring for over a century.

—*Defending Allegheny Forests*: A Special Publication
of the Allegheny Defense Project

The fire that ravaged the United States Forest Service Forestry Sciences Laboratory on August 11, 2002, did $700,000 worth of damage and threatened to consume seven decades of critical environmental research. Volunteer firemen from rural communities near the Irvine, Pennsylvania, facility extinguished the blaze before all was lost, but their efforts could not contain the flames of a much larger inferno: There is a new front in the great American timber war, and it could make the one that ravaged the Pacific Northwest look tame by comparison.

On August 14, officials confirmed that the suspicious blaze was deliberately set. The *Warren Times Observer* received an anonymous e-mail in early September claiming responsibility. Its author(s) declared allegiance to the Earth Liberation Front, a radical underground movement already responsible for more than $50 million in damage nationwide. The brief missive was jarring even by ELF standards. It promised to burn the facility again if the Forest Service rebuilt it and, for the first time in the group's history, threatened to shoot people who did not heed the call for environmental purity.

The attack was part of a disturbing trend in northwestern Pennsylvania.

In March 2002, ELF arsonists did $500,000 worth of damage to a highway construction site near Erie. In November, they set fire to an Erie mink farm. On January 1, 2003, they firebombed a Ford dealership in Girard. By January 2003, four of the five most recent attacks featured on the ELF's website were actions taken within sixty-five miles of the Allegheny National Forest.

The most radical form of environmental activism has finally migrated from the California redwoods to the Pennsylvania hardwoods, but that is only the latest manifestation of the Green movement's growing presence in the area. More peaceable activists have been battling for control of the Allegheny for almost a decade, shocking locals with a series of lawsuits, sit-ins, and protests. Perhaps that was inevitable. Many of the same questions that defined the West Coast timber wars have gone unanswered. What do citizens want from their national forests? Can logging coexist with recreation? How important are "noneconomic benefits" such as aesthetics? The Allegheny crisis is more than an eastward expansion of the West Coast's timber wars, however: It will ultimately test the limits of the American environmental movement.

The 1990s were heady times for environmentalists. One of their foremost achievements was convincing the average American that there is intrinsic value in "old-growth" forests. Protecting "the last best places on earth," a familiar Sierra Club mantra, has become a template for environmental activism, a movement fueled by the controversial albeit wildly successful effort to set aside millions of acres for the northern spotted owl. The current controversy surrounding oil drilling in the Arctic National Wildlife Refuge fits the script nicely. Critics oppose drilling because humanity has never sullied that landscape: As one of the last pristine places, it deserves special protection.

The Allegheny region, known to many locals as "Pennsyltucky" for its peculiar mix or rural and industrial cultures, is so intriguing because it stands much of that logic on its head. First, it brings the national environmental debate much closer to home. The Arctic National Wildlife Refuge—and the virgin forests of the Pacific Northwest, for that matter—are far removed from the seats of American power. Part of their presumed value resides in that very remoteness and their tenuous existence as the last, shrinking vestiges of an endangered environmental heritage. By contrast, approximately one-third of all Americans live within a day's drive of the Allegheny National Forest. It is less than five hours from Washington, D.C. And like it or not, the forest's long intimacy with the appetites of humanity has changed it forever.

Rather than one of the "last best places on earth," the Allegheny looked more like one of the "first worst" by the time anyone considered protecting it. Activists interested in saving western Pennsylvania's old growth are at least a century too late. Observers derided the scarred hillsides as the "Allegheny Brush Heap" by the time the Forest Service began buying the land in the

1920s. Unprecedented industrial exploitation had chased the deer, elk, turkey, and almost every other species out of the region. The trees were gone. Even the dirt was washing away. And therein lies what many consider an unprecedented environmental success story. A century later, those animals are back. They live in a forest so unique that foresters had to invent new term—Allegheny hardwood—to describe it.

That miraculous rebirth has been matched by an equally stunning economic conversion. The trees that grew to replace the original ones, particularly the region's unmatched black cherry, are so valuable that of America's 155 national forests, the Allegheny is one of the few with a timber program that consistently turns a profit. The forest is currently home to more oil and gas wells than all the other national forests combined. A paper mill on the forest's eastern border produced every page of every Harry Potter book ever printed.

Many locals thought that their efforts to balance the Allegheny's undeniable environmental improvement with the material demands of modern society would insulate them from the political upheavals playing out in the last of America's old growth. They were wrong. In fact, it is the very nature of their efforts to maintain that balance that makes the forest such an important tipping point in the battle for the American landscape. Activists do not want to simply save the Allegheny. They want to restore it. But restore it to what? At what cost? And why? People who view logging as a critical facet of the Allegheny's future are convinced that the answers to those questions lie in an environmental agenda far more radical than the one loggers faced in the Pacific Northwest. Some of the activists agree. On June 8, 1998, the *Pittsburgh Post-Gazette* quoted one of four Earth First! activists arrested during the group's first protest in the Allegheny region: "The Allegheny, because of its prized hardwoods, especially the black cherry, is the biggest timber moneymaker of all our national forests," he said. "If we can stop logging there, we can stop it everywhere."

I never suspected that the Allegheny National Forest would become that kind of environmental proving ground when I was growing up there. Ridgway, my hometown, is located on the southeast corner of the forest. Situated along the banks of the Clarion River approximately 120 miles northeast of Pittsburgh, the community is home to about 4,500 residents. It was a good place to grow up. Almost all of the fifty customers on my paper route instructed me to deposit the daily *Ridgway Record* inside their unlocked front doors. There were no bowling alleys, movie theaters, or fast-food joints, but we found plenty to do in the woods. Hunting and fishing were an integral part of the lifestyle—and so was logging.

Everyone learned about the Allegheny's history at a very early age. Gray-haired ladies at the historical society showed us pictures from the now unthinkable "brush heap" era. Grainy photos revealed streams full of mud and hillsides that were bare except for endless acres of stumps and slash. They showed us skies filled with smoke from the fires that regularly consumed huge chunks of the already devastated landscape. The only thing our young eyes could recognize were the names of the places involved: Hallton, Highland, Mill Creek, Bear Creek, the Clarion River. We knew them because those were the places we went to hunt and fish—only by the time we came along they were packed with lucrative hardwoods. The river occasionally stank like the Johnsonburg paper mill seven miles upstream, but other than that, we considered the area a natural wonderland. We were not alone. People from Pittsburgh, Buffalo, Cleveland, and beyond descended on the Allegheny to marvel in its cool trout streams, bright fall foliage, and plentiful white-tailed deer.

Ridgway always has been—and is struggling to remain—an industrial community. Founded in the mid-1800s, the town thrived on virgin hemlock during Pennsylvania's historic timber boom. Logs flooded enormous sawmills throughout the region. By the early twentieth century, Ridgway was home to the United States Leather Company, one of America's ten largest corporations at the time. My maternal grandfather worked at one of the huge tanneries when he arrived from Italy in the 1920s.

The tanneries were gone by the time my father graduated from high school in 1951, but other industries had risen to take their place. The Elliott Company made electrical motors for submarines in World War II. When my father signed on, the company was building components for enormous hydroelectric turbines.

The Elliott shut its doors in the early 1960s, but factory floors still seemed to offer a viable future when I graduated from high school in 1991. Many of my classmates' fathers worked at the paper mill. Others made a decent living at one of region's numerous pressed metal factories. The North Carolina-based Carlisle Companies employed a few hundred people in Ridgway at a plant called Motion Control, which manufactured automotive brakes. I landed a job there one summer during college. I made $10.60 an hour running a press line, a job that entailed hard physical labor in temperatures often topping 125 degrees. A few of my high school classmates worked there full-time. They made a few dollars more per hour, which amounted to a pretty good living.

Many of those jobs are gone now. Carlisle eliminated the Motion Control facility in 2001. The Johnsonburg paper mill still employs about four hundred people, but ninety people lost their jobs when new owners shut down one of its machines in 2003. Temple-Inland recently stopped production at its particleboard plant in Mount Jewett, putting more than a hundred people out of work. Keystone Thermometrics closed its facility in the same town a few months earlier, a move that sent 130 people to the unemployment office.

Towns surrounding the Allegheny National Forest have experienced a series of industrial upheavals over the past 150 years, but this time it is not clear that something is going to rise from the ashes. Forest County, Pennsylvania's smallest and least populated, contains the southwestern quadrant of the Allegheny. Its seasonal unemployment rate has gone as high as 22 percent in recent years. Statistics from the United States Census Bureau reveal the toll: in 1900, 134,231 people resided in the four counties that now contain the Allegheny National Forest. Over the next seven decades, the region was a study in demographic consistency. Population edged up to 141,000 residents by 1980, but the modest growth stopped there. By 2003 the regional head count had slipped to less than 128,000, a 10 percent decline over 23 years.

Times have been tough, but there was one resource that appeared recession-proof: timber. Roughly one-third of the world's veneer-quality black cherry stands on or near the Allegheny. Valuable oak and maple resources add to the potential. Furniture plants and other secondary concerns moved south many years ago, then eventually overseas, but the trees are literally rooted in the local soil, a fact that many people considered a critical economic lifeline.

The Forest Service created a long-range management plan for the Allegheny in 1986 that allowed for an annual timber harvest of 94.5 million board feet. Loggers and sawyers began gearing up for the timber, and for a few years, things proceeded according to plan. The booming economy of the 1990s sent the price of local hardwoods through the roof. In 1987, the highest bid for black cherry coming off the Allegheny was just over $600 per one thousand board feet. By 1995, it had risen to $2,276. Timber cut on state-, industry-, and family-owned lands saw similarly spectacular gains.

It is hard for people unfamiliar with the timber industry to understand exactly what these numbers mean. At one point during recent environmental struggles, the price for a thousand board feet of black cherry exceeded $4,000. John Lindgren from the Oregon and Washington Log Market Report gasped at the figures. "We don't have anything like that out here," he said. According to his records, a thousand board feet of premium old-growth timber was selling for around $1,000 in 1992, around the time environmentalists were struggling to save the last of the virgin forests there. Robbie Robinson from Starfire Lumber Company in Cottage Grove, Oregon, said that the very best old-growth timber was commanding approximately $2,400 per thousand board feet in 1994, the year after the spotted owl took national forest logs off the market. "That's an unbelievable number," he said when informed of the black cherry's value.

Such remarkable prices translated into serious money for communities in the Allegheny region. The Forest Service does not pay property taxes, but a federal law passed in 1908 requires the agency to return 25 percent of all receipts back to local communities for road and school expenditures. Timber sales generate almost all of that revenue. The four counties home to the Allegheny received a total of $2.66 million through the 25 percent payment in 1987. It soared to more than $5.3 million by 1995, but trouble was on the horizon.

Activists filed their first lawsuit against the Allegheny in 1997. The amount of timber sold off the forest plummeted by 95 percent within three years. The forest's timber program—once the crown jewel of the federal system—was in shambles. Mirroring the flare-up over the spotted owl, Allegheny residents discovered that the forest was home to an endangered Indiana bat. That alone led to a total moratorium on logging that lasted six months.

Those are not the only forces at work, however. Most if not all timber workers agree that huge multinational timber corporations have made life tough for the mom-and-pop operations that have survived on Allegheny timber for more than eight decades. At the same time, a series of devastating droughts and infestations have threatened the forest's health and called the sustainability of its timber program into question.

Charges that the Forest Service is operating the Allegheny as a "black cherry tree farm" aimed at benefiting the agency's corporate masters are more controversial, but activists make important economic and scientific arguments that deserve close attention. So do counterclaims arguing that the activists' old-growth vision for the Allegheny is not only unfair to local communities but impossible to achieve, given the forest's peculiar industrial history.

Unfortunately, the real issues have been buried in a cultural and political quagmire for almost a decade now, and they sank even deeper the day the Earth Liberation Front burned down the research lab in Irvine and threatened to kill anyone ambitious enough to rebuild it.

So how did the Allegheny become the center of such a rancorous debate? To fully understand its place in the national environmental dialogue, it is important to explore how a vast virgin forest became an industrial moonscape in the latter part of the nineteenth century; how eight decades of federal management and historical accidents turned that brush heap into a black cherry bonanza; and how the national environmental movement moved beyond America's "last best" places and developed even more ambitious plans for one of its "first worst." *The Agony of an American Wilderness* is a story about the characters, communities, and cultures that are caught in the cross-fire, but it is also a wake-up call for a nation. As wrenching as the spotted owl dispute was for the people involved, it was only one salvo in a much larger battle for control of the American landscape.

Chapter One

The Forgotten Forest: The Allegheny Experience, from Old Growth to Brush Heap and Beyond

New Group Wants to Turn Clock Back on Parts of Allegheny National Forest

—Headline in the *Erie Times-News*, October 15, 2001

The Allegheny National Forest is currently at the center of a critical political power struggle, but it was not always such a hot property. It was, in turns, an impenetrable expanse, a land of economic opportunity, an industrial waste-land, and a federal forestry experiment. How and why it progressed through that gamut defines everything from the people who live there to the trees that grow on its hillsides. That history also sets it apart from the virgin forests that have so far dominated the national discussion about logging. It is fairly easy to save an old-growth forest, after all: Just stop cutting it down.

The debate about logging in the Pacific Northwest was more complicated than that, of course. Native American culture, industrial pollution, and modern fire suppression efforts call into question how untouched that landscape really is. Economics, politics, and shifting social views about the environment also fuel the discussion. Unfortunately, casting it as a Manichean choice between loggers and pristine forests made for irresistible headlines. The *Time* magazine article that thrust old growth into the national spotlight on June 25, 1990, was presented as "Owl vs. Man: In the Northwest's battle over logging, jobs are at stake, but so are irreplaceable ancient forests."

The media's fascination with pristine landscapes continues to this day. On December 27, 2003, the *New York Times* aimed an angry editorial at a Bush administration plan to resume logging in the enormous Tongass National Forest in Alaska. Headlined "Tongass Travesty," it charged that the proposal "is essentially a holiday gift to Senator Ted Stevens and Gov. Frank Murkowski, both of whom have lobbied for the resumption of the clear-cutting that has already stripped the nation's only temperate rain forest of a half million acres of old-growth trees."

America's old-growth drama is still unfolding more than a decade after the spotted owl took center stage. In focusing so intently on it, however, the media have ignored equally important environmental developments elsewhere. Northwestern Pennsylvania's unique history has already eliminated the Allegheny's virgin forest, but that only serves to make discussions about its future even more complex.

Fourteen thousand years ago a glacier surging out of the north halted near the banks of the Allegheny River. It brought a pile of sediment that dammed the river's northerly flow and turned it south toward what is now Pittsburgh. The ice field covered a substantial portion of what would become Pennsylvania, but that was the extent of its flirtation with the high ground south and east of the Allegheny River.[1] That unglaciated plateau, known as the Big Level, is now home to the Allegheny National Forest.

Seneca Indians, members of the dominant Iroquois League, were following the glacier's lead and sticking close to the river by the time European trappers penetrated the region. Poor soil, steep slopes, and isolation hampered permanent settlement on the high ground. Apart from a few rough-and-tumble enclaves along the river, it remained largely off-limits to Europeans.[2] That hegemony did not last long. The Seneca sided with the English in the American Revolution and paid for that miscalculation with their land. Ambitious leaders in Philadelphia developed a system to sell and settle the untamed wilderness, but that plan was an abject failure for the better part of a century.

No government document could counteract the harsh geographic realities afflicting the Allegheny region. Apart from areas connected by navigable rivers, it was completely cut off from civilization. The growing season was short, and the winters were harsh. Anyone interested in establishing a homestead on the thin-soiled landscape had to clear a forest so thick that it blocked sunlight from the ground at high noon. Early legislators added to the dismal assessment of the region by referring to the wilderness east of the Allegheny River as "the waste lands."[3] They set the price at $80 per one hundred acres, a price few would pay. Wealthy speculators from Holland smelled an opportunity when the price plummeted to less than $14 for a hundred acres in 1792.[4] They controlled more than 995,000 acres east of the Allegheny River and more than 400,000 acres west of it within two years.[5]

They couldn't sell it, either. Census records show that by 1800, the white population of Warren County amounted to 233 people. In 1820, it was still home to fewer than two thousand pioneers.[6] McKean County proved even harder to settle. It was home to just 728 residents in 1820.[7]

American expansionism basically leapfrogged northwestern Pennsylvania. The Ohio Valley, which offered flat ground and fertile soil, opened to settlement in 1795.[8] The 1803 Louisiana Purchase steered hordes of land-starved pioneers even farther westward. By 1857, more than fifty thousand starry-eyed forty-niners were making it and breaking it in gold-crazed San Francisco.[9] Kane, Pennsylvania, near the heart of what is now the Allegheny National Forest, did not exist until 1864.

Taming the western Pennsylvania highlands required the same industrial force that eventually dragged the American West into modernity: a railroad. Businessmen eager to connect central Pennsylvania to the thriving lake port in Erie proposed laying tracks across the wilderness as early as 1837. They finally succeeded in 1864—just five years before dignitaries drove the famous golden spike in Promontory, Utah. Within twenty years settlers and speculators transformed northwestern Pennsylvania into a gargantuan industrial machine. Completing that transformation did not come easy, however.

Colonel Thomas L. Kane arrived in Elk County in 1856. His father, an influential federal judge in Philadelphia, had recently taken charge of a dead relative's estate that included 132,000 acres in northwestern Pennsylvania. The good judge and his associates put Thomas in charge of exploring the region and its resources. They were particularly interested in potential coal deposits, paying little heed to the vast tracts of ancient trees.[10]

Born in 1822, Kane was an accomplished young lawyer who gained national notoriety by championing the cause of the Mormons during their tumultuous western migration. When the United States raised an army to confront the Mormons in 1857, Kane traveled to Utah, mediated the dispute, and defused what appeared to be a hopeless situation. In Utah, the Mormons took to calling him their "Sentinel in the East." Today, a statue of Kane stands in the rotunda of the Utah capitol.[11]

His older brother Elisha Kent Kane had even more impressive swashbuckling credentials.[12] By the late 1850s, the naval surgeon had traveled extensively in China, India, and Africa. In 1848, he served in Mexico, where he saved an enemy general's son by repairing an artery in the wounded man's groin, performing the surgery with a bent fork. In 1850, he became the senior medical officer on an unsuccessful expedition to rescue an English explorer lost in the Arctic. He led another rescue expedition in 1853, but his company got frozen in at Rensselaer Bay, abandoned ship, and endured a brutal two-year trek to Greenland over land, sea, and ice. Kane, a savvy self-promoter, capitalized on the hardship with a two-volume set entitled *Arctic Explora-*

tions. It sold twenty thousand copies before being published in September 1856 and made him one of the most famous figures of the antebellum era.

The saga of the young Kane brothers serves as a fitting tribute to the end of an era—and the beginning of another. They had conquered China, India, Mexico, the Arctic, and the great American West by 1855, but neither of them had set foot in the remote forests of their home state. That changed when Judge Kane sent young Thomas into the wilderness in 1856. By 1859 he had selected a homestead in the densely wooded highlands near what is now Kane, Pennsylvania, and, a year later, began quarrying stones to build a proper home.[13] But that would have to wait.

Legend holds that Kane was the first man in Pennsylvania to volunteer for duty in the Civil War. He rose to the rank of brigadier general after a series of hardships that included a bullet wound in the face and a stint in a Confederate prison camp. In the meantime, his Pennsylvania holdings sat idle. According to an historian who chronicled the era, "During the war period, it seemed as if nature was about to repel the invading settler and the primeval forest would once more become unbroken over the Big Level."[14]

The war also delayed completion of the railroad until October 1864, the same year Kane returned from the war. When he arrived at the site of his future home, he discovered that someone had stolen the stones he had piled there four years earlier.[15] That was only a minor setback. The railroad was finally chugging across the Big Level, and the Industrial Revolution came billowing out of its stacks.

The main industry in the early days was maintaining the rails. A fire in Kane destroyed a sawmill and over $20,000 worth of lumber in 1865. Similarly disastrous fires struck in 1867, 1868, 1869, and 1871. Each time, critical timber resources needed for railroad maintenance—and homes for the railroad workers—went up in smoke. It all came full circle in 1874 when the railroad buildings burned.[16]

The hemlock boom years were still a generation in the making. Pennsylvania was America's timber leader throughout the mid-1800s, but activity was concentrated farther east along the Susquehanna River, which flowed to large markets in Philadelphia and Baltimore. Pioneering lumbermen began cutting white pine near Williamsport and rafting it downstream as early as the 1790s.[17] Harvesting was limited until the 1830s, when loggers finally depleted the white pine they had been cutting in Maine. The rapidly expanding nation screamed for more wood, making Pennsylvania trees an irresistible cash crop by the mid nineteenth century. The age of exploitation had only just begun, however, and the Susquehanna watershed remained the locus of American timbering for decades.

Communities such as Kane were growing—but in a different direction.

Industrialists like General Kane's son Elisha Kent ignored the timber surrounding them because they were gripped by another pursuit: oil fever.[18] The history of the Allegheny National Forest is inextricably linked to the fossil-fuel deposits that teem below its surface. Edwin Drake drilled America's first commercially successful oil well near Titusville in 1859.[19] The site is less than fifteen miles west of the Allegheny River and the current border of the national forest. Towering trees quickly gave way to oily derricks as aspiring millionaires stampeded across the virgin landscape.

Bradford, Pennsylvania, was a typical timbering community in 1870. Situated approximately seventy miles east of Titusville and twenty-five miles north of Kane, it was home to just six hundred settlers. All hell broke loose after prospectors found oil there. Contemporary observer John McLaurin noted that "rigs multiplied like rabbits in Australia. . . . The valley soon echoed and re-echoed the music of the tool-dresser and rig-builder and the click of the drill, as well as the vigorous profanity of the imported teamster." In 1878, drillers working in the Bradford Oil Field completed 2,026 wells and produced 6,500,000 barrels. Production peaked in 1881 at more than 25,000,000 barrels. The numbers seem quaint by modern standards, but at the time the Bradford Field was producing almost 94 percent of the world's oil.[20]

The Bradford oil boom ended even quicker than it started. Production decreased by half within three years as productive wells in the "Middle Field" came online. Located between the Titusville and Bradford fields, it occupied large portions of what is now the Allegheny National Forest. The speculative craze reached Kane in 1885, devouring everybody's attention and acting as a catalyst for other pursuits. Prospectors looking for oil often struck natural gas instead. At first this was considered a nuisance, but in 1884 Elisha Kent Kane (the son, not the brother, of General Kane) and a few associates established the Kane Gas Light and Heating Company. They sunk a well in town that was so productive that "Before means could be devised for confining the gas, the roar of its escape could be plainly heard at a distance of eight miles, and the company were threatened with suits for damage on account of loss of sleep by the neighbors."[21] A dangerous and unsightly problem, to be sure, but the discovery ushered in a host of modern conveniences such as gas light and heating. Those in turn drew more settlers, not to mention industries that required heat, such a glass manufacturing.

The tanneries spun an even more intricate industrial web. When Timothy Barnes moved near to what is now Sheffield in 1832, he had to hack his own road out of the forest. The area remained an isolated backwater until workers completed the railroad and industry moguls realized that the region gave them access to a critical resource: hemlock trees. Hemlock didn't float as well as white pine, which made it more difficult to raft downstream. It was also inferior as a building material. What the hemlock did have was bark extremely rich in tannin—an essential element in converting hides into leather. The Horton and Crary Company, incorporated in 1867, bought fifty thousand acres of timberland within twenty years. The fact that the land was never divided between numerous settlers—a primary failure of the initial program to develop the area—was suddenly driving industrialization. Land was available in huge chunks, and it was cheap. Horton and Crary employed three thousand workers in the area by the late 1880s.[22]

Tanneries controlled almost all of Pennsylvania's hemlock by 1890. The largest facility was in Wilcox, nine miles south of Kane. Three hundred men worked at the enormous complex. Four hundred more toiled throughout the summer peeling bark from the trees. The tannery devoured 63,000 tons of bark and produced more than 6 million pounds of leather every year.[23] Approximately twenty-five of these tanneries operated in the four counties that are now home to the Allegheny, and their vast output rocked the American landscape.[24]

Richard Kandare, a historian for the United States Forest Service, estimates that the Wilcox tannery processed one million buffalo hides between 1866 and 1876. The effects were predictable. According to the United States Geological Survey, the last bison killed in North Dakota fell in 1888.[25] By that time almost all of the hides tanned in Sheffield were coming from South America.[26]

The destruction of the buffalo herds was lamentable in many ways, but there was an undeniable upside. American prosperity was born, at least in part, in the vats of northwestern Pennsylvania's tanneries. The nation was exploding with immigrants in the late 1800s, and every one of them needed shoes. More importantly, those shoes carried them to factories that used leather belts to drive their machinery. Belts seventy feet long and three feet wide were common, with countless other pieces connecting smaller machines.[27] The buffalo never stood a chance.

Neither did the hemlock. It shocks modern environmental sensibilities, but many of the tanneries in the initial burst of industrialization simply let the felled logs rot in the woods. Aside from the bark, they had no use for them. That changed as the trees that had kept Williamsport in business for so long began to disappear. Northwestern Pennsylvania's hemlock timber was suddenly a marketable resource.

Historians refer to the years after 1885 as the "railroad logging era," and the mill at Kushequa exemplifies its ruthless efficiency.[28] In the late 1880s, a lumberman convinced Elisha Kent Kane to take advantage of the vast sea of virgin timber. Kane completed a mill on a site near Mt. Jewett in 1889 and secured almost fifteen square miles of surrounding timberland. He built a railroad to get the bark to a tannery in Mt. Jewett and another one to get sawed lumber to major rail lines. By 1896, a new mill built on the same site was producing 200,000 board feet of lumber a day. It operated at that rate until 1908, when the hemlock in the area finally disappeared. Similar operations began taking hold throughout the region. By 1904, a mill in St. Marys was cutting 200,000 board feet a day. Two locomotives brought in forty rail cars of logs every day. Another operated at night to supply a tannery with bark. The operations consumed three thousand acres of timber every year before shutting down in the early 1920s.[29]

In 1890, a regional historian lamented the dark side of industrialization: "Up to 1875 wild animals existed here almost as numerously as in the first years of the century; but the oil prospector, wild-catter, scout, railroader and farmer came, and acting like the Irishman at Donnybrook, struck at everything, upsetting the institutions of the wilderness. The great tan-yards, the saw-mills which were built on every stream, the stream of wasted oil which for 25 years has floated down the waters of the county, have all contributed to thin out the finny tribe." His only solace was that, despite the thinning, "fish are still found in sufficient quantities to entertain the angler. . . ."[30]

The outlook for other creatures was grim. Seneca Indians regularly camped near Kane to trap pigeons as late as the 1860s. A display at the Seneca-Iroquois National Museum in Salamanca, New York, estimates that flocks stretched for two miles and contained up to a billion birds. They were gone by 1880. In 1929, a historian guessed that the birds were "apparently exterminated by some fatal disease or great storm which may have swept them all out to sea."

A more likely explanation came later in the same book, when a settler who had trapped as many as three hundred pigeons per day noted that the birds sold at market for between fifty cents and three dollars per dozen. Trains to New York and Philadelphia had to add extra cars to carry all the dead birds.[31] Similarly, the last of Pennsylvania's native elk fell sometime in the 1870s. Whitetail deer were almost entirely extirpated by the turn of the century. Smaller animals such as fishers and beaver followed suit.[32]

The state established the Pennsylvania Game Commission in 1895 to halt the shocking destruction of local fauna, but the flora kept falling to the ax. The lumber and tanning industries continued thrashing their way through the forest, and the small trees they left behind were perfect for making methanol, acetate of lime, charcoal, wood alcohol, and other increasingly essential industrial inputs. The process required extensive heat, but that was an afterthought for tycoons already operating vast oil and natural gas facilities. In the late nineteenth and early twentieth centuries, more than seventy large wood-chemical plants operated across Pennsylvania's northern tier. Any tree wider than the blade of an ax constituted a marketable resource.[33] In 1975, a researcher with the United States Forest Service called Pennsylvania's railroad logging era "the highest degree of forest utilization that the world has ever seen in any commercial lumbering era."[34]

The current battle for control of the Allegheny is not about deciding what to do with a brush heap, however. The Big Level is one tough piece of land. A forester encapsulated the local sense of respect for its resilience when I asked him if modern loggers were destroying the forest. "What are they going to do, cut the whole thing down at once?" he asked. "They already tried that. It didn't work."

Northwestern Pennsylvania's transformation over the past eight decades is one of the strangest events in environmental history. It has been largely ignored in the national environmental debate, but the Allegheny National Forest is an integral part of the story. The United States Forest Service began purchasing denuded land in the 1920s. Today, the ANF covers more than 513,000 acres south and east of the Allegheny River. That is not particularly impressive by national standards. The Tongass National Forest, the largest in the system, covers 17 million acres.

The Allegheny is more notable for its trees. It was originally part of a much larger forest type known as "northern hardwoods" that extended into New England. There were also elements of the oak forests that predominated to the south. The coveted black cherry that occupies more than a quarter of the canopy today probably made up less than 1 percent of the pre-settlement forest.[35] The current mixture of trees is so unique that foresters have coined a new term to describe the forest type: "Allegheny hardwoods." Activists call that a linguistic aberration designed to lend legitimacy to an artificial environment. That is not entirely untrue. The Allegheny is home to a forest that has been buffeted by humanity since the late nineteenth century. The desire to replace the "brush heap" with valuable timber is not the only factor that led to the black cherry bonanza, however.

Forest Service rangers did not walk around planting black cherry seedlings in the naked soil when they arrived in 1923. At the most basic biological level, the lucrative trees invited themselves to the Allegheny's restoration party. Black cherry, like many of the valuable hardwoods that have thrived along with it, is relatively "shade intolerant." Put differently, they need a lot of light to grow. The species could not dominate the pre-settlement forest because enormous beech, hemlock, and white pine trees shaded the ground. Black cherry trees survive by lying in wait and growing quickly when exposed to light. When fires or tornados eliminate the older trees, the wily cherry beats other species to the punch and dominates the stand. The last substantial tract of old growth on the Allegheny—approximately four thousand protected acres in the Tionesta Natural Research and Scenic Areas—offers a case in point. A tornado that devastated Kane in 1985 cut a huge swath through the ancient stand. The afflicted area—untouched by logging, salvaging, or any other active management—is so thick with young black cherry trees today that walking through it is nearly impossible.

The explosive-growth strategy works, but not for long. More "shade tolerant" species such as hemlock eventually retake the forest because they can grow, ever so slowly, in the shadows cast by other trees. By the time the black cherry dies, perhaps 120 years after its life began, there is a hemlock waiting to take its place and shade the ground for another three hundred years, if not longer.

The black cherry can only emerge from the darkness if another fire or tornado sweeps through the area and puts light on the ground. Mankind hurried that process along by cutting down every tree in sight between 1885 and 1930. The tanneries and sawmills were destroying the hemlock, but by exposing hundreds of thousands of acres to sunlight, they were laying the groundwork for a hardwood paradise.

The black cherry got its next assist from another unlikely source: the deer. Habitat loss and market hunting nearly eliminated them by the end of the nineteenth century, but the budding conservation movement intervened. The Pennsylvania Game Commission began importing deer from other states in 1906. In 1907, the legislature made shooting doe illegal, a move designed to increase birthrates and speed repopulation. Even more importantly, the Game Commission was placing the deer in an increasingly denuded landscape. Whitetails devour tree seedlings, which grow abundantly in clearcuts. And so they ate and mated. In fact, they ate and mated so much that forest regeneration was in danger by the 1920s because the deer were eating the saplings as soon as they broke the soil. By the mid-1930s, the second-growth trees that survived were too tall for the deer to eat anymore. Winter browse was so limited that forty thousand deer died of starvation during winter of 1935–1936. Pennsylvania hunters harvested more than 186,000 in 1940.[36]

It hardly seems possible that hordes of famished deer could have helped any of the trees in the forest, except for the simple fact that deer do not particularly care for black cherry. As the Allegheny began to recover, the abundance of light on the forest floor brought the cherry to life, and the hungry deer herd devoured the competition.

If a kicker was necessary, it came in the form of fire. Historically, Pennsylvania forests never suffered overmuch from fire because of consistent rainfall throughout the year. That changed when the whole area was clear-cut. Water swept down the bare hillsides and into rising streams instead of soaking into the dirt. The sun baked the ground, which was conveniently covered with spindly brush. Fires unlike any the region had never seen scarred the Allegheny throughout the latter stages of the railroad-logging era. Again, the advantage went to the hardwoods. Their seedlings can resprout after being burned. Coniferous trees—hemlock—cannot.[37] If the Big Level's conversion to the "Allegheny hardwood" forest type was a timber conspiracy, Mother Nature was in on it.

Local foresters insist that they are simply playing the cards history dealt them. But what a hand! They refer to the miraculous second-growth hardwoods as their "cherry nuggets" and "acres of diamonds." They also believe that they can perpetuate the lucrative timber and still be responsible stewards of the land. Recreation opportunities, wildlife habitat, and other indicators have all improved right along with the black cherry since the brush-heap era. That is proof enough for them.

Environmental activists say that amounts to dirty poker. They warn that the "timber beasts," meaning large forestry corporations, are coming back to rape the land again now that it is ripe and ready. They insist that the Forest Service is using destructive tactics such as herbicides, fencing, and clearcuts to turn the Allegheny into a "black cherry tree farm," a listless monoculture that will eventually implode on itself. They concede that the current forest was created by a host of interrelated forces, but they do not see it as something worth keeping. Leave the forest alone, and it will mostly manage itself—it did fine for thousands of years without help from the federal government. Portions of the activists' plans that do not call for wilderness or old growth stress outdoor recreation and scenery. They say that the ensuing natural bounty will improve local communities, lure tourists with fat wallets, and free local workers from the oppressive yoke of Big Timber.

All of the issues surrounding the Allegheny's future are mired in controversy. For instance, some evidence suggests that the natural progression of black cherry back to hemlock and beech—which is what foresters would expect in a landscape untouched by man—has been ruptured beyond repair. Timber supporters point to that research and insist that if activists stop timber harvesting for good, the forest will become an ocean of worthless ferns and scrub brush instead of the promised old growth. Zero-cut advocates disagree, countering that it is continued cutting that will doom the forest. Resolving that debate requires a fair and honest assessment of the best available science. Unfortunately, a decade of wrangling has produced more animosity and suspicion than meaningful headway, and it has thrust reluctant Allegheny communities onto the front lines of America's still-raging environmental wars.

NOTES

1. E. Willard Miller, ed., *A Geography of Pennsylvania* (University Park, Pa.: The Pennsylvania State University Press, 1995), 39–41.

2. J. E. Henretta, *Kane and the Upper Allegheny* (1929; reprint, Baltimore: Gateway Press, 1998), 21.

3. *History of the Counties of McKean, Elk, Cameron and Potter, Pennsylvania, with Biographical Selections*, vol. 1 (Chicago: J. H. Beers and Co., 1890), 96–97.

4. Donna Bingham Munger, *Pennsylvania Land Records* (Wilmington, Del.: Scholarly Resources Inc., 1991), 153–165.

5. Henretta, *Kane and the Upper Allegheny*, 113; *History of the Counties of McKean, Elk, Cameron and Potter*, 96–97.

6. H. L. Blair, *Warren County Review of Its Historical-Political-Social Development, 1739–1950* (Warren, Pa.: Warren Public Library).

7. *History of the Counties of McKean, Elk, Cameron and Potter*, 53.

8. North Central Pennsylvania Regional Planning and Development Commission, *Lumber Heritage Region of Pennsylvania Management Action Plan*, vol. 2, appendix B (Ridgway, Pa.: 2001), 6.

9. *The New Encyclopedia Britannica*,15th ed. vol. 27. (Chicago: Encyclopedia Brittanica, 2002), 4–5.

10. Thomas T. Taber III, *Sawmills Among the Derricks*, vol. 7 of *Logging Railroad Era of Lumbering in Pennsylvania* (Williamsport, Pa.: Reed Hann Litho Company, 1975), 701–702.

11. Henretta, *Kane and the Upper Allegheny*, 23–28.

12. The Elisha Kent Kane Historical Society offers a tremendous wealth of information about the explorer at www.ekkane.org. Of particular interest is a master's thesis written by Mark Horst Sawin and submitted to the University of Texas at Austin in 1997. Entitled "Raising Kane: The Making of a Hero and the Marketing of a Celebrity," it explores Kane's place in American history, his Arctic adventures, and a few of his more salacious antics, such as his high-profile affair with a spiritualist named Margaret Fox.

13. *History of the Counties of McKean, Elk, Cameron and Potter*, 315.

14. Henretta, *Kane and the Upper Allegheny*, 24, 28.

15. Henretta, *Kane and the Upper Allegheny*, 24; *History of the Counties of McKean, Elk, Cameron and Potter*, 315.

16. Henretta, *Kane and the Upper Allegheny*, 25, 31, 36, 37, 45 and 47; *History of the Counties of McKean, Elk, Cameron and Potter*, 316.

17. NCPRPDC, Lumber Heritage Region, 10.

18. Taber, *Sawmills*, 702.

19. Phillip Ross, *Allegheny Oil* (USDA Forest Service Eastern Region, Allegheny National Forest Heritage Publication No. 1, 1996). The following account is taken from its pages, except where noted.

20. Ross, *Allegheny Oil*, 18. See also *History of the Counties of McKean, Elk, Cameron and Potter*, 85.

21. Henretta, *Kane and the Upper Allegheny*, 54; *History of the Counties of McKean, Elk, Cameron and Potter*, 320.

22. J. S. Shenck, *A History of Warren County, Pennsylvania* (Syracuse, N.Y.: D. Mason and Company Publishers, 1887), 511–520.

23. Elk County Historical Society, "The Wilcox Tannery," *Elk Horn*, 38, no. 3, (2002): 6.

24. Thomas T. Taber III, *Tanbark, Alcohol, and Lumber*, vol. 10 of *Logging Railroad Era of Lumbering in Pennsylvania* (Williamsport, Pa.: Reed Hann Litho Company, 1974), 1083.

25. United States Geological Survey, "What Is Prairie? History of Humans on the Prairie," Northern Prairie Wildlife Research Center, www.npwrc.usgs.gov/announce/prairday/poster/history.htm.

26. Shenck, *A History of Warren County*, 520.

27. NCPRPDC, Lumber Heritage Region, 36.

28. Taber, *Sawmills Among the Derricks*, 702–721.

29. Taber, *Tanbark, Alcohol, and Lumber*, 103–108.

30. *History of the Counties of McKean, Elk, Cameron and Potter*, 56.

31. Henretta, *Kane and the Upper Allegheny*, 26, 51, 186–187

32. Information about these and other native Pennsylvania species can be found in "Wildlife Notes," a series of pamphlets published by the Pennsylvania Game Commission.

33. Phillip Ross, "Allegheny Lumber Heritage: The Historic Wood Products Industry on the Allegheny National Forest" (Warren, Pa.: Allegheny National Forest, n.d.), 35–39. See also NCPRPDC, *Lumber Heritage*, 65–67.

34. David A. Marquis, *The Allegheny Hardwood Forests of Pennsylvania, USDA Forest Service General Technical Report NE-15* (Upper Darby, Pa.: Northeastern Forest Experiment Station, 1975), 11.

35. H. J. Lutz, "Original Forest Composition in Northwestern Pennsylvania as Indicated by Early Land Survey Notes," *Journal of Forestry* (1930): 1098–1103. See also, G. G. Whitney, "The History and Status of the Hemlock-Hardwood Forest of the Allegheny Plateau," *Journal of Ecology* 78 (1990): 443–458.

36. Marquis, *The Allegheny Hardwood Forests of Pennsylvania*, 26–28.

37. Marquis, *The Allegheny Hardwood Forests of Pennsylvania*, 24.

Chapter Two

Meet the Activists: History, Culture, and Politics Collide at the Annual Gathering

In August 2002, a fire consumed the Forest Service research lab in Irvine. The message e-mailed to the *Warren Times Observer* office was startling, even by ELF standards.

> The Earth Liberation Front is claiming responsibility for the 8/11/02 arson attack on the United States Forest Service Northeast Research Station in Irvine, Pennsylvania.
>
> The laboratory was set ablaze during the early morning hours, causing over $700,000 damage, and destroying part of 70 years worth of research. This lesson in "prescribed fire" was a natural, necessary response to the threats posed to life in the Allegheny Forest by proposed timber sales, oil drilling, and greed driven manipulation of Nature.
>
> This facility was strategically targeted, and if rebuilt, will be targeted again for complete destruction. Furthermore, all other U.S. Forest Service administration and research facilities, as well as all DCNR buildings nationwide should now be considered likely targets.
>
> These agencies continue to ignore and mislead the public, at the bidding of their corporate masters, leaving us with no alternative to underground direct action. Their blatant disregard for the sanctity of life and its perfect Natural balance, indifference to strong public opposition, and the irrevocable acts of extreme violence they perpetrate against the Earth daily are all inexcusable, and will not be tolerated. If they persist in their crimes against life, they will be met with maximum retaliation.
>
> In pursuance of justice, freedom, and equal consideration for all innocent life across the board, segments of this global revolutionary movement are no longer limiting their revolutionary potential by adhering to a flawed, inconsistant [sic] "non-violent" ideology. While innocent life will never be harmed in any action we undertake, where it is necessary, we will no longer hesitate to pick up the gun to imple-

ment justice, and provide the needed protection for our planet that decades of legal battles, pleading, protest, and economic sabotage have failed so drastically to achieve.

The diverse efforts of this revolutionary force cannot be contained, and will only continue to intensify as we are brought face to face with the oppressor in inevitable, violent confrontation. We will stand up and fight for our lives against this iniquitous civilization until its reign of TERROR is forced to an end—by any means necessary.

In defense of all life,

—Pacific ELF

In a perfect world, preparing for the Allegheny Defense Project's ninth annual gathering would have been easy. In the world of environmental politics, however, even a simple walk in the woods can be an adventure.

The ADP has been the primary anti-logging group on the Allegheny since 1994. The annual gathering brings supporters up to speed on forest issues, recent accomplishments, and the current plan of action. Staffers sweeten the pot with a few nature hikes, vegan delicacies, and other attractions that highlight any respectable activist confab.

Coming to terms with the political rhetoric that surrounds the gathering was a more difficult process. Timber supporters warned me that the gathering has become a breeding ground for radical activism. They said the ADP has conducted workshops on tree-spiking, road blocks, and other underhanded tactics. The ELF firebombing at the Forest Service Research Station a few weeks earlier took tension to a whole new level at the 2002 gathering. Nobody had the audacity to publicly accuse the ADP of setting the fire, but people grumbled in private. "Let's hope they don't burn your tent down," one industry backer quipped when he learned I was attending.

Activists also spoke of violent tactics, but in their minds it stemmed from radical factions on the other side of the fence. They said that in previous years drunken loggers had descended on the campground in the wee hours, honking their horns, hurling insults, and occasionally lobbing rocks. I packed my gear despite the dire warnings and headed for Marienville on an overcast September Friday. I left the riot gear at home; in retrospect, that was a good decision. The liquor-crazed timber thugs never materialized. Neither did the tent-burning eco-terrorists. Instead, the weekend offered a glimpse at a dedicated activist group that is simultaneously stronger and more vulnerable than its opponents realize.

I drove through the woods along a rough dirt road until I encountered a small truck parked on the berm. A muscular middle-aged woman and an older female companion were gathering stones for a fire pit they were building twenty yards into the woods. From what I could see, that made three of us.

This was hardly the eco-conflagration everyone warned me to expect. Then I noticed an aging white pick-up off to the right. A wiry thirty-something with a burly red beard was hard at work rigging a canopy over the vehicle. A mountain of buckets, camping stoves, and other supplies were spilling out the back. I figured he might know where everyone was, so I introduced myself. "Jim Kleissler," he replied. "I didn't expect you until tomorrow."

Finally, Jim Kleissler—the driving force behind the Allegheny Defense Project. His detractors paint him in various turns as a socialist blowhard, a loud-mouthed monkey-wrencher, and a dangerous pagan, but he dispelled a few of these charges by granting my request to attend the gathering. Politically savvy Green radicals—another one of the charges levied against the ADP faithful—do not typically tolerate journalists at their annual strategy session. Some of the misconceptions surrounding Kleissler stem from his often unforgiving manner: What supporters consider a frank approach to environmental issues strikes others as smug and dismissive.

Few people in the region really know Jim Kleissler. He has lived in the area for about a decade, but it takes a lot longer than that to achieve insider status in a place as insular as the Allegheny. He was born and raised in New Jersey. His family is devoutly Catholic. His uncle, Monsignor Thomas Kleissler, founded RENEW in Newark, New Jersey, in 1976. The nonprofit encourages parishioners to pursue spiritual growth and community service. Jim admits wrestling with the faith but laughs at the charge that his environmental stance is fueled by a radical pagan agenda.

Kleissler enrolled at Drexel University in Philadelphia after high school and became increasingly involved in environmental activism. The spotted owl had recently brought national attention to logging practices in the Pacific Northwest. Words like "old growth," "clear-cutting," and "endangered species" quickly colonized the soccer-mom lexicon and a galvanized activist movement began to solidify its gains and spread the good word. Kleissler's new passion led him to the Allegheny. It had such a profound impact on him that he dropped out of a five-year engineering program after four and a half years and dedicated himself to saving the forest. Kleissler allied himself with a fellow activist named Susan Curry, and in 1994, they established the Allegheny Defense Project as "the only group focusing on the protection of Pennsylvania's sole national forest."[1]

The momentum was there, but gaining a toehold in backwoods Pennsylvania was an uphill battle. Kleissler recalls the early days with pride. "We were just a bunch of college kids, really," he said. "And so, literally, we were ignored. That's what it comes down to. We were basically ignored. We got memos from the Forest Service through FOIA that were pretty funny because they used to talk about how misguided we were, that if they just had one more chance to sit down with us, they could set us straight."

Nobody ignores the ADP anymore. A snippet from the group's literature, which it proudly disseminates to this day, indicates why: "Since the ADP formed, the amount of timber sold from the national forest has decreased from 65 million board feet in 1994 to 2 million board feet in 1999."[2] That statistic is only part of organization's success. In 2001, a Montana-based national organization called the National Forest Protection Alliance put the Allegheny National Forest on a larger stage by naming it number one on its list of "America's 10 most endangered national forests."[3]

The listing indicated progress on two levels: First, it pointed to Susan Curry's rise through the environmental ranks. By the time the National Forest Protection Alliance issued its list, she had left the Allegheny for Charlottesville, Virginia, where she became NFPA's eastern field coordinator. It also spoke to how effective she and Kleissler had been at drawing national attention to an otherwise forgotten national forest.

The ADP's early years were also marked by internal progression toward a harder environmental line. Kleissler and Curry did not publicly embrace zero cut—an end to *all* commercial timber harvesting on *all* public land—until 1996. The move mirrored a similar shift by national environmental groups at the time. The most tumultuous and highly publicized shakeout happened within the Sierra Club. An upstart coalition of members proposed an internal ballot initiative forcing the organization to adopt the zero-cut agenda in 1996. Club leadership opposed the measure as too radical, but members passed it by a two-to-one margin. The following year a group of three zero-cut advocates won seats on the club's fifteen-member board—a coup that was followed by an even testier election in 1998. In November of that year *Mother Jones* characterized the fray as "downright raucous" in an extensive online article entitled "Mutiny at the Sierra Club."[4]

The political transition to zero cut was much smoother for the Allegheny Defense Project. The *Mother Jones* article noted that one of the first Green Party candidates that the Sierra Club endorsed for national office was Bill Belitskus, a Kane resident who also happens to be a member of the ADP's board of directors.

Kleissler admits that the ADP's move to zero cut was not unanimous, but he says that widespread refusal to cooperate with the group made for a strong consensus. "The forest protection movement, which started before the ADP came here, it didn't start out as a zero-cut movement," he said. "But we got there how? We got there out of efforts to work with the industry, to work with the Forest Service, to reform the Forest Service, to adopt more selective cutting, and the industry has fought that tooth and nail for decades. This is nothing new."

People who oppose Kleissler disagree. They point out that the Forest Service, citing concerns about forest health, reduced the allowable sales quantity on the Allegheny by 45 percent in 1995, a year before the ADP went zero cut. Sue Swanson, head of a regional timber group called the Allegheny Hardwood Utilization Group, remembers when the ADP shifted gears. "We held a couple forums to try to understand what they were concerned about," she said. "Initially, their concerns—we probably could have come to an understanding on some of them. Then they became part of the national environmental groups that were more radical. They've gone from being issue-oriented to being zero cut. At that point the opportunity to deal with them pretty much flew out the window."

A local mill owner expressed the local sense of frustration succinctly. Referring to the Kinzua Dam, an enormous flood control project built on the northern border of the forest in the 1960s, he said, "I'd like to see them drain it down and plant cherry trees in the bottom of it. But it's a multiple-use forest. I have to realize that other people use the forest for other things. We're solution-oriented people, so we'll compromise. But they're anchored at zero, so we're not going to move."

This disagreement highlights an inevitable point of contention. No amount of education and outreach is going to make a sawmill owner agree with Kleissler about an appropriate harvest level. There might have been some wiggle room before 1996, but since the ADP went zero cut, it is hard to see how any discussion can move forward. It draws attention to the very heart of the dispute over the Allegheny: Why not harvest a few trees? Most environmental activists were not even calling for zero cut in the spotted owl case. Why would the Allegheny need even more protection than those "last, best places"? Ideally, both sides would come to the table, present their case and accept the decision as a political compromise. It is never that easy, of course, and many of the disagreements are as much about personality and perspective as they are about science.

The worldview that separates the Allegheny Defense Project from the larger Allegheny community became clear as soon as the activists began unpacking their gear at the gathering: These people actually camp. It is not that people who live and work in the Allegheny region do not camp; they simply have different ideas about what that word means.

Very few people that I grew up with had the time, gear, or inclination to walk deep into the woods, pitch a tent, and sleep under the stars. When people say they are going camping, they usually mean they are heading to a hunting camp. For those not so privileged, a case of beer and a truck with a working heater will suffice. Teenagers sometimes even forgo real firewood in favor of broken pallets stolen from outside one of the area factories. They do not require chopping, and they burn better.

There are folks more "in tune" with nature, to be sure. But even people with tents tend to pitch them alongside their vehicles or use developed campgrounds along the road. Many avid outdoorsmen are handy with a fly rod, quick to identify one tree species from another, and eager to track deer in the most remote places. But even the most gung-ho among them see no need to trek into the woods the night before opening day. They can sleep in the comfort of their own homes and walk or drive into the forest in the morning.

Kleissler recognizes that many locals use the Allegheny differently than the way his followers do. "At first it upset me," he said. "My analogy is, they take it for granted. It's part of the reason why it's harder for people to understand our goals. They don't understand the woods. They have never lived without them. They don't have an appreciation for the potential."

They don't understand the woods? Maybe residents don't spend days at a time contemplating their spiritual connection to the land, but that does not mean that they do not love the forest. Local affection for the Allegheny is colored by a distinct and passionate familiarity. They don't need to wander through the woods. They live there. Moreover, the forest provides more than an isolated retreat. For many families, the trees pay the mortgage and feed the kids. It is similar to native New Yorkers who have neither the time nor the desire to spend every waking hour admiring the Statue of Liberty and the ice skaters at Rockefeller Center. Those things help define the character of the place, but only tourists and passersby have the luxury of obsessing over them. Locals on the Allegheny even have a term for the urban outsiders who come to admire the forest when it suits them: Flatlanders.

One of the recurring points of contention in the Allegheny debate is whether or not it is fair to lump activists together with that outsider contingent. In addition to the backwoods camping gear, various items at the 2002 gathering hinted at a cultural disconnect. Bumper stickers on many of the cars advocated Ralph Nader for president. A few of the activists boasted multiple piercings and strange facial hair. T-shirts proclaimed the virtues of underground bands unknown to local ears. And what exactly is a vegan, anyway? Apart from the occasional youngster who went off to college and came back with a funny haircut, the only time many locals had experienced such a strong dose of the activist aesthetic occurred when the Rainbows came to town.

In June and July 1999, the Rainbow Family of Living Light held its annual gathering near Ridgway. Instead of sixty activists, the event drew approximately twenty thousand people from all over the world. Held in a different national forest every year, Rainbow gatherings beckon to commune dwellers, Hare Krishnas, street urchins, and anyone who might be interested in easy access to LSD. The ADP's activist culture is far removed from the Rainbows' unfettered far-outness, but some locals either cannot or will not make that distinction.

The charge that the ADP is a group of radical hippies infuriates Kleissler, and not without reason. He emitted a low sigh before agreeing to discuss the Rainbow gathering. He went to the event planning to distribute literature and meet a few like-minded people. Instead, he found what he considered a large, messy party. "I went down there when they were in Ridgway, and I could only take it for about four hours," he said.

In some ways the ADP's 2002 fall gathering supported Kleissler's claim of a straight-laced, grassroots base. In addition to a few concerned citizens from the Allegheny region, there were lawyers from Pittsburgh, activists from Ithaca, and other environmentalists from near and far. The event was a bit touchy-feely by local standards, but there was nothing over-the-top about it. A few people rolled joints, but most of the folks around the campfire stuck to the beer that someone fetched in Marienville. Nobody mentioned a radical anarchist overthrow. There did not appear to be any free love being asked or offered. In all it was a sober, educational experience with a group of activists who line up, predictably, left of center.

Kleissler said the lack of hippie fervor is by design. "We don't organize the gatherings that way," he said. "Sometimes people who come want to do things like that and if you want to do it—we've had people come out who want to have a mass-type thing, like a Christian mass. We really can't take a position on religion. It's not really part of what we do. And there's people like that. We get Rainbow types. We get anarchists. We probably get communists. I thought the Red Scare was over, but anyway."

Kleissler recognizes that the easiest slam against the gathering is the age distribution of its participants. When someone at a location removed from the event asked me how many people were attending, I said that there were probably fifty. Kleissler quickly interjected that he thought it was more like sixty. Even if that was the case, at least half were college students or recent graduates. "The proportion of college students over noncollege is unbelievable," Kleissler admitted. "For that reason we have been trying to organize a more accessible gathering."

Kleissler cites available time and youthful enthusiasm as possible reasons for the discrepancy, but he says that financial concerns hamper the group's efforts to conduct an event with wider appeal. People resisting the ADP suspect that the group's problem is far more basic. Jack Hedlund, executive director of the pro-timber Allegheny Forest Alliance, explains it this way.

"Here's my opinion of it," he said. "The Susan Currys and Jim Kleisslers and even the Bill Belitskuses aren't natives, see? They are outsiders looking in. Had they been here and lived through all this stuff—you can go back clear to when my father was born and lived through the slash [of the brush-heap era]. His early childhood was working in the woods when the place was basically raped. But his contention is that it's much better off now than it was then. He has seen the transition."

Kleissler lives in nearby Clarion, but he seems to realize that his New Jersey roots give his detractors a valuable rhetorical device. The same holds true for Belitskus, who hails from the Pittsburgh area. Josh Raisler Cohn, one of the first activists arrested on the Allegheny, was a student at Oberlin College in Ohio. The ADP is closely affiliated with Heartwood, a zero-cut group based in Indiana. The ADP's summer 1999 newsletter listed eighteen "coordinators." Of those, only one resided anywhere near the Allegheny. There were three in Pittsburgh, two in Philadelphia, and three from elsewhere in Pennsylvania. The others were in Ohio, New York (including two in New York City), Indiana, and Michigan. The most far-flung was a Ruckus Society representative from Berkeley, California.

That hardly conjures up the image of a vibrant local movement. To be fair, ADP Forest Watch Coordinator Ryan Talbott was born and raised in Marienville. Literature that mentions him regularly emphasizes that "Ryan's family roots in the Allegheny region go back to the seventeen hundreds." Several other well-spoken locals such as Sheffield's Janis Trubic also actively support the group. Still, those connections have done little to shake the popular notion that the ADP is an outside force. Kleissler counters that he gets tarred as an intruder while huge corporations like Willamette seem to come and go with impunity. A small sidebar on the ADP website recently made the point: "Many of the companies cutting the Allegheny are not locally based. Examples are Kane Hardwood (a subsidiary of Collins Pine, based in Portland, Oregon) and Bradford Forest Products (The Danzer Group, based in Germany)."

Kleissler got particularly angry when discussing an oil refinery in Bradford. "And why aren't we upset that American Refining Group is here?" he asked, before launching into an impression of what locals might sound like if they ever attacked the refinery the way they lambaste the ADP. "'Damn Philadelphians! They should go back to Philly where they fucking came from.' I mean, talk about the biggest, most hypocritical thing I've ever heard. It's OK for some guy from Germany to come in and decide what we should do with our timber, but God forbid Ryan [Talbott] from Forest County looks up one day and wants to have some say. He just doesn't have enough money."

Kleissler could supposedly deflect charges that he has no local support by providing a list of members, but he claims that no such list exists. There is a button on the group's website labeled "Join" that details how you can get the quarterly newsletter for a $15 donation.[5] The group has also run the "ADP Activist Corps" since at least 1999.[6] The summer newsletter from that year promises that you can "join the ADP by working for the forest. Become an ADP member by volunteering your time."

Kleissler still insists that the ADP is not a membership organization. And even if there is a list, there is nothing that says Kleissler has to disclose it. The Allegheny Defense Project is a controversial organization, and people who belong might prefer to work from the sidelines. Until ADP leaders decide to better quantify their local support, however, they can expect the "outsider" label to stick.

Name-calling aside, the whole question of flatlanders versus locals is ultimately beside the point, at least politically. For better or worse, the Allegheny is a national forest governed by national laws, not the needs and desires of local communities. "It's not an island that belongs to the people in Kane," Bill Belitskus explained. "It belongs to everyone."

Kleissler treasures this argument. He might be a flatlander, but he is also a United States citizen. As such, he has a right to criticize how the Forest Service manages the Allegheny. Timber supporters agree, but they say that the national laws that Kleissler uses to fuel his litigious strategy are actually on the loggers' side. Jack Hedlund argues that zero cut would be a breach of the Forest Service's congressionally mandated multiple-use mission, and he presents documents to bolster his case. The federal government established the first designated forest reserves in 1891. The 1897 Organic Administration Act defined their function, in part, as such:

> No public forest reservation shall be established, except to improve and protect the forest within the reservation, or for the purpose of securing favorable conditions of water flows, and to supply a continuous supply of timber for the use and necessities of citizens of the United States.[7]

The Allegheny was in the throes of its heaviest cutting when Congress passed the Organic Administration Act. By the time the Forest Service established the Allegheny in 1923, the agency was managing land—and promising things to local communities—under the auspices of the 1911 Weeks Law. That law provided funds for the Forest Service to purchase private land for inclusion in the national forest system and decreed that:

> The Secretary of Agriculture is hereby authorized and directed to examine, locate, and purchase such forested, cut-over, or denuded lands within the watersheds of navigable streams as in his judgment may be necessary to the regulation of the flow of navigable streams or for the production of timber.[8]

So what about that timber? Jim Kleissler insists that it was never part of the plan. He conducted a workshop at the 2002 ADP gathering detailing his take on history. At least twenty eager college students sat around the campfire drinking it all in: The Allegheny National Forest, according to Kleissler, was established for watershed protection and watershed protection only. He pointed out that the Weeks Law did not promise anything. It simply decreed that the Secretary of Agriculture *may* engage in harvesting. I interviewed Kleissler a few months later and asked if the area's history might make it a poor choice for zero cut. "Why didn't they create the Allegheny for timber production then?" he reiterated.

Some people argue that they did, pointing to an essay entitled "The Allegheny National Forest—PA: What, Where and Why."[9] L. L. Bishop, the Allegheny's first forest supervisor, compiled the document in 1925. It offers a sense of what the Forest Service was promising local communities in the early days, and it makes one thing abundantly clear: If the federal government intended Pennsylvania's only national forest to function without logging, Bishop never got the memo. He groaned that a productive stand of hardwoods might be a long time in the making and promised other benefits such as clean water and recreation, but the list of timber-centric zingers is enough to make an environmentalist weep sawdust:

> Upon the forest will be produced and made available for use such timber products as the industry may require.

> Timber that is produced upon the forest is for use and can be obtained under reasonable provisions.

> The aim of the Forest management plan will be the production of the greatest amount of material of the highest class in the shortest length of time.

> If the Forest comes to be made up of 500,000 acres, . . . then there could be sold each year 250,000 cords of wood and 125,000,000 feet of logs.

Even without the cordwood, Bishop's production estimate is more than twice the revised harvest limit established for the Allegheny in 1995. Kleissler said he was familiar with the report, but dismissed Bishop as a renegade. "He's a bureaucrat, an agency guy," Kleissler said. "But why did they create the Allegheny National Forest? He didn't create the Allegheny National Forest. He was put in there after the Allegheny National Forest was created."

Not exactly. Bishop played an integral role in buying land for the forest, concocting a plan for its future, and selling the idea to local residents. Two years before the Allegheny's official proclamation, the *Warren Morning Mirror* ran an article hailing Bishop's arrival and the benefits he promised to bestow. "Care will always be taken to provide watershed," the paper reported, "and thus prevent erosion and rapid run off, which means floods." It also went on to detail other benefits, however: "[The] [p]olicy of [the] Forest Service is the establishment of permanent Forest communities, partly dependent on agriculture and partly on woods work. Local settlers always favored, and local industries catered to. The class of forest products needed by local plants will be the kind of material grown."

The first forest supervisor came to town before the federal government purchased a single acre and promised to continue providing timber. Does that mean that logging has always been part of the bargain? Kleissler still thinks not. "Well, go to the source," he instructed. "The Allegheny National Forest was created in 1923 by presidential proclamation. It doesn't say anything about timber production. Now, maybe that supervisor had different ideas. You know, he's not law. His opinions aren't law."

What about that presidential proclamation? Kleissler and other activists mention the document a lot, sometimes delivering the damning evidence verbatim. According to the proclamation, the Allegheny was established "to enable any State to cooperate with any other State or States, or with the United States, for the protection of the watersheds of navigable streams, and to appoint a commission for the acquisition of lands for the purpose of conserving the navigability of navigable rivers."

And there it is in black and white, sealed by President Calvin Coolidge. The one-page proclamation does not mention a single word about cutting trees. That would appear to be game, set, and match for Kleissler, except the proclamation does not really say anything about watershed protection, either. The full clause in question reads:

> Whereas, certain lands within the State of Pennsylvania have been or may hereafter be acquired by the United States under authority of the Act of Congress approved March first, nineteen hundred and eleven (36 Stat. 961), entitled "An Act To enable any State to cooperate with any other State or States, or with the United States, for the protection of the watersheds of navigable streams, and to appoint a commission for the acquisition of lands for the purpose of conserving the navigability of navigable rivers"; and . . .

Note that the excerpt favored by activists follows the word "entitled" and falls completely within quotation marks. It only uses phrases such as "watersheds" and "navigable streams" because they are part of the title of a law passed on March 1, 1911: The Weeks Law, legislation that specifically mentions timber as a legitimate pursuit in the national forests. In fact, the proclamation does not recommend watershed protection as the Allegheny's solitary purpose. It merely references the law that gave Coolidge the power to issue the proclamation in the first place.

So do logging communities have a legal or historical "right" to the timber growing on America's national forests? The argument is nothing new. It failed in the Pacific Northwest, where a federal court decided that an endangered bird and the old-growth forest in which it lived was more important. Then what are national forests for? Who are they for? What is the best way to manage them? Who should decide? Those are all serious questions that still propel the national debate.

Yes, a federal judge put a limit on logging in the spotted owl case, but Kleissler and like-minded environmentalists across the country have raised the stakes immeasurably since securing that victory. Zero-cut activists argue that any cutting, even one-tenth of 1 percent of current levels, is unacceptable—and not just in dwindling old-growth forests that comprise the last refuge for threatened species in the American West. The Allegheny is critical test case because, in the activists' own words, if they can stop logging there, they can stop it everywhere.

Understandably, the people who live and work on the Allegheny do not relish their role as political guinea pigs.

NOTES

1. This assessment, used extensively in the group's literature, can be found in the "Project Overview" section of the Allegheny Defense Project's website at www .alleghenydefense.org.

2. www.alleghenydefense.org.

3. National Forest Protection Alliance, *America's 10 Most Endangered National Forests*, 2001.

4. www.motherjones.com/news/feature/1998/11/sierra.html.

5. www.alleghenydefense.org.

6. Allegheny Defense Project, *Hellbender Journal* 5, no. 1 (1999): 18.

7. Ch. 2, 30 Stat. 11, as amended; 16 U.S.C. 473–475, 477–482, 551.

8. 61 P.L. 435; 61 Cong. Ch. 186; 36 Stat. 961.

9. L. L. Bishop, "The Allegheny National Forest—What, Why, and Where," 1925. Available at Allegheny National Forest headquarters, Warren, Pennsylvania.

Chapter Three

Mom and Pop Go Bust: The Complex Plight of the Allegheny Sawmill

In a report issued earlier this month, U.S. Magistrate Judge Ila Jeanne Sensenich said the Forest Service was attempting to clear large sections of the national forest of native woods with the primary goal of fostering the growth of black cherry trees. Lumber from black cherry is much more valuable than the native hemlock and beech.

—Associated Press report published in the
Kane Republican on September 17, 2002

The Earth Liberation Front's attack on the Forest Service research lab in Irvine sent a chill through the Allegheny timber industry. The note that eco-terrorists sent to the *Warren Times Observer* assured readers that "innocent life will never be harmed," but it never bothered to define the difference between an "innocent life" and a guilty party.

The growing battle for control of the Allegheny National Forest has turned Timothy J. Spilka's life upside down, but he can take some solace in the fact that he is probably off the ELF's mysterious hit list. He owns and operates Spilka Wood Products, a tiny sawmill located just off Route 6 in Ludlow. At least he used to operate it, before shutting down indefinitely. The ELF threat did not intimidate him into submission: He silenced his saws three months before the research lab went up in flames.

The Cochran mill in Ludlow, the Mitchell mill in Ridgway, and the Bennett mill in Russell City are just a few of the other operations that had either shut down or sold out by early 2003. Susan Swanson, executive director of a state- and industry-sponsored economic development organization called the Allegheny Hardwood Utilization Group (AHUG), estimates that at least a dozen small mills in western Pennsylvania have met the same fate. She warns that medium-sized mills are next. Don Payne's mill in Kane, which employs approximately twenty, was down to just one day a week by 2003. The McMillen mill in Sheffield, a regional stalwart for sixty years that at one time employed more than fifty, issued pink slips to its last sixteen workers in late 2002. At the same time, mills operated by large corporations are expanding. Why?

Environmental activists grumble about corporate greed and the inherent instability of the timber industry. Industry flacks fume about litigation and other tactics that activists have used to hamper harvesting on the national forest. All that finger pointing does little to illuminate the intricate interplay of interest and influence that has afflicted the smaller mills. That requires a closer look at who is selling out, who is shutting down, and why.

In the late 1980s, David Kiehl was working for Hammermill, a major player in the Allegheny region and one of the largest wood-and-paper companies in the country. He stayed on board after International Paper swallowed Hammermill, but after a year he decided to strike out on his own. He and two coworkers bought ten acres of land near Marienville in 1988 and called their new venture Northeast Hardwoods. With forty years of experience between them, they started buying and marketing veneer-quality logs. Within a year, they had bought 150 acres along with an old mill that adjoined their property.

The operation was booming when I visited in October 2002. A heavy frost had hit the night before, leaving a thin blanket of icy condensation on a huge stack of logs behind the wooden office building. The pile stood fifteen feet high and stretched at least a hundred feet more toward the mill. The deep-red cross section of the logs offered a glimpse at the region's most lucrative cash crop—black cherry. Tidy stacks of less valuable species filled the rest of the log yard, enough to supply the mill for four weeks. Heavy-equipment operators shuffled logs toward a series of hulking green structures in the distance. Lumber handlers bundled in sweatshirts and flannels grappled with the boards that exited the mill, organizing them in series of neat stacks. Trucks arrived carrying freshly cut logs as trucks loaded with freshly sawed boards exited the facility. Dave Kiehl runs a tight ship.

But that ship is no longer his own. The sign in front of Kiehl's office introduces visitors to Highland Forest Resources, not Northeast Hardwoods. Many locals refer to the operation as "Seneca." Both Seneca and Highland are wholly owned subsidiaries of National Fuel Gas, a diversified energy company based in Buffalo, New York, that sells natural gas to more than 700,000 customers. It also pumps oil throughout the United States and owns major heating and power systems in the Czech Republic. Highland bought the Marienville operation from Dave Kiehl and his partners in 1998. Today, he runs a much bigger version of that mill on the same site, as a Highland employee.

In October 2002, Seneca owned more than 150,000 acres of forestland in the region. Plots were scattered in and around the Allegheny, providing high-quality hardwoods to mills in Hazen, Kane, and Marienville. Together, the mills sawed approximately 20 million board feet per year and employed approximately 160 people.[1]

Why did he sell it? Kiehl explained his decision to an Associated Press reporter in September 2001. "I definitely didn't want to sell," he said. "If we would have held on, within six months we would have been laying off and within a year we would have had to close our doors. The way I see it, the small- to medium-size operation is going to be extinct. We just can't compete."[2]

Kiehl says Northeast Hardwoods was a thriving local operation in the mid-1990s. Twenty people worked at the mill, which sawed approximately 3 million board feet per year. The mill contracted with another twenty independent loggers and skidders who worked in the woods. Kiehl says the economic crunch started when activist litigation slowed harvesting on the Allegheny. As a small operation without its own land, Northeast got most of its timber off the national forest. Kiehl had to make a decision when those logs stopped coming. "I had a couple offers to sell the mill, and I decided it was the best thing to do," he said. "Looking back on it, it was the best thing to do. Ninety to 95 percent of what we used came off the national forest. It would have choked us."

Kiehl admits that the highly cyclical timber market has always made it tough on small operators, but says he and others like him could have survived if activists had not intervened. "If you don't have size and volume you can hardly withstand the normal economics," he said. "Then add what these people are doing. It would have put us under."

The historical context in which those lawsuits are unfolding makes Kiehl even more furious. His grandfather was a logger during the early 1900s when almost all of the original beech and hemlock disappeared. Kiehl has pictures on his office walls documenting that era's brutally denuded hillsides. Forest Service efforts to nurse the Allegheny back to health began in 1923. "Do the math," Kiehl said. "If hardwoods take eighty to a hundred years to mature, where are we?"

By that calculation, the Allegheny should be at the very beginning of a timber boom, and that's exactly what Kiehl expected when he opened his mill. "The actual 1986 [Allegheny National Forest management] plan called for 94 and a half million board feet," Kiehl said. "The sickest thing is, I can remember sitting in the meetings and [the Forest Service] told us in the industry, 'You better get prepared to use this.' We geared up for it and [the actual harvest] kept dropping. It's disgusting what happened."

Activists are disgusted, too, but for entirely different reasons. Jim Kleissler attacks the notion that the mom-and-pops are going under because of the declining Allegheny harvest. "You know what he did?" Kleissler explained when confronted with Kiehl's argument. "He expanded. In the middle of all that, he expanded. You know how big that mill was six years ago? It was like a quarter of the size it is now. When Northeast Hardwoods goes complaining I have a real issue with that because they expanded that mill before he sold out and after he sold out. That's all he's been doing throughout the entire decade of the 1990s, making the mill bigger and bigger so it chewed up more and more forest."

Kleissler attributes the decline in local mills to his favorite bogeyman— corporate America. In his view, the incessant drive for profit has led corporate owners to rip through more logs with faster machines. Efficiency is the name of the game, and the mom-and-pops simply cannot keep up. He mentioned the Spilka mill in Ludlow. "We predicted he was going to go out long before he did because he had an old saw-blade system," Kleissler recalled. "He never upgraded, so he couldn't compete with the Danzer mill, for example, in Bradford." (Danzer, a large German corporation, owns Bradford Wood Products.)

"What they're doing is trying to blame something that's happening in the timber market on us." Kleissler said. "And if you talk to the companies in the timber market, except the ones who have grudges against us for whatever reason, what's happening in the timber market is exactly what's happening in most other industries. It's called acquisition and takeover.

"International Paper. Willamette. Weyerhaeuser. Georgia Pacific. MacMillan Bloedel, now Temple-Inland. Which one of those companies was here in 1980 operating plants in the Allegheny? None of them. That's your acquisition process. They started coming in in the mid-1980s when they doubled the cut on the Allegheny. . . . Those acquisitions were taking place, that process, that's something that started long before we came along. At this point, unfortunately, I don't think there is anything we . . . or anyone can do about it."

Kleissler also bristles at the notion that the plummeting Allegheny harvest is costing jobs. His take on Northeast Hardwoods directly contradicts the one Kiehl outlined. "To suggest that any problems he might have . . ." Kleissler said—pausing before resuming—"which he doesn't have, because if you look at what happened in the middle of the alleged crisis, the amount of wood being processed in the four counties increased after we stopped logging on the national forest in 1999."

Kleissler was referring to a 2000 study conducted by Charles H. Strauss and two associates at the Penn State School of Forest Resources.[3] The Pennsylvania Hardwood Development Council, a branch of the Pennsylvania Department of Agriculture, commissioned Strauss to examine the role that the hardwood industry plays in the regional economy. "They did the numbers in 1997 and 1999," Kleissler said. "They did an economic analysis. They showed what happened was, they weren't processing less wood in this area. They were processing more. They went from 90 million board feet, not 90 million, I don't know, it went from 90-something to 110 million."

Kleissler has an excellent memory. Strauss polled all the hardwood producers in the region. (The study actually included five counties, the fifth being rural Cameron County, which is east of the Allegheny.) The study shows that 92 million board feet poured into area mills in 1997. In 1999, the total input was more than 105 million board feet. Those statistics certainly call Kiehl's claims into question. He said he sold his mill to National Fuel in 1998 because he couldn't get any logs, but the amount of timber zipping through area sawmills was increasing at that time. According to Kleissler, corporatization of Kiehl's mill illustrates his point quite nicely: The corporation did not buy it to shut it down. They bought it to expand capacity. The mill produces more today than ever. It employs eighty people instead of twenty.

Like everything else in the debate over the Allegheny, the truth might be a bit more complicated than either environmental activists or their detractors will admit. First, the Strauss study hardly gives a complete picture of the harvest decline on the Allegheny. The annual harvest on the forest averaged more than 79 million board feet between 1987 and 1996. The harvest in 1997 was approximately 57 million board feet. By 1999, the second year of the Strauss study, the cut had plummeted to 21 million board feet. It fell even further to approximately 14 million board feet in 2000.

The Strauss study therefore tracked the Allegheny harvest decline from 57 million to 21 million board feet, when in reality the 1990s saw it tumble from almost 80 million to less 15 million. Those numbers are abstract statistics to the casual observer, but as far as Kiehl is concerned, they sealed his fate.

Nobody knows how much local mills are producing today. Finding out requires the kind of complex analysis that Strauss employed in his study, and nobody has footed the bill for it since. Paradoxically, this ambiguity might help clarify the situation by focusing attention on a much more telling statistic: Local mill owners are less concerned with how much timber is available than they are with where it originates. Those extra logs that Strauss noted had to come from somewhere, and in every case the shift favored larger corporate mills over mom-and-pop operations.

Timber coming off private land increased from 21 million to more than 36 million board feet during the period studied. A substantial portion of that private land belongs to the large corporate mills. Collins Pine owns 125,000 acres. National Fuel had more than 150,000 acres. Both operations increased harvesting on their own lands after litigation threw them off the Allegheny. Without their own timber to cut, small operators had no access to that kind of ready substitute. Kiehl says that explains why a large landowner like National Fuel can still operate a mill in Marienville, while he never stood a chance.

And he is not alone. Payne Enterprises, which employs approximately twenty people on the outskirts of Kane, specializes in black cherry lumber and veneer. Until recently, it relied almost exclusively on Allegheny timber. It is similar in size to the mill Kiehl sold in 1998, but owner Don Payne has remained independent. In January 2003, he told me that times are tough. "This thing with the Forest Service hit us pretty hard," he said. "We have to go to the state forests, private forests. It was a hell of a thing for us."

The mill was operating just one day a week when I spoke with him. Even though the mill is a specialty operation that relies on high-quality hardwoods instead of mass production, Payne said his biggest hurdle now is finding logs. Kleissler rejects that claim, arguing that there is still plenty of wood available. "Payne has access to the Susquehannock State Forest, OK?" Kleissler said. "And the cut on that has—it's out of the world now. It more than makes up for what was being cut in McKean County on the Allegheny. Really small operations have been able to get bids on there, comparatively speaking. I find it hard to believe that Payne can't get wood."

The Strauss report again confirms that local mills managed to make up for the decline on the Allegheny by securing "out of region" timber. Payne acknowledges that he gets some timber from the state forests, but therein lies the problem. The nearest section of the 260,000-acre Susquehannock State Forest is fifty miles east of Kane. Oleona, in the heart of the Susquehannock, is more than ninety miles away from Payne's mill. Shipping logs that far costs money, and Payne said that the combination of fewer logs and higher transportation costs has created a serious problem.

Besides, it seems strange for Kleissler to suggest making up for timber formerly coming off the Allegheny by cutting on a state forest. The ADP's zero-cut strategy applies to all public land, not just national forests. If Kleissler were in charge, any harvesting that Payne did on the Susquehannock would come to a quick and decisive end.

Asked where logs would come from if not the Allegheny, Kleissler pointed to a large map detailing the state and private inholdings located within the national forest's boundary. He focused on lands controlled by the Pennsylvania Game Commission and argued that those acres see substantial cutting.

The logical next question is whether those acres would be off-limits if his policy suggestions became law.

"We are zero cut on state game lands," he confirmed as he continued pointing at the map. "That is these two tracts right here. But that's not likely to happen any time in the next twenty years. Until somebody can prove to us otherwise, you know, that's sort of our position with that. On the state lands we still have a lot of, you know, we still haven't fully explored the issue to the extent that we're not budge-able, in one direction or the other, you know what I mean?"

Don Payne thinks he does know. In his mind, it is just another step toward the ultimate demise of his livelihood. Born in Kane in 1948, he has seen the forest transform from a stand of immature timber into an incredibly valuably resource. As a boy he tagged along with his father, who harvested pulpwood for the paper mill in Johnsonburg. He won his first Allegheny timber contract in 1972 and opened his mill two years later. That Kleissler would point to state lands as an economic refuge for the mills while working to cut them off to harvesting only solidifies Payne's opinion: People like Jim Kleissler and his Kane-based ally Bill Belitskus will do anything to control the Allegheny. "Those two people have no credibility with me, as many untruthful statements as they've spoken," Payne said. "I don't trust a single word they say."

Payne even theorized that the economic woe purportedly visited upon the local timber industry by litigation is more than an unfortunate by-product of their environmental ideals. "We're on partial layoff," he said. "We're only running one day a week. I think it's really had the desired effect the ADP was looking for."

Kleissler is equally free with the harsh rhetoric. He said that Payne seems to think that, since he has spent years thinning the forest and letting the black cherry grow unabated, the federal government owes him a shot at the timber. "Excuse me?" Kleissler intoned. "We owe you something in the future? As if, it's like a welfare mother saying you owe me something in the future. No. It's public land. You have no ownership over what we cut or what we don't cut in the future."

"To what extent is providing a subsidy to a private timber corporation—a millionaire like Donald Payne—how much of a public service is that, when that's a service that's already being provided on a large scale on private land in Pennsylvania?" he asked. "I don't have a lot of sympathy for Don Payne. He's a wealthy multimillionaire who can afford to have his workers paint his building ten times over."

The last remark is a rip on Payne's attempts to keep his workers busy while he waits for the judicial smoke to clear. Tim Spilka did not have that luxury. His Ludlow mill was a six-man operation. The saws have been quiet since

April 2002. Did he shut down because of growing competitive pressure from large corporate mills, as Kleissler argued? Or did activists tie up his supply lines through litigation? His take on the situation does not provide consistent ammunition for either side.

Physically, Spilka is straight out of central casting. At forty years old, he has dark hair and a burly beard. His belly indicates a penchant for fine living, and his thick forearms a history of hard physical labor. His mill is equally rugged. The parking lot, empty for months by the time I saw it, was overgrown with weeds. Three large wooden sheds covered small stacks of aging boards and a few pieces of idle machinery. The mill doors stood wide open, revealing the blades and conveyor belts inside. The office stood at the other end of the parking lot. It was a small structure made of brown boards with a single window. The only decoration was a small placard that said "I [heart] St. Francis" and three notices from UPS detailing failed attempts to deliver a package.

Spilka conveys a surprisingly thoughtful demeanor, even as he details the demise of the business that his father opened in the early 1960s. "Well, that's complex," he said when asked why he shut down. "Right now the best way to describe it is market conditions. From my point of view, the lumber business is bad right now. The last timber sale we had was a private sale, which is what we've been doing. It wasn't so much poor quality. We paid too much for it. We lost a considerable amount of money. It just didn't seem like things were getting any better."

Further elaborating, Spilka offered an explanation approximating Kleissler's: The large corporate mills have become increasingly active, forcing him into a competition that he cannot win. "I can't say it's an intentional effort," he said, "but it seems like some of the big mills are trying to make it hard on us."

Conventional wisdom says that small mills lose out to the corporate owners because of technology and economies of scale, but Spilka is not so sure. "That might be part of the possibility," he said, "but it's hard to believe. I don't know how that works. It almost seems like their overhead, even as a percentage, is higher than mine. . . . I don't know if they just can't shut down and have to keep going no matter what the cost. I don't know if they are losing money or not. I would be if I paid what they paid."

Spilka is far more concerned with another advantage that corporate mills have over the mom-and-pops: Small operators have a limited amount of money to spend on timber. "I look at it this way," he said. "If I lose $100,000, oh my God, that's half the money I have available to buy timber. Now, if Georgia Pacific loses $100,000 on a timber sale, that's one-tenth of 1 percent of the timber budget for the month. For me it's a disaster. For them, it's, 'Oops, we made a boo-boo.' It really makes me reluctant to jump back in."

Dave Kiehl confirmed that this cash-flow disparity is part of what convinced him to sell his mill to National Fuel in 1998. "I treat this company like it is my home, but size makes a difference," he said. "If I made a mistake in my own company it would do us in. Here, it's just a mistake."

The fabulous value of the region's black cherry works as a double-edged sword. The highest bid for Allegheny black cherry in 1998 came in at $2,500 per 1,000 board feet, up from $600 a decade earlier. Much of that was due to increasing demand for the product. That explosion put tremendous pressure on small mills like Spilka's. They were getting more for the lumber they sold, but they also had to pay more to get it.

Things got worse when activist litigation took hold. From 1998 to 1999, the harvest off the Allegheny dropped from 51 million to 21 million board feet. The amount of that which was black cherry plummeted from more than 14 million to less than six million board feet. This decrease in supply, coupled with the still-strong market for timber, sent prices through the roof. In 2000, the highest bid for black cherry on an Allegheny timber sale soared to $4,626 per thousand board feet.[4]

This was a clear concern for mill owners such as Payne and Kiehl who cut heavily on the Allegheny. As a smaller operation, Spilka was on even shakier ground. "It used to be we were completely for cherry, when we would cut 95 percent cherry," he said. "We didn't buy logs. We bought standing timber. For quite a long time, I would say for the first fifteen years we worked, we cut almost exclusively off the ANF, and before I worked my dad did for ten or fifteen years."

Spilka acknowledged the role that the litigation played in decreasing the available pool of timber. "It makes you mad," he said, revealing a hint of anger for the first time before adding, "Sometimes you want to laugh. There they go again. I don't want to say those people, referring to the environmentalists, don't have a right to do what they're doing. But it's a shame it affects so many people."

Spilka complained that in addition to reducing the pool of Allegheny timber, litigation makes him think twice about bidding on what is for sale. When a mill wins a sale on the national forest, the owner has to pay the Forest Service a deposit and a down payment up front. Spilka said he was working an Allegheny sale in the late 1990s when activists filed a lawsuit and began seeking a court injunction to stop the cutting. He said he and his father worried that if the judge ruled against the Forest Service, the mill would be left holding the bag while the case proceeded, minus their deposit and a substantial portion of their timber budget. Spilka would have been barred from cutting timber for which he had contracted, and too broke to bid on any more. That did not come to pass, but he said it soured him on Allegheny sales for a few years.

Once that suit cleared the courts, he tried again. "I could smell more lawsuits," he said. "We waited a while, and it seemed like this was a little problem, but people were being allowed to cut. On the fourteenth of June last year we bid on a sale . . . and apparently we were the only bidder. So we were the high bidder. Later we got a letter [from the Forest Service] saying, 'We can't award the sale because we have a lawsuit.' In the meantime, they had our deposit, which I think was around $60,000. I asked them, 'What's the deal?' They said, 'We think we're going to be allowed to award the contract but we don't know when.' I asked, 'What's the status? Do we get our money back if we don't want to wait?'"

Spilka said there is a clause that allows bidders to withdraw at the 90-day mark, but not after. He was lucky enough to find out right before the deadline, and he withdrew. If the money had been tied up, he would have faced the prospect of bidding on another sale and having both approved simultaneously. With a limited budget he would not have been able to cover both deposits and down payments. That would have landed him in default.

Activists argue that they are not to blame for Forest Service policies that keep money tied up during litigation, and they are right. On the other hand, timber supporters point out that activists are responsible for the litigation, which is what gums up the works in the first place. Spilka does not seem interested in refereeing the grudge match. He said he supports industry groups such as AHUG but generally stays out of the political fray. "I haven't become very actively involved," he said. "I don't know. It's kind of tough. What more can you say?"

Spilka has seen tough times in the past. In fact, this is not the first time the mill has shut down. Seasonal slowdowns sometimes prompt small owners into a temporary hiatus. Still, this time he is beginning to wonder. "It's been more common the last few years than in the past," he said. "I couldn't tell you when it changed. But for many years I had no familiarity with the unemployment compensation system."

He is familiar with it now, just as he is familiar with endangered species, litigation, and competition from corporate giants. So far he has taken each in stride, revealing a surprisingly measured outlook on his own situation. Spilka even took a level tone with regard to the increasing number of ELF attacks in the region, refusing to lump all the environmental groups together: "I don't think there is a 'they,' one environmental group," he said. "I think, unfortunately, there are some you almost want to say are crazy. Extreme, I guess."

When asked if thought he would ever open the mill again, Spilka thought a moment before answering.

"I don't know," he said. "It's getting harder. It's getting harder on the small mill."

NOTES

1. Highland has diversified much of its forest holdings since this interview.

2. Mike Crissy, "Lack of logging taking toll around Allegheny National Forest," Associated Press, September 2, 2002, http://forests.org/archive/america/lackoflo.htm.

3. C. H. Strauss, B. E. Lord, M. J. Powell, M. Shields, and T. W. Kelsey, "Economic Impact of Pennsylvania's Hardwood Industry: Current Status and Proposed Growth" (University Park: Pennsylvania State University School of Forest Resources, 2000).

4. United States Department of Agriculture, "Allegheny National Forest Statistics 1since Forest Plan Implementation," January 2001, www.fs.fed.us/r9/allegheny/forest_management/timber/timstats.pdf [accessed April 9, 2004].

Chapter Four

I Work in the Woods: Fear and Logging on the Allegheny

Logging Project Targeted: Magistrate Recommends ANF Timber Sale Be Halted.

—Headline in the *Warren Times Observer*, September 9, 2002

Chuck Novosel was not born with a chainsaw in his hands, but it didn't take him long to find one. Novosels work in the woods. Everybody knows that. The same has held true for generations of Buehlers, Carlsons, Cochrans, Kocjancics, Mitchells, and other logging families in the Allegheny region. The profession still offered a viable alternative for young men a decade ago. They envisioned a hard but honorable life that might soon put enough money in their hands to buy a home and support a family. Most hoped to eventually get some equipment, hire a crew, and go into business for themselves.

The past decade has crushed much of that optimism. The timber market has soured along with the rest of the economy. Large corporations have overtaken many of the area's smaller mills and pressured loggers to buy bigger, more expensive skidders. Automated feller-bunchers have replaced some of the skilled woodsmen who used to cut trees by hand. A dysfunctional workers' compensation system devours as much as a third of the logging crew's payroll. Rising fuel costs and spates of foul weather have only made matters worse.

Logging has never been easy. It is dangerous. It is dirty. It is expensive. It offers a notoriously uneven paycheck. But those are all challenges that loggers in the Allegheny region have overcome for more than 120 years: Work harder, work faster, and try to jump out of the way when something comes crashing down from overhead. The formula for success is not that simple anymore. Many loggers are left to ponder why, as they put their equipment up for sale or watch the repo man swing into action. They grumble among them-selves—almost always among themselves—about the weather and the fuel and the mills. But a different challenge has added an angry edge to their mus-ings. Loggers insist that "tree huggers" have made life harder than it has ever been by decimating the Allegheny's timber program. The activists beg to differ, of course. They say that independent loggers are falling prey to the same corporate profiteers that are stalking the beleaguered mom-and-pop sawmills.

The truth is not an easy thing to discern. It is difficult to talk about "log-gers" in the wider sense. Some of them are doing well. Others have sold all their equipment and moved on. Whatever the root cause of their woes, one thing remains certain—making a living in the woods is getting more difficult all the time, and the people who have done it for years do not know what to do about it.

Novosel Logging is located in Kane. When Chuck answered the door in summer 2002 he was wearing cut-off jeans, work boots, and a muddy t-shirt. Just twenty-eight, he was already a successful independent businessman. His short-cropped blond hair and youthful enthusiasm are rare commodities in the modern world of Pennsylvania logging, where the people who cut, skid, and haul timber grow grayer every year. Chuck's decision to take up the trade speaks volumes about his family's history in the woods. His increasingly anomalous success says even more about what it takes to make it.

Novosel launched into a colorful monologue about life in the woods, using four thick photo albums to document a clan defined by its economic and cul-tural ties to the timber business. Page after page showed enormous stacks of lumber crowding the old Novosel mills. Instead of birthdays and vacations, the images captured countless skidders, backhoes, and other heavy equip-ment. Very few included the people who operated them. The oldest photos were in black and white. Newer ones tracked Chuck's growth as he posed in front of logs, lumber, and machines with his two sisters. One album included a newspaper article titled "Novosel Land." It detailed the ambitious family's exploits in purchasing more than six thousand acres of timberland for an unbelievable price: "Legends of the colorful 'lumbering era' are being rewritten in our area today by an even more colorful band of lumbermen who take a 'million dollar deal' casually—punch a half hundred miles of roads through unbroken forest and pack more power at their fingertips than hun-dreds of men and horses in the by-gone days." The story appeared on Decem-ber 8, 1962.[1]

The sense of continuity that the albums convey—three generations in the business—has been ruptured in recent years. His predecessors did very well and the family still owns timberland, but they have sold their skidders, trucks, and mills. Chuck is the last Novosel in the business. Still, his success is linked to his family's history in the woods. He worked for his father during high school. His mother put the house up as collateral to help him get a loan for his first skidder after graduation. "I graduated in June 1992," he recalled. "I graduated on June 9. By June 15, I had my first machine."

In just six days, Novosel went from a carefree teenager to a dangerously indebted entrepreneur. A proper chainsaw costs $800, but a new skidder can run well over $100,000. To the uninitiated, a skidder looks like a large tractor with a series of cables jutting out the back. Loggers attach the cables to felled trees and drag them out of the woods to the landing. Those who do not own one have to work for somebody who does. That was not part of Novosel's plan, so he took the risk and started making payments: $1,900 a month.

The key to staying above water is to keep the machine running. Mills contract with loggers to harvest trees growing on company property or timber they have bought elsewhere. There is a set rate for every thousand board feet they cut and skid. Less valuable pulpwood pays by the ton. A select few loggers have enough cash on hand to buy standing timber on private or public land, but that is becoming a thing of the past. Novosel detailed why it is so hard for the few remaining independents to operate on the national forest. "The sales are way too big," he said. "A million dollars is nothing."

The Novosel clan could swing million-dollar deals in the early 1960s, but by the early 1990s, Chuck was more worried about paying for his skidder. He hired one man to work with him, but he often went into the woods by himself. Working alone is part of the logger machismo. It drives wives and safety advocates crazy. OSHA documents reveal that "By many measures, logging is the most dangerous occupation in the United States."[2] Creditors are not interested in sob stories, however, so loggers continue to work solo when necessary. "It was sink or swim," Novosel said. "I'd get a load a day and I'd make my payments. . . . For the first four years I really struggled."

That hard work paid off. Novosel has thrived while others have hit hard times. He traded his skidder in for a new one in 1996. By 2002 he owned three of them, plus a dozer, a log truck, and a mechanized harvesting machine called a Timco. He had five employees running the equipment along with him. He was younger than all of them. That success would seem to put the lie to complaints about environmental monkey-wrenching. If Novosel can find trees to cut, make a living, and invest in several hundred thousand dollars worth of equipment, why can't everyone else? The answer to that question points to the complex interaction of corporate interest, environmental litigation, and simple luck on the Allegheny.

Novosel is a hard worker and he has shown a keen sense of business acumen, but his last name certainly hasn't hurt. He made the payments on his first skidder by staying busy—a fact that he attributes at least in part to family connections. "I started in 1992," he said. "I bought a skidder thanks to my uncle. He put me to work." Novosel is referring to his uncle Carl, a well-connected, well-respected logger who knew the business inside and out. He owned his own timberland, and he knew everyone else in the area who did. So he helped his nephew. Far from blind nepotism, the decision made good business sense. He knew that Chuck was well trained. He knew that he could trust him. And he was right.

Ironically, Chuck Novosel got an even bigger break when litigation hit the Allegheny. With skidder payments ballooning to more than $2,000 a month, many loggers took a beating when the discovery of the Indiana bat led to a six-month shutdown. It did not affect Novosel, who cut his last tree on the Allegheny in 1995. After that he began contracting with a large corporate mill that had its own timberland. "I was lucky," he said. "When all these guys were taking a hit because of the bat, I was expanding. I probably wouldn't have been able to do that if the company I was working for was dependent on the ANF."

Novosel has made the most of his good fortune. He is even flirting with the idea of bidding his own timber. He admits that will be difficult, however. "The bigger companies, you can't compete with them," he said. "I look at a lot of jobs and we bid on the timber. These companies will come in and put the bid down and double it. They're just buying it to keep the mills running."

That might support claims that loggers' difficulties stem from the influx of corporate heavies, but Novosel has a slightly different take. He says independent loggers never faced such stiff competition from the national powerhouses until litigation threw everyone off the Allegheny. "That's when it changed everything," he said.

Novosel replied in the negative when I asked if he knew any young loggers who had gone under. That's not because business is thriving. It is because for the first time in Kane's 150-year history, residents doubt whether there is a future in logging. "As far as loggers, I don't know anyone who really took a hit because I don't know anyone who's young who's getting in the business," he said. Later, he added, "Ninety-five percent of my friends, they're gone. And as far as I know, they're not coming back."

Sue Swanson agrees with Novosel's assessment. As director of the Allegheny Hardwood Utilization Group, she has seen what has happened to the current generation of loggers who have tried to take up the family trade. "Just in Kane, I probably know of at least six young men who have left," she said. "[They] were working in the forest products industry either as cutters or skidders. When you look at that, six doesn't look like very many, but when you look at the total population, I mean, it's a pretty large segment. And I'm sure I don't know of all of them.

"There are a few younger men who are trucking, but the cutting and skidding population is kind of my age," she continued. "It's scary. I can't imagine encouraging someone who is young and wants to be able to support a family to do this right now, not with all the pressures that are involved."

Jim Kleissler insists that the Allegheny Defense Project is not adding to that pressure. He says timber supporters such as the Allegheny Forest Alliance and the Allegheny Hardwood Utilization Group are attempting to protect their powerful industry allies by ignoring the real economic threat. "I find it ironic that they try to portray themselves as good for loggers," he said. "What position have they taken that is good for labor? What have they done about automation of the timber industry to preserve manufacturing jobs and logging jobs?"

According to this theory, corporations obsessed with efficiency force loggers to buy equipment they cannot afford. Kleissler again refers to the study Penn State professor Chuck Straus conducted in 2000. "The amount of timber that was cut in 1999 in the four counties was not less than what was cut in 1997 in the four counties," he said. "The contractors, the guys with their own skidders and everything, they are not bound by who owns what. Their services are still in demand."

Mike Miles is not so sure. He got into the logging business the same way Chuck Novosel did—by following his father. The elder Miles was one of the last truly independent operators. Mike tried to follow suit after graduating from high school in 1996. He bought a skidder, went to work, got married, and had two kids. By the time I spoke to him at the Ridgway Elks lodge in February 2003, he was in the throes of bankruptcy. The bank had taken the skidder, not to mention his house. His family was living in an apartment while he tried to piece his life back together. Is that Kleissler's fault, or is corporate America to blame? Miles's experience is telling because it highlights how hard it is to answer questions like that.

His roller-coaster ride through the logging business amplifies the larger ups and downs that have rocked the industry in recent years. He graduated from high school in 1996, a year before activists began filing lawsuits on the Allegheny. But Chuck Novosel upgraded his skidder that same year and he is still making it. Novosel had family connections, but so did Miles. Neither of them cut heavily on the national forest. So what happened? Miles recalls that things got tight when litigation kicked the large timber companies off the Allegheny and his dad started having trouble competing for bids. "[Shane, his older brother] didn't even have his own skidder at the time," Mike said.

"He worked through my dad working private timber. The problem was my dad couldn't buy enough private timber to keep me busy."

Sitting idle is certain doom for a logger trying to pay for a new skidder, so Mike signed on to work for National Fuel, the company that purchased Northeast Hardwoods from Dave Kiehl in 1998. That's when Miles traded his machine in for an even more expensive model. "I bought the first new one when me and my dad were still buying private timber," he said. "Then I went to work for the gas company. I wanted more production, so I traded my new one in on this one, because it was bigger and you could produce a little more with it. That's how that come about, because they want more production because they're a mill. So that's what I did."

That was a bad decision and one that inspires derision rather than sympathy in many of his fellow loggers. Faced with the same market conditions, the same environmental movement, and the same corporate pressure, most made do with their old skidders or bought cheaper used equipment to minimize their monthly payments. Miles did not. His new machine cost $135,000, which translated into $2,400 a month. He said he was making it, though, largely because he was allowed to keep the "junk"—the wood used to make paper. National Fuel only wanted the trees it could sell as veneer or saw into boards. Miles sold the pulpwood to the International Paper facility in Erie. That mill closed for good on October 16, 2001. The shutdown threw almost eight hundred workers onto the street. It also left Miles in deep financial trouble.

"I always relied on selling my wood, softwood, because the gas company just gave me that wood for free," he said. "[National Fuel] didn't bid on it [because they owned the property]. So that was free money to me. But me not being able to [sell] it, that's how I lost—I guess in a sense I didn't lose the money, but I wasn't making it no more. That's more or less how I lost that money."

Then the weather turned against him. "It was so wet last winter we couldn't even work," Miles said. "I was working maybe two days this week, off the rest of the week. . . . So more or less the money I was making, I was just feeding my family. I couldn't pay nothing."

He had owned the new skidder for a year and a half when the bank came and took it back. Far worse, he inexplicably failed to incorporate his business or in any way protect himself financially, so his house went along with the machine. Dejected, Miles packed up his family and headed to Georgia, where he found work doing odd jobs for a real estate company. He still had a few connections in Pennsylvania, however, and he eventually found someone who needed his services. He says the bank offered to give him another chance if he came back and started making payments on the skidder, but reneged when he and his family arrived.

Miles says he will never consider working inside, despite the world-class beating he has suffered at the hands of the logging industry. His response shows how incredibly strong the desire to work in the woods can be. "No," he said. "No way. It's boring. I've done it. My dad was in cahoots with a mill down in Sykesville and on our rain days he'd tell us to go work [there] and run the resaw. I won't ever do it again. I was there two days and I had enough. I, just, [have] no time for it. I won't work in a plant. I don't like being inside."

The disdain for factory work is coupled with something more positive and, in the end, more important: Miles puts up with the danger, noise, and uncertainty of working in the woods because he *loves* it. He enjoys putting chain to wood and watching the timber fall. He looks forward to hooking trees up to the skidder and dragging them to the landing. He is addicted to the sense of independence that he derives from the work. "It's a passion," he admitted. "That's why I came back from down south. I missed it."

That passion has proven irresistible. By early 2003, Miles was working in the woods near Lock Haven, just over a hundred miles away from his apartment and family in Ridgway. A friend in the business landed the contract and hired him. Most nights they were staying in a hotel, although they usually made it home on weekends. Miles did not have his own equipment yet, but he was working on a plan to regain his footing. That outlook is more cautious optimism than unbridled enthusiasm. "I hope not," Miles said when asked if his children might follow him into the business someday. "I don't think there's a future in it. I mean, I might be able to make a future for myself in it, but to drag them down in it, unless something changes, I don't see it."

Miles readily admits that bad luck, bad timing, and his own bad decisions played a role in his travails. "No," he replied when asked if he was bitter how those factors played out. "I can say, you know, a lot of things. But, I mean, I learned through the whole process of what happened. You can't trust what people say. I learned that you just have to grit your teeth and make money however you can."

Miles is less measured in his response to what he considers the activists' role, however. "Bitter," he said when asked about his view of the Allegheny Defense Project. "It just seems that they ain't got nothing better to do. Everywhere in the world ain't like our counties are, from here north, and rely on logging like we do. So, bitter."

That animosity is a telling reaction. Miles did not cut on the Allegheny, but he still sees the national forest shutdown as a contributing factor in his financial crisis. In fact, it is the only factor that appears to have raised his hackles. Miles is especially angry with Kleissler's suggestion that loggers can survive by working in other forests where harvesting might continue. He was trying that at the time of the interview but doubted that the work would make ends meet. "If I drive to Lock Haven everyday, it costs me $35 in fuel just for my pickup," he complained.

Miles might be more forgiving if he could grasp why activists are so adamant about stopping the Allegheny timber program. Like everyone else who grew up on the Allegheny, Miles has heard tales about the brush-heap era and views the current crop of hardwoods as a real improvement. "I look at some of [the ADP's] stuff and I think, yeah, I guess in a rain forest where they slash and burn, you know, stop some of that," he said. "But what we do, we try to protect the forest. So I can't see any of their concern. If the regeneration is there, what's the difference? I can remember seeing pictures down there by the Clarion River bridge [in 1920s Ridgway]. There wasn't nothing on that hillside."

There is something on that hillside today—a stand of lucrative hardwood trees. Miles likes the way they look. He likes hunting the animals that live in and around them. And he likes making a living harvesting those trees. He is finding that to be more difficult than he ever imagined, and despite all the forces that have gone into creating that reality, the only group against which he appears to hold a grudge is the Allegheny Defense Project. Fair or not, it is a popular sentiment among local loggers. And it is even stronger among those who actually cut on the Allegheny and suffered the effects of litigation more directly.

Fritz Kilhoffer made a living cutting trees on the Allegheny National Forest, but it did not start out that way. He was born and raised in Wilcox. After graduating from Johnsonburg High School in 1969, he went to work at Keystone Carbon in Saint Mary's. He worked there for nine years until the stress of life on the floor finally got to him. Very few loggers migrate into the field in their late twenties. Even fewer do so with an eye toward improving their health. But that's how he did it, and for years he never questioned the decision. He started in 1978. In 1986, he purchased a skidder and broke out on his own. In 1991, the Allegheny Hardwood Utilization Group and the Pennsylvania Forestry Association both named him logger of the year. He was selected three times to compete in the Pennsylvania Game of Logging, an annual statewide event that measures speed, accuracy, and safety. He had two skidders, two mechanized feller-bunchers, and five employees he was paying as much as $13.50 an hour. He had become another success story in the world of Allegheny logging, until circumstance beyond his control forced him back to work on the factory floor.

Kilhoffer cut for Larry Buehler, a Ridgway mill owner and local bigwig whose family name is synonymous with timbering on the Allegheny. The

Buehler clan owned land in the area, but most of the timber for the mill came from the national forest. "Why did I get out of the logging business?" Kilhoffer mused when I asked him in February 2003. "Well, I was working for Buehler Lumber Company all the time I was in the business, and when the Allegheny National Forest stopped the timber sales, [Buehler] more or less stopped the loggers logging."

Jim Kleissler says loggers did not suffer when the Allegheny cut back on harvesting because cutting on private and state land increased accordingly. Things were not as tidy as that, however. "I really blame them for myself getting out of the logging business when I did and selling my equipment," Kilhoffer said when asked about the Allegheny Defense Project. "At the time, we was cutting on the Allegheny National Forest and Larry had just bought a sale out in Highland. They protested it and shut the sale down. At the time Larry's forester told me that, you know, there's enough work for me there for over a year. It was probably one of the closest jobs [to home] I had and pretty decent cutting. And they shut it down. That was it. Larry just sort of stopped buying it. And that hurt my business big time."

Kleissler says the loggers had plenty of time to adjust—even when the Indiana bat forced the Forest Service to stop all logging on the Allegheny for six months in 1999. "You know how that lawsuit went?" Kleissler asked. "We filed that lawsuit in November, OK? There was a preliminary injunction hearing in January. At that hearing in early January, the Forest Service said that cutting would stop on April 1. Cutting stopped on April 1. That's not all of a sudden. That's pretty much six months' notice."

That might seem like a lot of time to Kleissler, but it was not enough for Kilhoffer. Close to 90 percent of the cutting he did for Buehler was on the national forest. The shutdown flooded the market with loggers looking for work. Kilhoffer could not wait for the moratorium to lift. He was a successful businessman, but he was making payments on a lot of machinery. At one point, his monthly outlay for equipment was more than $4,500. "We went and cut private, whatever we could find," he said. "Larry had some private stuff. It wasn't near the cutting we had on the Allegheny National Forest."

Kilhoffer started selling his equipment piece by piece, eventually paring the operation down to a two-man crew. The timing was particularly harsh because he was on the verge of having everything paid for. "If I could have got one more good year in, I could have been sitting pretty well," he said. "But I didn't get that last year because of the shutdown. From there I had to downsize and keep downsizing."

Kilhoffer admits that the drive for efficiency has been a contributing factor, and says he may have even played a role in that regard. "I feel that the thing that sort of hurt the smaller loggers—and in a way I'm a little bit to blame, too—is the mechanized logging in this area," he said. "I was like the second person to buy a Bell feller-buncher. Then bigger companies moved in. Even Larry got Timcos and grapplers and chippers. They can go through a bunch of timber in a hurry, and they can put a lot of the smaller loggers out of work."

Still, he was making it until the activists shut down the forest, and he sees their lawsuits as the root cause of his exit from the industry. In fact, he said the lawsuits made the pressure to buy more expensive equipment even worse—and hurt the environment in the process. "The reason why I think that is, if you can keep cutting on the Allegheny National Forest, the Allegheny National Forest has regulations in place that does not allow a lot of this mechanized logging, which would leave a lot of room for the smaller logger to go in and cut," he said. "The Allegheny National Forest, I think, manages their timber very well and protects the land very well. Where the mechanized logging is hurting—cutting on private timber where you can get away with a lot more—you can go in and, in my opinion, in a lot of places they're not doing it right. They're making way too much of a mess."

Kilhoffer fought to keep a grip on his business, but he eventually sold all of his equipment, cut his last employee loose, and signed on with a factory after working in the woods for thirteen years. In his late forties, he was too young to retire. He risked sliding into debt if he continued making payments on idle equipment, and every year he delayed the decision he became less attractive to potential employers. "I was Larry's number one veneer cutter for years, you know?" he said. "It was a hard thing to take, and I just got disgusted with it and got out for a while."

The clock Kilhoffer began punching belonged to the Temple-Inland particleboard plant in Mount Jewett. The Texas-based company employed about 130 at the facility, a hundred more at its adjacent medium-density fiberboard plant. Kilhoffer was at home on February 13, 2001, when an accidental explosion killed three of his coworkers. OSHA cited numerous safety violations and fined the company $248,000.[3] Kilhoffer stayed with the company for another two years before quitting just in time on January 25, 2003. Six weeks later, on March 7, Temple-Inland announced a "temporary curtailment of production" at the particleboard plant that continues to this day. Kilhoffer saw it coming. "They did some layoffs," he said. "My job got bumped back and it seemed like I was going backwards instead of ahead up there. And I didn't like the condition of the plant anymore. They were sort of letting it deteriorate. They weren't taking care to clean up and there was dust building up. To me, I felt safer going back in the woods than staying there working at the plant."

For the second time in his life, Kilhoffer turned to logging to keep himself healthy and employed. Things were different, however. He did not have any of his own equipment. He joined a crew with his son-in-law, who was still in the business. They contracted with RAM Forest Products, Inc., an operation that cuts on the national forest when possible but also retains substantial land holdings in the area. "If we stay with RAM, they have their own timber, fortunately," Kilhoffer said. "That's why you have to go with a big company. Collins Pine has their own land. Seneca Resources. If you're not in with somebody like that and they shut the Allegheny National Forest down, you're in trouble. You're in big trouble."

Like Miles, Kilhoffer's anger stems from his inability to comprehend why activists want to get rid of the black cherry. "I'm sure there are other national forests that have the pine and the hemlock and what they want in it," Kilhoffer said. "We have the best black cherry in the world growing here. If this land is suited for that kind of tree and it does well, why not take advantage of it? Why plant a hemlock tree when a cherry tree does super here? Go down to [Pennsylvania's] Cook [State] Forest. They have a lot of virgin timber down there. Why do they gotta have it all? Why do they want to see it all that way? I don't understand the reason."

Loggers obviously have a hard time accepting the activist mindset. The feeling is mutual. Kleissler says he wants to help the loggers, but fears that they will always question his every word. "I'm saying the reason I don't try is because, if I walk up to these guys and say, 'Hi, I'm Jim Kleissler with the Allegheny Defense Project,' I think that because of everything that's going on, there's an inherent distrust there," he said.

The plan Kleissler says he would like to propose to help loggers speaks volumes about the cultural disconnect. "One of their biggest problems is, I think they would do very well if they were labor organized somehow," he said. "You know, it's funny how anti-union all the corporations are, even the small guys like [Kane mill owner Don] Payne and them. They are all anti-union to the teeth. . . . The workers, the loggers, the independent logging crews, they need to be better organized because AHUG is supposed to represent them. But AHUG clearly has a close association with management at the mills and so forth. What the loggers need is, they need an association that represents their interests. . . . Loggers have no voice."

Kleissler believes that a union would give them that voice. Since loggers work for themselves rather than the mills, they have to provide their own workers' compensation. In recent years those payments have become immensely expensive. Loggers who own a skidder and hire a crew have had to shell out more than $40 in comp payments for every $100 they pay their workers. "That's really a screwed-up system to begin with," Kleissler said. "The bottom line is, one of the main reasons they're independent is so that corporations that are buying the timber don't have to deal with liability issues." He added that loggers would be better off on the company payroll "because they'd get unemployment insurance."

Local reaction to the idea of a logging union—from both inside and outside the industry—usually falls somewhere between a guffaw and a blank stare. It took a minute for it to register when I posed Kleissler's idea to Fritz Kilhoffer. "No," he said, then paused before proceeding slowly. "I don't foresee that ever happening in the logging business. I never heard of anyone wanting to start a union at all. What good did he say a union could do for the logger?" I detailed the proposal. He was not enthused.

Mike Miles laughed when I asked him if loggers would be better off working directly for the mills and forming a union. He knows that money is not going to magically appear if the big companies start paying benefits. It is probably going to come out of his production rate. In his mind, that is a slippery slope leading to something even worse—an hourly rate. "If you're making production, most guys don't want to get paid [benefits] because they can make $1,000 bucks a week," he said. "Well, if [the mills] have to start paying unemployment, [they are] not going to pay you no twenty bucks a thousand board feet. They'll give you eight bucks an hour, right? So then they're going to be set at one wage, making three hundred, three-fifty a week when they could have been making a thousand."

His other fear is that working for the mill would mean using company equipment. Avoiding such large payments might seem like a real benefit, but it could also have a downside. "I guess if they did away with the contractors, and I could go to work for a mill like that, I would, to stay in the business," he said. "But what's going to happen? If they go that route they're going to buy Timcos because the mills can afford them, and they're only going to employ ten guys instead of there being two hundred logging crews, you know, four hundred jobs."

Kleissler argues that Miles's automation nightmare is already unfolding and that a union would give loggers enough bargaining power to resist. They disagree. Fair enough. What is more telling is Kleissler's theory that loggers might like things arranged that way even if it would put them further ahead financially. He admits that, as a group, loggers are "an independent breed," but he does not appear to grasp the full import of that reality. Most of the loggers I know would rather join the ADP itself than align themselves with a union.

It is important not to sentimentalize the loggers' storied independence. They are, after all, involved in the timber industry, which loudly and frequently decries free trade—especially imports pouring in from timber-rich Canada. Groups like AHUG and the Pennsylvania Hardwood Development

Council receive state money to flog Allegheny products overseas. At the personal level, loggers are no less likely than other people to send their kids to public schools and state colleges. In short, members of the logging community are scarcely more libertarian than their neighbors who work indoors. On the other hand, there is an almost maniacal entrepreneurial drive that pushes them into the woods—that convinces them that they can make it on their own despite the weather, the costs, the competition, and the growing environmental movement.

That independent spirit might benefit Kleissler as much as anyone. If loggers ever did organize, they likely would consider zero-cut activists their foremost adversaries. As it stands, many loggers do not even know the environmentalists or their organizations by name. They know that there are "tree huggers" pushing for zero cut, and they know that the Indiana bat shut the Allegheny down for six months, but most of them stay out of overtly political discussions. Miles did not recognize Kleissler's name when asked if he paid any attention to the larger debate. "I try to," he said. "I just really quit keeping up with it because you're so sick of hearing about it."

Chuck Novosel offered a similar take on Kane activist Bill Belitskus. "I think he's just going a little overboard," he said. "To be honest, I don't know a whole lot about where he's coming from."

That does not mean that loggers do not care. They are outraged, in fact. They just are not the type to take to the streets. There is not a whole lot they can do about the financial pinch other than keep going to work when they can find it. As for the question of zero cut, the courts are going to make that decision. Or Congress. Or the Forest Service. Besides, anything that can be done probably already has been done by one of the influential foresters in the area or the people at AHUG. That's what those people do.

AHUG director Sue Swanson has spent years coming to terms with that sentiment. She would rejoice if loggers rose up, crowded public meetings, and engaged elected officials with letters and telephone calls. She knows loggers, however, and she doubts that is going to happen. She rejects Kleissler's charge that AHUG ignores the loggers in favor of mill managers, and says that his view betrays a fundamental misreading of the local mindset. "I would agree that the loggers don't have a specific organization that agitates for them," she said. "But they have chosen not to do that. They are not the kind of people who join organizations, number one, or speak out on their own behalf."

Loggers highlighted Swanson's point on April Fools' Day, 2003. The 35th annual Loggers and Sawmillers Safety Meeting drew almost two hundred industry workers to the Kane Armory for a buffet dinner, informative fun, and awards. Tickets, which cost one dollar, automatically enrolled participants in a series of raffles. Four local workers performed a brief safety skit, and two safety specialists discussed the best ways to avoid getting crushed by "hazard trees." As asides, they both warned people for the umpteenth time about two common logging bugaboos—cutting alone and drinking heavily the night before work.

The festivities provided a few hours of interesting diversions, but they paled in comparison to the day's political developments. Before the meeting got under way, Swanson informed me that she was going to make an important announcement. She had just learned that a federal magistrate in Pittsburgh had rescinded an earlier recommendation in the ongoing East Side litigation. Issued the previous autumn, the recommendation could have doomed logging on the Allegheny had it been allowed to stand. After waiting months to hear whether the presiding judge would accept that decision, Swanson told me that the magistrate had surprised everyone by agreeing to reconsider and hear oral arguments. It was the best news timber supporters had heard in over a year.

Swanson approached the podium about halfway through the meeting and quickly shifted to the big announcement. Addressing the loggers, who were arranged in neat rows of folding chairs on the armory's gymnasium floor, she detailed the magistrate's reversal and proceeded to explain why it was so important. The assembled loggers and sawyers greeted news of the victory with a round of silence. No hoots, no hollers, no "Way to go!" Swanson was not nearly as taken aback as I was. She quickly segued into the rest of the program.

Swanson gave a knowing chuckle a few days later when I asked her about the loggers' apparent indifference. She attributed it to a few factors, one of which mirrored Mike Miles's complaint about being sick of the whole debate. "I think they all realize this has been going on for six years," she said. "It really doesn't change a lot. You don't really see a resolution to it. Even when you get good news, [the activists] just file another suit the next week."

"It's not cheering crowds and jumping up and down," she said of the loggers. "They're totally opposite of the people Jim represents. They work in the woods because they don't want to be around gobs of people. Jim has no idea what loggers are like. They seem to have an inherent interest in [the larger debate], but they don't get involved. They don't come to the meetings. They just go to work every day and hope it gets better."

"Better" is a loaded term, of course. It means different things to Jim Kleissler and Fritz Kilhoffer. Like all environmental disputes, partisans in the Allegheny timber war inevitably turn to science to support their vision of the future. Unfortunately for observers searching for a clear-cut "answer" to the crisis, science is never quite as definitive as it is cracked up to be. That was true with the spotted owl (Is it really endangered?), oil drilling in Alaska (Will it hurt the caribou?), and other well-publicized imbroglios. (Global warming? Fuel efficiency standards? And so on.)

The Big Level's unique place in American environmental and industrial history only makes matters worse. For a moment, set aside debates about legislative intentions, economic fairness, and how many trees to cut: Biologically speaking, what will the Allegheny look like in a hundred years if the activists get there way?

The uncomfortable answer is that no one really knows.

NOTES

1. Novosel still has the original clipping, but the paper in which it appeared is unclear.

2. United States Department of Labor, "Logging eTools" (Washington, D.C.: Occupational Safety and Health Administration, 1998; revised December 2003), www.osha.gov/SLTC/etools/logging/mainpage.html.

3. Associated Press, "Families Sue Over Deadly Plant Explosion," *Warren Times Observer*, August 21, 2002.

Chapter Five

Restoration, Reality, and the Perils of Science: Can the Allegheny Become a Wilderness Again?

> Wilderness is a resource which can shrink but not grow. Invasions can be arrested or modified in a manner to keep an area usable either for recreation, or for science, or for wildlife, but the creation of wilderness in the full sense of the word is impossible.
>
> —Aldo Leopold[1]

Pity the American forester. Experts do their best to predict what a proposed management plan will do to a given landscape, but diseases, droughts, floods, fires, pollution, tornadoes, and a host of other forces regularly send them back to the drawing board. The process becomes infinitely more complex when economics, politics, and changing social views come into play. That was true in the Pacific Northwest, where new opinions regarding the value of old-growth forests combined with controversial theories about a threatened owl to spark a rancorous national debate. The same thing is happening today with regard to fire suppression in the American West. The debate over the "science" of managing the Allegheny National Forest has failed to garner the same sort of headlines, but it poses many of the same questions in ways that might prove even more intractable.

On an overcast Sunday in March 2003, an activist named Kirk Johnson led twenty eager hikers on a four-mile walk that highlighted the perils of scientific forestry. He organized the event to detail his proposal to turn the area—which he refers to as "Chestnut Ridge"—into a federally designated wilderness area. That plan would ban logging forever on the 5,000-acre tract. Johnson and his proposal figure prominently in the larger Allegheny debate, but for the moment it helps to focus on the profoundly ambiguous notion of "restoration."

Johnson began the hike with an optimistic account of his reasons for creating the wilderness area. One of them was, "So people can see what the forests were like when the settlers came in here." Whether that is compelling or not is open to interpretation, but one thing is not: There are no chestnut trees on Chestnut Ridge, at least none that will survive. An Asian fungus began killing the New World's American chestnut in 1904. By mid-century, a primary species in forests like the Allegheny had been devastated. Johnson named the area Chestnut Ridge after finding a few young ones in the area, but their prospects are grim. Mighty efforts to develop a blight resistant strain have consistently failed.

That is not the only hurdle Johnson faces if he wants to recreate the presettlement forest for contemporary society. Like the rest of the Allegheny, Chestnut Ridge was cut heavily during the railroad-logging era. It is currently home to a stand of relatively shade-intolerant hardwoods, including black cherry, that all started growing at approximately the same time. Logic argues that those trees will eventually die and give way to slow-growing, shade-tolerant species such as hemlock growing in the dark understory, but that fails to address a crucial truth: On huge swaths of the Allegheny, including portions of Chestnut Ridge, that understory simply does not exist. If foresters stand back and let the hardwoods die, there is no guarantee that a forest approximating the long-lost "virgin landscape"—or anything else, for that matter—will emerge. Explaining why and proposing a solution requires overcoming a messy environmental reality.

Jack Hedlund is not a professional forester, but he knows quite a few of them. He counts many of them as friends. As head of the Allegheny Forest Alliance, he naturally turns to them for their views on forestry. They insist that the activist vision for the Allegheny is not only ill advised, but impossible to achieve. Hedlund is furious with activists like Jim Kleissler for refusing to heed those dire warnings.

"They're not foresters," Hedlund fumed. "They don't understand the science of forests. They want to say they understand it. They don't understand it. They haven't been trained in it or anything else. So how can [Kleissler] legitimately claim that he knows what's best for the forest when he, Bill Belitskus, and the whole damn crew have no credibility in forestry management?"

Hedlund is not alone. Sue Swanson from the Allegheny Hardwood Utilization Group added her own voice to the substantial local chorus. "Part of the thing that frustrates me . . . is that people who have no expertise in forest management or any of those things are assuming it, and that we put them on the same level as people who have that expertise," she said.

Kleissler says those charges amount to a diversion perpetrated by people eager to talk about anything other than the issues at hand. "OK, I know I am not a scientist," he said. "I am not trying to be a scientist. It's all about credibility."

Activist Bill Belitskus agrees. "I'm not a consulting forester?" he said in response to complaints that he has no professional credentials. "Yeah, that's right. But I'm not dumb."

Environmentalists claim that they do not need PhDs in forestry to prove that the Allegheny's reliance on even-aged management is an ecological disaster. There is no question that many of the management techniques used to perpetuate the current crop of Allegheny hardwoods can impact the forest. But activists have moved beyond arguing that the Forest Service undertakes these efforts because federal foresters fail to understand good science. To them, the Allegheny's current management plan suffers from greed and political corruption. Any perusal of literature prepared by the Allegheny Defense Project yields a steady dose of that opinion, but a press release issued on May 21, 2001, captures it nicely. Prepared to highlight the filing of a landmark lawsuit, it details the activists' vision of malfeasance:

> "The Forest Service is attempting to manage our public national forest as a black cherry tree farm for the benefit of private timber interests," said Jim Kleissler, Forest Watch Director for the Allegheny Defense Project. . . .
>
> The primary complaint brought by the groups is that the Forest Service, through the East Side sale, is using clearcutting in order to maximize the greatest dollar return. The groups contend that through clearcutting, herbicide spraying and fertilizer application, the Forest Service is attempting to unnaturally propagate the high-value black cherry tree at the expense of other uses of the forest such as wildlife, recreation and watershed protection.
>
> Absent extraordinary measures, such as clearcutting, followed by fertilization and the construction of hundreds of miles of fencing, extensive herbicide use and thinning to eliminate hardier species of trees, most of the forested areas of Northwestern Pennsylvania would eventually revert to a native tree species mix such as American beech and Eastern hemlock," explained Tom Buchele, attorney for the conservation organizations.

Activist Kirk Johnson wrote an article titled "Profits over Ecology" for the ADP newsletter at about the same time—just a few months before splitting with Kleissler to form his own organization focusing on wilderness instead of zero cut. In it, he argued that "the Forest Service, by intensively clearcutting for black cherry, is consciously creating a profoundly disturbed wasteland which the black cherry weed is wont to colonize."

The dispute over clear-cutting is, technically, a misnomer. The Forest Service manages most of the Allegheny as an "even-aged forest" through prescriptions such as shelterwood cuts. Instead of clear-cutting, loggers enter a stand and remove enough trees to put light on the forest floor. A few years later, after enough seedlings have taken hold, they go in again to remove the rest of the mature trees—minus a few that they leave for seeding and wildlife purposes. Furious activists point out that loggers are cutting down most if not all of the trees; it just takes them a bit longer to do it. In that view, "even-aged management" is just a kinder, gentler name for clear-cutting.

Forest Service officials point out that they did not invent the even-aged forest. Timber companies made that decision for them by basically mowing the entire Allegheny Plateau in the railroad-logging era. The Allegheny is an even-aged forest today largely because its 513,000 acres started recovering from that experience at roughly the same time. "A lot of it has to do with what we inherited, if you will," forest supervisor Kevin Elliott said. "The hillsides, the condition, the age, the structure and the composition of the hillsides, we inherited."

Kleissler agrees that the denuded landscape was an even-aged forest upon the Allegheny's creation, but that is not the problem he is trying to address. He charges that the Forest Service has abandoned responsible environmental stewardship by *maintaining* the forest's unstable even-aged condition through intensive management. Forest Service officials counter that even-aged management not only supplies high-value timber to local industries, but also provides the best way—and maybe the only way—to move forward in a landscape already so heavily impacted by the hand of man. They are not alone.

Jim Finley has researched the forests of northwestern Pennsylvania extensively as a professor of forest resources at Penn State. He also conducts frequent workshops for private landowners through the university's cooperative extension program, toiling mightily to convince them that they should sacrifice short-term profit for long-term stability when managing their timber. In July 2003 I met him in a comfortable rustic cabin just outside of Ridgway, where he and his wife own 280 acres of timberland. They face many of the same dilemmas confronting the Forest Service on the Allegheny, and they have come to many of the same conclusions regarding even-aged management.

"Well, it's pretty high-impact, but it's the only alternative we've got if we're going to manage it," Finley said. "I feel really comfortable, and I guess I am saying this as a forester, I feel really comfortable that there is good management being done on whatever portion of that national forest that is being managed."

If we're going to manage it is the operative phrase. Activists argue that if left alone, it would revert to the forest of old, plus a few complications, such as the absence of the American chestnut. Finley is not so sure, and his concerns are not limited to areas of the forest that have been cut. He even has doubts that the four thousand acres of protected old growth in the Tionesta Natural Research and Scenic Areas can retain the pre-settlement attributes they have not lost already.

"Whether we want to blame it on whitetail deer or we want to blame it on acid precipitation, whatever events have happened have changed the nature of the forest," he said. "And those areas that were not harvested, the natural processes that took place in the understory of those forests aren't taking place the way they did. So can that forest replace itself? I don't think so. Just this summer they reported the occurrence of the hemlock woolly adelgid in Centre County. So how long is it going to be before that ends up moving to the Allegheny National Forest? When is the hemlock that you see in this forest, out this window, going to die? We already have the beech bark scale that's been here, what, thirty-five years? And it's killing beech like crazy. So is beech going to remain a component of that forest? It's going to remain a small component, but it's not going to look like some people perceive it ought to. So two of the dominant species that they often talk about—the hemlock and the beech—have become increasingly less likely to reestablish themselves. And so human-caused problems—because both of those things we brought to this continent—changed the character of that forest. Can we keep that old-growth there? I'm not sure. Can it replace itself? I don't think so."

Finley was equally concerned about the Hickory Creek Wilderness Area, approximately nine thousand previously cut acres already off-limits to management. Will nature turn it into something approximating the virgin landscape—or anything else worthwhile—now that the national forest has locked loggers out? "Being that kind of soothsayer of what it's going to look like two hundred years from now is going to be difficult," he mused. "But I can reflect back. Have you ever walked the power line behind the Kane Experimental Station? You know the one that's just full of ferns? That power line was put in, in 1923, I think. So it's eighty years old. And the dominant vegetation in there is what? Ferns. And I speculate that as these forests fall apart and those fern patches begin to develop, the ability of other things to invade those fern patches will become increasingly difficult. I can take you right past this façade of trees here, and I don't have to take you very far to get to a full canopy forest with a fern understory. We're not capable of capturing that vertical structure that should be here."

Activists are not calling for the whole Allegheny to be an unmanaged wilderness. Some proposals call for active restoration, including replanting, on some of the most afflicted areas. Finley doubts that even the most aggressive efforts could ever convert the Allegheny into what it was, however. "I don't think you could do it," he said. "You might be able to expand the hemlock. I don't think you're going to expand the beech."

One complication is the explosion of ferns that Finley mentioned. Light floods the forest floor when a dominant tree in the canopy falls over, whether it is due to wind, fire, or a chainsaw. That light brings the forest floor to life. Unfortunately, modern efforts to grow trees of any species on the Allegheny have run into difficulty. The ferns blossom into a lush green carpet which is strangely beautiful to the untrained eye, but they suck up so much light, water, and nutrients—and grow so quickly—that trees saplings never stand a chance. In some areas, like the old power line near Kane, the ferns have hampered regeneration for eight decades.

Jim Finley hates ferns. But if were to make a list of threats to forest regeneration, they would register a notch or two below the creature I once heard him refer to as the "eastern mountain maggot": the white-tailed deer. He made the reference tongue in cheek—Finley has a profound respect for the whitetail's vital role in the Allegheny ecosystem—but it illustrates how seriously foresters view the ubiquitous animal's impact.

Researchers estimate that the deer population on what is now the Allegheny National Forest stood at approximately 10 to 15 per square mile in pre-settlement times. That fell to almost zero by 1895, a downfall that led to substantial reintroduction efforts. The era's massive clear-cutting provided abundant food for the new deer. The extirpation of predators such as wolves and cougars gave them free rein while hunters pressured legislators to enact laws to increase the population.

It worked. By 1938, there were approximately 42 deer per square mile on the Allegheny.[2] The number has fluctuated since then, but recent estimates put the number close to 30 per square mile—at least twice as many deer as the pre-settlement forest contained. That helps explain why there is no understory in the second-growth forest at Chestnut Ridge, nor in the old growth in the Tionesta Natural Research and Scenic Areas: The deer ate it.

If the Allegheny is turning into a black-cherry tree farm, the deer are also at least partly to blame. Deer will browse on a whole host of plants before turning to black cherry. Ferns are one of the few plants they like even less. So what is growing on the Allegheny? Black cherry and ferns—not to mention other less tasty species such as the black birch, a tree that neither loggers nor zero-cut activists admire.

So how should responsible foresters respond? Researchers conducted a ten-year study and discovered that fenced areas with low deer densities tended to develop more diverse understories. That is, trees such as hemlock and beech, species that activists want to promote, had a chance to grow unmolested. Fenced areas with high deer densities, on the other hand, tended toward the "black cherry tree farm" that activists despise. They concede that the deer pose a problem, but the zero-cut crowd argues that the Forest Service is overplaying it to divert attention away from other serious issues, such as soil compaction caused by logging and acid rain. The Earth Liberation Front was so frustrated that its adherents burned down the Forest Service research lab in Irvine, where much of the most current research was conducted. Deer are not the only complicating factor on the Allegheny, to be sure, but all the Molotov cocktails in the world cannot overcome a simple fact: When foresters put up a fence to keep the deer out, the land inside it develops an understory. The land outside the fence—with the same soil problems and the same acid rain—does not.

Timber supporters say that turns the familiar environmental discussion about old growth and logging upside down. The Allegheny is not the Pacific Northwest, where activists successfully argued that the last of America's virgin forests and the animals living in them needed to be saved from industrial exploitation. Turn off the chainsaws on the Allegheny, they say, and you will end up with something that is not much better than the brush heap that the Forest Service encountered in 1923. Managing it—cutting the timber, fencing it for a while to keep the deer at bay, and spraying herbicides to kill the ferns—is the only way to make sure that there is a forest for future generations to enjoy. That is a simplified version of a complex point of view, but it serves as a base for people who think that logging in at least some form is in the best interest of the Allegheny National Forest.

Zero-cut activists at the Allegheny Defense Project view it as so much corporate doublespeak. Yes, the deer are a problem. Why, then, does the Forest Service use even-aged management to promote whitetail habitat? The Final Environmental Impact Statement for the Allegheny's 1986 management plan says as much:

> The long-term, forest-wide effect of even-aged silviculture on vegetative patterns is to create horizontal diversity, which results from differences in vegetation between stands. . . . Different wildlife species benefit from the habitat types available at different times during the growth cycle of trees. For example, the regenerating stage, which is present from 1 to 10 years following final harvest cutting, benefits the white-tailed deer.[3]

In layman's terms, cutting big trees leads to young trees that deer can eat. That, in turn, leads to more deer. "[T]he Forest Service acknowledged that . . . heavy deer browsing is the key factor responsible for the escalating difficulties and failures in forest regeneration," Jim Kleissler wrote in the ADP's autumn 2002 newsletter. "Yet the Forest Service continues to apply essentially the same even-aged timber management practices that were, at the turn of the century, and continue to be, the major cause of deer overpopulation."

Whether the Forest Service's reliance on even-aged management is "the major cause of deer over-population" is open to debate. Federal authorities do not regulate hunting in Pennsylvania. The Pennsylvania Game Commission does and only recently began a systematic effort to decrease the number of deer. That was a highly contentious maneuver. Pennsylvania consistently sells more hunting licenses than almost any other state, and the people who hunt constitute a powerful political force. Many of them are accustomed to seeing a lot of deer, and they immediately cry foul when they catch wind of any proposal to change that. Quite a few of the older hunters I know in the Allegheny region remember hunting in the mid-1970s when the deer density on the national forest was estimated to be forty-five per square mile. It has decreased by a third since then. Try telling them that there are too many deer.

Is the Forest Service acting irresponsibly when it creates habitat on the Allegheny for those users? Should officials convert the Allegheny to an old-growth enclave and presumably starve the herd to bring numbers down? Is that even possible, given the fact that private and state owners with huge tracts in and around the national forest would still be using even-aged management? How would a zero-cut Forest Service proceed if those deer hampered proposed restoration efforts? Those are just a few of the complications involved in the Allegheny deer issue, and they all point to the difficulty in relying on "good science" to resolve environmental disputes. The science cannot be separated from the cultural, economic, and political worlds in which it operates.

The Forest Service used what it called "the best available science" to create the Allegheny's 1986 management plan that established the allowable annual sales quantity at more than 90 million board feet. That science was deemed obsolete by 1995 when the same agency published a report called "Analysis of Timber Harvest Program Capability" that adjusted the allowable sales quantity to 53.2 million board feet, a reduction of more than 40 percent. That is a pretty large error in scientific circles. Part of it was due to uncontrollable events such as droughts and insect infestation, but there were also miscalculations such as overestimating the acreage suited for commercial timber production.[4] Do those miscalculations indicate that the Forest Service cannot be trusted to steward the land responsibly? Or do the reduced timber goals prove that the agency is willing to adjust to new research as it develops? That depends whom you ask.

"The fact that the Allegheny National Forest dropped from 93 million board feet and said we have to readjust our rate, well, that was responsible science," according to Jim Finley. "You don't look at that and say, 'You don't know what in the hell you're doing.' You look at that and say, 'Hey, you looked at what you know, and things are not as you thought they were. And you're being prudent in adjusting it.' One of the things about science and about management is that it's not absolute."

Activists might be forgiven for being less sanguine. The Forest Service, once considered a paragon of bureaucratic efficiency, has taken a beating in recent years. Its accounting system for tracking timber sales, known as TSPIRS, has been a debacle.[5] That is, anyone asking how much the Forest Service makes or loses on its timber sales usually has a hard time getting an answer. More disturbing are charges that the Forest Service, either willfully or through ignorance, fails to manage its lands responsibly. In one instance, some of the agency's workers staged a revolt in the 1980s, forming the Association of Forest Service Employees for Environmental Ethics to change its outlook from within.[6]

The agency's travails have led to national concerns about its ability or willingness to make good decisions based on science, and that has filtered down to the Allegheny. Activist Bill Belitskus expressed frustration that people involved in managing the Allegheny seem to have such a cozy relationship with state and local officials. He noted that Susan Stout, head of the Forest Service research station that ELF activists burned down, was heavily involved in the Warren County League of Women Voters. As such, she coordinated the public presentation of a study that a Cornell University graduate student had conducted on the nature of the Allegheny debate. Belitskus is convinced that the Allegheny Defense Project did not get a fair hearing at that presentation. He is even more suspicious of Stout's relationship with Republican Congressman John Peterson, an avid timber supporter. "Her son got an appointment to a service academy by John Peterson," Belitskus fumed. "Everything is so interconnected."

He stopped short of charging a direct connection between Stout's research conclusions and the academy appointment, but it fascinated him enough that he mentioned it again at the federal courthouse in Pittsburgh when he directed a reporter from the *City Paper* to ask Stout about it.[7] So much for a debate about hard science.

Science certainly has a place, but calls to use it as the last and only arbiter in any environmental dispute are fundamentally misguided, anyway. Jim Kleissler can cite voluminous studies warning that the herbicides, clear-cutting, and other aspects of even-aged mangement are destroying the environment. Foresters who support logging weigh in with research arguing the exact opposite. If the Pacific Northwest is any guide, those disputes will continue long into the future. People are still arguing whether or not the northern spotted owl was ever really threatened in the first place.[8]

Jim Finley understands the complexities of western forests, but argues that, in the end, scientists studying them faced an easier task than foresters on the Allegheny. "It's been there for tens of thousands of years," he said of the last old-growth forest in the Pacific Northwest, "but it's a simpler forest. I could walk through this forest here and identify, just in dominant tree vegetation, twenty to twenty-five species. And if I walk through a stand on the Base of Mount Saint Helens, the side that didn't blow off, or Hurricane Ridge in the Olympic National Forest? Five species."

Old-growth forests also have a discernible if controversial history—one that scientists can try to study and compare with current conditions. Are the trees healthier than they used to be, or less so? Is the soil wetter or drier? Is the fauna more or less diverse? In fact, the ability to track that kind of data served as one of the primary reasons for saving the last of the virgin forests. Gauging their progress allows scientists to use them as an indicator for the health of the larger ecosystem, much in the same way that the spotted owl was seen as an indicator for the health of the old growth. In that view, ancient forests are a living, breathing canary in the coal mine of modern civilization.

The problem with making those determinations on the Allegheny is that, for a long time, northwestern Pennsylvania *was* the coal mine. And the tannery. And the lumberyard. The Allegheny is not what it was five hundred years ago. In fact, it is not even what it was last year. The second-growth forest is still maturing. And in some cases it is dying. Researchers on both ends of the environmental spectrum can make predictions, but forces such as acid rain and political machinations within the Pennsylvania Game Commission cloud the crystal ball. Yes, western old growth has felt the impact of pollution, fire, logging, and other encroachments, to be sure, but nothing on the scale that the Allegheny suffered in the fifty years prior to 1923. The lack of an established blueprint against which to gauge the forest's health makes it all the more difficult to manage. "I think one of the problems foresters have is, we've never seen this forest before," Finley said. "It's never happened before."

Making objective, scientific assessments about the Allegheny might be hard, but disturbing biological developments began to call for action by the late 1980s. Deer browsing had been hampering regeneration for decades; then a series of droughts and insect infestations started taking a toll in the crown structure across huge swaths of the Allegheny. The Forest Service responded by slashing the estimated amount of timber that it could sell off the Allegheny, but it also formulated a massive program of even-aged management to deal with the dying trees: Cut them down, fence the areas to keep the deer out, spray herbicides to kill the ferns, and fertilize when necessary.

The legality and scientific merit of that proposal is still tied up in court almost a decade later. Timber supporters naturally resent the economic disruption brought on by that delay, but there is also a great deal of angst over the issue of forest health. Many well-educated, well-meaning foresters believe that the Allegheny cannot survive without active management, which in their mind includes logging. They look at the deer research conducted by Susan Stout and others at the Northeastern Research Station. They look at forest's woefully inadequate understory. They look at the beech trees, which continue succumbing to infestation. They take all that into account and conclude that the forest—for better or worse—is simply too far gone to become a wilderness again.

Even Jim Kleissler admits that his vision for the Allegheny is problematic. "The main problem with our goals is that the ANF is too deteriorated," he said in a January 2003 interview. "I think that's the most legitimate critique of our plan."

Is there a scientifically proven way to manage the Allegheny that takes the Big Level's peculiar history into account? Timber supporters hoped that the answer might lie in "certification." Certification became an international buzzword in the early 1990s when environmental groups and timber interests began searching for a way to affix a stamp of approval on the very best forestry practices. In 1992, they established the Forest Stewardship Council to act as an independent, third-party auditor. Timber companies can petition the Germany-based FSC for certification. If granted, they can use it to market their products to ecoconscious consumers. In 1994, the Kane Hardwood Division of Collins Pine became the first company in Pennsylvania to pass the strict FSC audit. The Forest Service will not actively seek third-party certification, but it welcomes the process if initiated by outside forces.

The Allegheny Forest Alliance seized on the idea in 2001. Eager to prove that the controversial East Side project was based on good science, the organization began seeking "Green Tag" certification from the National Forestry Association—an American alternative to certification offered by the international Forest Stewardship Council. East Side received that certification in early 2003 after a long and costly process. Ecstatic timber supporters considered it an enormous victory over zero-cut activists who insist that any cutting on the national forest, no matter how limited, amounts to an environmental calamity. In fact, the audit found that one of the few problems with the East Side project was that the Forest Service was not implementing it because of activist litigation.

Case closed? Hardly. Activists pointed out that the National Forestry Association is an industry group and charged that its certification requirements are less strict than the Forest Stewardship Council's. They also questioned the purported "independence" of Ken Kane, the forester who conducted the audit. Kane works for Keith Horn, Inc., a prominent operation in the Allegheny region. He was also a member of the Kane School Board when he completed the certification process. He later became president of that board, an entity that happens to be member of the Allegheny Forest Alliance. As such, activists charged that he had a vested interest in maintaining the Allegheny timber program and the 25 percent payment that it contributes to local schools.

Ultimately, the certification process failed to provide an answer to questions about science. Concerns about independence and credibility will almost certainly doom any other efforts to do so in the future. What is the best way to manage the Allegheny? Is even-aged management destroying the landscape? Can it revert to pre-settlement conditions after 150 years of industrialization? If so, would that make it a better forest?

Kleissler has reached his own conclusions. In his mind, the Allegheny will never reach its full potential—ecological or economic—until the lure of the lucrative black cherry is removed from the mix. Maybe the forest will never look like it did when settlers arrived. Fine. He says that he is not trying to make that happen. Rather, he simply wants the Forest Service to stop cutting down trees, compacting soils, dirtying streams, and spraying toxins all over the landscape so a more natural ecosystem can take hold.

Kleissler is passionate in his convictions—so passionate, in fact, that some of the tactics he has used to convey them have rattled locals on the Allegheny. That comes as no surprise. He is an agent of change in a region married to its forestry heritage. He is challenging decades of carefully researched science, and in doing so, he is calling into question the integrity and wisdom of proud communities that have stewarded the Allegheny since the brush-heap era. That aggressive style of activism only adds to suspicions that he and his supporters intend to seize the Allegheny and ignore local economic concerns no matter what the science says.

The fact that a few activists are starting to agree with that assessment might be the zero-cut movement's Achilles heel—on the Allegheny and beyond.

NOTES

1. Aldo Leopold, *A Sand County Almanac* (1949; reprint, with a preface by Carolyn Clugston Leopold and Luna B. Leopold, New York: Ballantine Books, 1970), 278.

2. There are numerous studies detailing the impact that deer have on the Allegheny's ecosystem. They include: John P. Butt, "Deer and Trees on the Allegheny," *Journal of Forestry* 82, no. 8: 468–471; Stephen B. Horsley, Susan L. Stout, and David DeCalesta, "White-tailed deer impact on the vegetative dynamics of a northern hardwood forest," *Ecological Applications* 13, no. 1 (2003): 98–118; Jim Redding, "History of deer population trends and forest cutting on the Allegheny National Forest" (Warren, Pa.: United States Forest Service Northeastern Forest Experiment Station, General Technical Report NE-197), presented at the 10th Central Hardwood Forest Conference, Morgantown, W. Va., March 5–8, 1995.

3. United States Department of Agriculture, "Final Environmental Impact Statement: Land and Resource Management Plan Allegheny National Forest (Warren, Pa.: United States Forest Service, 1986), section 4, 22.

4. United States Department of Agriculture, "Analysis of Timber Harvest Program Capability: 1995 through 2005" (Warren, Pa.: United States Forest Service, 1995).

5. Linda M. Calbom, "Financial Management: Annual Costs of Forest Service's Timber Sales Program Are Not Determinable" (Washington, D.C.: Government Accounting Office, GAO-01-1101R Forest Service Timber Costs), September 21, 2001.

6. Paul W. Hirt, *A Conspiracy of Optimism: Management of the National Forests since World War Two* (Lincoln: University of Nebraska Press, 1994), xv, 315.

7. I have met Stout's son. It seems to me that he would make a fine officer. He is bright, ambitious, and well spoken. More importantly, he is putting those attributes to use as a journalism student at Northwestern University. He says he neither sought nor received an appointment to the Naval Academy. He was a congressional page, but it seems a stretch to think that would call his mother's professional integrity into question. Charges like that one are not limited to activists, of course. Accusations regarding Jim Kleissler's alleged pagan and communist aspirations strike a similar note. Neither have anything to do with the actual research guiding management on the Allegheny, but they quickly overtake the debate.

8. Patrick Moore, *Green Spirit* (Vancouver, B.C.: Greenspirit Enterprises, Ltd., 2000), 41–43; Gregg Eastbrook, "The Birds," *The New Republic,* March 28, 1994, 22.

Chapter Six

Take It to the Streets: Radical Activists Battle Pre-Teen Satirists for Control

> Just because the preservationists have a culture different than ours doesn't mean they should come up here and interfere with ours. They appear to want to come up here and see the trees and not allow us to live our lives as we wish and our ancestors before us lived. They want to ruin our way of life then go back to their own way of life until the next weekend. We're supposed to sacrifice our way of life to give them pleasure?
>
> —Letter to the Editor, *Warren Times Observer*, October 7, 2002

On June 20, 1998, *The Washington Post* ran an article featuring a six-day "direct action" workshop conducted by, among others, the Ruckus Society. A Montana-based organization that promotes civil disobedience, Ruckus schooled more than a hundred activists in the fine arts of banner painting, blockades, and sit-ins. "Washington, be warned," the *Post* advised. "Guerrilla boot camp has arrived in the suburbs."

And it eventually filtered down to rural Pennsylvania. Tucked away in the middle of the article is this nugget: "Jim Kleissler, a 26-year-old activist from Pennsylvania, came to prepare for his next round in the state's logging wars."

Kleissler makes no effort to hide his affinity for the "active" aspects of activism. "I have no problem with nonviolent civil disobedience," he told me. "I think it's noble. I thought it was noble when Martin Luther King did it. I still think it's a noble thing to try to do."

"We find that if we do street theater, one nice element is, it's empowering to the activists," he continued. "It's hard enough getting people to step out of their lives and care about the forest when they have bills to pay. . . . Students, even with classes, if it's not a little bit fun it becomes even harder to get people to step out of their life and volunteer."

75

That quest for empowerment infuriates many locals. People in the Allegheny region write letters to the editor. They go to public meetings. They run for the school board. They do not march through the streets and chain themselves together in government offices. People have been trying to paint Kleissler as an outsider ever since he arrived. That job gets a little easier every time collaborators decide to empower themselves with a little street theater.

A protest at a chip mill Willamette built a few miles east of Kane in 1994 offers a powerful case in point. The facility processes trees into woodchips for the paper mill in Johnsonburg. A machine dumps logs into a debarking drum that is 90 feet long and 12 feet in diameter. From there, the logs zip though a powerful chip mill and emerge on the other end in enormous piles. The facility employs six full-time and two part-time workers. According to manager Norm Asel, the mill provides work for another eighty people who cut, skid, and haul the logs. He says it usually runs about twenty-five hours a week, never operating before 7:00 a.m. or after 4:30 p.m. At that rate, it consumes 200,000 tons of wood every year.

The controversy over the mill centered in part on the noise it makes. People who support the facility insist that it is barely audible from the road. People opposed to it say that the mill emits an earsplitting howl that will shake the coffee out of a cup a half-mile away. The truth is somewhere in between. You can definitely hear it from the end of the mill's long driveway, emitting a deep hum akin to a tractor-trailer running in the distance. Asel admits that it was worse when the facility opened. "So we did some testing, and we said, well, yeah, it's not over OSHA limits, but we decided to do something about it," he recalled. "We spent $350,000 to put a special building over the top of our drum."

That was not nearly good enough. Current ADP board president Bill Belitskus moved from Pittsburgh into his 25-acre woodlot in the early 1980s. It includes a modest home, a lovely garden, and a stand of relatively young timber that he is managing for wildlife and watershed values. All of that less than a mile from the chipper, which arrived more than a decade *after* Belitskus did.

Belitskus is still furious about the facility. In a July 2002 interview, he told me that the proper planning permits were never in place but construction moved ahead because industry clout carried the day. "It was a cover-up," he said. "All the people knew. [Local forester] Ed Kocjancic knew. [AHUG Director] Sue Swanson knew. We got snowed. The planning commission lied. The Hamlin Township supervisor lied."

It is impossible to fully understand the Allegheny debate without exploring the intriguing character that is Bill Belitskus. Trim but powerfully built, he stands over six feet tall. His full shock of snow white hair is matched by a similar beard and mustache. A Vietnam veteran who served in military intelligence, he also has a bachelor's degree in psychology and a masters in special education. But all those pursuits have taken a back seat to his passion: Belitskus is a full-time activist. He regularly attends meetings at the McKean County courthouse with a video camera in hand. He blasted commissioners for deciding to charge citizens for copies made on the county's machine. He once threatened to file a formal complaint against planning commissioners for starting a meeting at 5:28 instead of 5:30.

Many of his charges surround allegations of secret meetings. As a reporter for a local online newspaper called the *Mountain Laurel Review*, Belitskus berated the commissioners for deciding to raise the real-estate valuation rate without detailing their deliberations in full. The sprawling three-part series came complete with one subhead that screamed: "COMMISSIONERS ACT LIKE THUGS, CHANGING MEETING ROOMS WHEN IT SUITS THEM." More recently he charged that every cost-of-living pay raise the commissioners have received since 1979 was illegal. He filed an unsuccessful lawsuit demanding that they pay $1.2 million in restitution out of their personal accounts.

Residents are accustomed to Belitskus's litigious ways, but they took notice when he turned his critical eye on Willamette's chipper in 1998. Claiming that the noise had reduced the value of his home by a third, he started an all-out campaign against the corporation. He and a neighbor who lives even closer to the facility erected handmade protest signs in full view of traffic along Route 6. The fight was on, adding fuel to a fire that had been flickering on and off for several years.

The ADP's zero-cut agenda took hold in 1996. The group and its Indiana-based allies at Heartwood filed their first lawsuit against a national forest management project in June 1997. A judge ruled in the activists' favor in October, forcing the Forest Service to withdraw seventeen already-awarded logging contracts totaling $10.7 million.[1] Even before that ruling, activists issued a Notice of Intent to File Suit against other projects in July 1997. It involved efforts to protect the Indiana bat, an endangered species with a possible presence in the area. A judge eventually rejected the suit on procedural grounds, but things were just getting started.

The first organized "direct action" aimed at the Allegheny National Forest hit on May 20, 1998. Four activists in their late teens and early twenties, all of them from either New York or New Jersey, forced their way into the Allegheny supervisor's office in Warren. They chained themselves together and refused to budge until local police arrested them. A dozen or so supporters picketed the street in front of the building. The four arrested activists claimed allegiance to a group that people in the area associated with a whole different world—Earth First! Three months later a researcher managed to trap an Indiana bat in the forest. Kleissler and his colleagues at Heartwood immediately reiterated their intent to file a lawsuit under the Endangered Species Act, and everyone in the timber industry knew that things were going to get bad. That's when the chipper took center stage.

Before dawn on October 20, 1998, Oberlin college student Josh Raisler Cohn charged the front gate of the chipper property along with Shannon Hughes, a senior at the Indiana University of Pennsylvania. They erected a 30-foot-tall tripod, which Raisler Cohn climbed and occupied for six hours. Hughes attached herself to the front leg of the stand with a lock around her neck. Earth First! issued a press release that morning, happily reporting that "It's hardly business as usual at Keystone Chipping, a Willamette Industries wood chip mill located near Kane, Pennsylvania."

They were right about that. The two activists, along with a small cadre of supporters, were blocking the only access road to the mill. Mill manager Norm Asel remembers it vividly. "There were quite a few loggers here that morning and we had to corral them," he said. "Things could have gotten ugly real quick."

The police eventually showed up and carted the two activists away after a brief standoff. It was an enormous victory, according to the environmentalists. The December issue of *Threshold*, the "Movement Magazine of the Student Environmental Action Coalition," put the action on its front cover. The story detailed the eight log trucks and police cruisers backed up at the protest site. It also noted that the loggers and mill employees were furious: "Their attitude was pretty clear from the start when, within a few minutes of the commencement of the protest, one enraged trucker began threatening videographers with a crowbar."

The article also clarified the activists' attitude toward local concerns:

> Confrontations are expected to increase as Earth First!ers, SEACers, and other activists continue to pursue their agenda in spite of some local resistance. . . . The level of tension and antagonism between people opposed to logging in the Allegheny region and those in support of it is extremely high. Many residents perceive that their economy will take a big hit without logging on public lands. But the activists from the Student Environmental Action Coalition, the Native Forest Network, and Allegheny Earth First! had a decidedly zero-cut agenda in mind.

None of the press surrounding the protest mentioned the Allegheny Defense Project by name. Bill Belitskus says that is because it was not an ADP action. The group did not officially plan or sanction the event, so he is technically correct. However, Raisler Cohn had been an active ADP supporter for years. He even lived with Kleissler for a short time. The *Threshold* article listed Jim Kleissler as a contact for more information. The Earth First! press release directed interested parties to call ADP cofounder Susan Curry.

Maybe the activists felt empowered, but it is hard to see what the protest accomplished apart from that. It does appear to have solidified Belitskus's position as town pariah. Asel won't talk to him anymore. When I ask people around Kane about the incident, they tend to get personal. "That chipper only runs from eight till four," one guy said. "If Bill Belitskus had a fucking job he wouldn't have to worry about the noise." Other people joke about how Belitskus, the zero-cut activist, heats his house with wood. Some launch into tirades about how his wife is paying the bills through her job as a local teacher while he works to slash Allegheny logging and, they argue, the school funding that comes with it.

Direct actions like the one at the chip mill have virtually eliminated any possibility that locals will accept the ADP as the grassroots, bottoms-up organization that Kleissler claims it to be. Sawmill owner Dave Kiehl says he went to witness the protest and found where the activists' supporters parked their cars. He noted license plates from Missouri, Indiana, and a few other states. The *Threshold* article proudly noted participants from Oregon and Montana. Jack Hedlund, director of the Allegheny Forest Alliance, has been arguing for years that the ADP consists of radical activists from outside the area. The chipper protest made a lot of other people see it that way, too.

"The common citizen doesn't see that as being appropriate," Hedlund said. "I mean, I wouldn't do it. I think if you went out and basically interviewed any number of people, you would find that, who knows what the percentage would be, but the vast percentage would say that, no, I wouldn't go out and chain myself, climb up a tree and live in it or chain myself to a fence or something like that. But therein lies the problem. Their ideas are so much in the minority in this region that they have to get press however they can. . . . It has to be sensational in order for them to get it. Just going to a meeting and speaking doesn't get them the sensational press that they feel that they need."

ADP activists certainly attend meetings and public forums, but even when they do, things often take a confrontational turn. Kleissler had scheduled a nature hike for the 2002 gathering in September but changed the agenda when the Forest Service announced plans for a public tour of the proposed Spring Creek Project for the same day. After a morning workshop in which Kleissler detailed what he considers a few of the Forest Service's most egregious offenses, about thirty activists hopped into cars, formed a convoy, and headed to Marienville.

Things quickly got off on the wrong foot. Forest Service officials were already discussing the tour route with a dozen attendees when Kleissler's group, which never bothered with the requested RSVP, burst onto the scene ten minutes late. The people already seated included a logger, a few people concerned about horse trails, some snowmobile enthusiasts, and Jack Hedlund. The contrast between the crowds was striking. Most of the people who came with Kleissler were college students. Several had bits and pieces of campsite detritus on their clothes. One of the kids had electric-blue hair.

Once the tour got under way, everyone hopped into cars and headed to the first site—a stand of red pine planted on the Allegheny decades earlier. Tour leaders pointed to the large number of trees blown over in recent windstorms and detailed how they hoped to address the problem. Bill Belitskus, sporting a baseball hat that detailed his enthusiasm for hemp products, was not satisfied with the presentation. He repeatedly tried to turn the discussion toward the East Side project, a separate management plan already in litigation. Forest Service spokesman Steve Miller informed Belitskus that the tour was going to focus on the Spring Creek proposal and that questions about larger forest issues could be better addressed at a different time. Belitskus growled that the Forest Service was avoiding those issues, angrily shook his head, and quipped, "Thanks for pointing out the forest, though, Steve."

The next stop was worse. A Forest Service employee described plans to decommission a short piece of road but maintain it as part of the Allegheny's snowmobile trail system. He seemed friendly to the conservationist cause, discussing how much damage a road can do to nearby streams. Belitskus slammed the proposal anyway, insisting that the proposed decommissioning would be insufficient because officials could easily reopen the road to cars. He demanded that the Forest Service consider a slew of alternatives and hire a landscape artist to depict how each would look once finished.

There was also a dispute about a recently implemented $35 permit fee charged to all-terrain vehicle riders. The Forest Service admits that ATVs can damage the environment, but officials consider riding a legitimate use that they have to accommodate. The permit system is supposed to help pay for enforcement, track how many people ride, and ensure that users stay on official trails. A Forest Service employee estimated that approximately four thousand had already been issued. Another noted that the Allegheny had collected approximately $90,000 from permit fees. Kleissler immediately smelled a rat. By his calculations, four thousand permits at $35 a pop would have generated only $12,500. The $90,000 figure led him to believe that there were far more ATVs operating on the Allegheny than the Forest Service would admit. His followers nodded their heads to show their shared concern. During the ride to the next stop I noted that four thousand times $35 is actually $125,000. Kleissler did a quick tally in his head and admitted the error. "I guess I spoke to soon," he said.

At another stop Belitskus confronted a young recreation specialist who was recounting her efforts to improve horse trails on the Allegheny. Belitskus grew tired of the discussion and accused her of establishing policies at a secret meeting in Sheffield. She explained that she had invited representatives from various user groups to meet with her so that they could understand their concerns before embarking on the official planning process, but Belitskus failed to appreciate her methods. "That's not the way to do it," he barked. "No more secret meetings on recreation, OK?"

At the last stop, a wildlife specialist and a forester stood in front of a large fenced enclosure and explained how even-aged management works: Loggers entered the stand in 1992 and removed enough trees to allow more light to hit the forest floor. They fenced the area to keep the deer out and let the remaining trees reseed the stand. In their eyes it was working. A thick understory crowded the enclosure. They said it was time to remove most of the remaining timber so the young trees could suck up more sunlight and become the Allegheny of tomorrow. "This is not a clearcut," the forester said. "We don't do that anymore."

Kleissler pounced. He argued that the harvesting technique—in this case a shelterwood cut—is clear-cutting with a kinder, gentler name. The forester countered that not all of the trees would be removed. He said that concerns over wildlife habitat—roosting trees for the Indiana bat, for instance—required foresters to leave a quarter acre of standing timber for every five acres harvested. He added that when cutting more than one acre, foresters concentrate the remnant trees in a single grove to provide a substantial patch of habitat. To top it all off, they leave it on the edge of the harvested area so the trees to do not fall victim to high winds. Kleissler listened to this explanation, thought for a moment, then made an interesting observation. "So what you're saying is, instead of a twenty-acre clearcut, we have an eighteen-acre clearcut."

Without hesitating, the forester replied, "No." The wildlife biologist responded, "Yes," at the same time. This was an embarrassing but illuminating gaffe. Kleissler was making some very strong points about the nature of even-aged management. This was the kind of open debate the tour was designed to encourage. Unfortunately, it didn't last long. The ADP contingent broke into open laughter when the two Forest Service employees gave conflicting answers. Kleissler kept hammering them about it. When he did not like the answers he was receiving, he basically called the forester a liar: "It just appears to me that you're being openly deceptive," he said.

At that point Jack Hedlund had enough. He tried to come to the rescue by repeatedly—and heatedly—interjecting a simple question: Do you take all the trees in a shelterwood cut? The answer was no. He asked it again, only differently: If you drive through here, there will be trees? The forester answered in the affirmative. Then one more time: So they won't all be stumps? The answer was no.

Hedlund's effort in turn drew fire from Belitskus. He approached Hedlund with a wide smile and loudly counseled, "Don't get too tense, Jack," as he passed. Some of the student activists tried to ask a few more questions after the exchange but nothing came of them. Eventually a Forest Service official ended the tour in understated fashion. "Obviously we don't see the world the same way," he said. "The Forest Service mission is meant to be a controversial mission."

Activists were still talking about the dual answer to Kleissler's clear-cutting question months later. Conversely, timber supporters continued chuckling over the notion that hyperactivist Bill Belitskus would consider telling anyone to avoid getting "too tense." The moment—potentially the most productive during an almost comically contentious four-hour presentation—had devolved into another series of glib talking points for both sides. Rather than an isolated incident, this sort of rhetoric has come to characterize even the most serious elements of the Allegheny crisis.

On September 5, 2002, the *Warren Times Observer* ran an article about local responses to the Earth Liberation Front's attack on the Irvine research lab. Congressman John Peterson, a vocal timber supporter whose district includes almost all of the Allegheny, offered his take on the root cause of eco-terror in the region: "The ADP has highlighted and attempted to stop all forestry on the national forest and in doing so they've made it a target for these more radical groups," he said. "Whether they endorse it or don't, their radical approach . . . is what attracts these other groups to try and stop good forestry research."

Kleissler was furious about the charge during an interview months later. "Obviously it pisses me off because, you know, it's an attack on our credibility, and that's all Peterson is ever about," he said.

Kleissler is exasperated by questions suggesting his involvement in the Irvine fire but indulges them as a necessary hazard of his profession. "It's so stupid," he said. "It's like, well, why would we? Why would people even think that we have? Because if you look at what we do, how stupid could we possibly be? What if we did do it and we got caught doing it? It would make all our other efforts go down the drain. It would be such a huge waste of our credibility. . . . You know, it all becomes about the tactics and not about the issue. I want to talk about the issue. That's what annoys me about John Peterson when he does his attacks."

Peterson did not dream up his comments in a vacuum, of course. Kleissler weighed in on the ELF attack in the same *Times Observer* article. "We condemn these kinds of activities, period," he said. "We're an organization committed to nonviolence. We condemn any kind of action that would destroy property, just as we condemn the Forest Service's destruction of our public property."

Critics were furious at Kleissler for attempting to equate well-meaning Forest Service professionals with violent eco-terrorists. They were even angrier about another quote in which he opined that timber supporters could have set the fire. Kleissler was still toying with that theory five months after the attack. He based it on the unprecedented threat of violence in the ELF's message to the newspaper. "That made me very suspicious," he said. "I am less paranoid than I used to be, but knowing a little bit of the history, especially what happened, I'm sure you're familiar with the stories of Judi Bari[2] and stuff like that out in California. . . . This is just personally, I suspect that, I suspected at the time, and I'm not sure entirely what to think now, that ELF had nothing to do with that fire. And that sentence is sort of what gives me that suspicion. It sort of suggests to me that someone is trying to pin it on the ELF and make ELF look more extreme than they really are."

Kleissler's theory is as close as anyone has come to making a direct accusation in the case. When asked if he thought Kleissler was involved in the firebombing, Jack Hedlund said, "No." I also asked if he thought Kleissler could do anything to prevent future attacks. "No," he said again. "If the FBI can't even find the jerk, the jerks that are doing it, what the heck can he do about it? There's nothing he can do about it. He can't expose them. He doesn't know who they are any more than I do."

That is where the agreement ends, however. Hedlund sees Kleissler's conspiracy theory as further proof of a radical agenda. "I view that as a result of ideological likeness," Hedlund said. "He's defending a position that in my estimation is indefensible. He's on the same side of the fence as ELF. Maybe not so far removed from the fence, but he's on the same side. So he's going to do what he can to, in essence, lighten or shed less light on what ELF has done. But you can't discount the fact that you have the [ELF] incidents in the Philadelphia area, you have SUVs in the [Erie] area being burnt, you have the construction equipment being burnt, then the lab being burnt. To say that someone is trying to pin it on ELF is, to me, ludicrous."

The Earth Liberation Front—or at least its anonymous press officer—agrees with Hedlund. I sent an e-mail to the ELF website in January 2003 seeking information about the Pennsylvania attacks. The shadowy organization issued an illuminating response to a question about whether the threat of violence indicated that a timber supporter was trying to frame the ELF:

> This is a concern that gets raised time and time again in the ELF because of it's [sic] unstructured nature—and in this case it was something we heard a lot. Of course

there is always the concern that law enforcement or the industry might construct a scenario in order to paint the ELF in a much worse light—but we have no evidence that they have ever done that. With the exception of this one communiqué, every single communication we have had from ELF cells since 1997 has always fallen within the guidelines for action. There have been no acts of violence or other non-ELF style actions claimed by supposed ELF cells (which we think would be consistent with an attack by law enforcement or industry).

In the case [of] the Allegheny fire, we believe it to be the work of an ELF cell who misjudged the direction they thought other cells would be willing to go. There is a chance that this communiqué was released as a way of "testing" the response in other cells, since the only way to garner that type of information is by releasing a publicized statement. ELF cells have no contact or knowledge of each other except what they read through the media, so this is the only way to see what the sentiment inside other cells might be. Again, this is just speculation—it's hard to know what exactly the reasoning was behind trying to force a shift inside the ELF by a single cell.

Regional outdoor columnist John Street lambasted Kleissler's conspiracy theory in the September 27, 2002, *Kane Republican*, labeling it the work of "sympathizers who attempted to explain away the incident as subterfuge." He lauded local citizens for "not stooping to the loutish behavior of their extremist adversaries."

Environmental activists argue the exact opposite. They see the Allegheny Defense Project as a peaceful organization that has fallen victim to radical tactics perpetrated by timber goons. Belitskus is particularly adamant about the allegations. He's quick to point out several smashed anti-chipper signs and a few more that had been torched on his neighbor's property. "These signs are going to stay up," Belitskus vowed. "Every time we put them up, the timber thugs tear them down."

Kleissler says the intimidation goes beyond vandalism. "We have gotten death threats in the past," he said, focusing on a series of incidents involving Josh Raisler Cohn, the activist arrested at the chipper in 1998. Raisler Cohn was already an accomplished protester at the time. The year before, he used a makeshift hammock to suspend himself from the roof of Oberlin's Mudd Library to protest live vivisection in the college's introductory neuroscience class. The action drew plenty of media attention around campus. Kleissler said Raisler Cohn got noticed in Pennsylvania, too, but by all the wrong people. "I don't know why they singled Josh out for harassment, but somebody singled Josh out for harassment," he said. "It was, ah, professional, I guess is the word I would use."

"He came out one weekend," Kleissler continued. "The first weekend he came out, he went out to Minister Creek and went camping. Anyway, he went camping, and when he got out of the woods the next morning, he came back to his car, and somebody had spray painted his car, 'Fuck off tree hugger.' Which was a really interesting greeting because he hadn't done anything."

Kleissler said Raisler Cohn was living with him when the second threat came. A female friend who was visiting her father in Maryland reportedly got in touch to say that someone had mailed her a picture of Raisler Cohn driving his car. Kleissler said the perpetrators had drawn crosshairs over the activist's head and scrawled, "Tell your friend to get the fuck out of our forest before he gets hurt." How did the anonymous goons know that the girl was Raisler Cohn's friend? How did they know she would be visiting her father? And how did they find the father's address? Kleissler thinks those questions point to a very sophisticated surveillance and intimidation campaign.

Raisler Cohn's hard luck reportedly continued once he got back to Oberlin. The summer 1999 issue of the ADP newsletter indicates that on May 19 of that year someone firebombed his van while it was parked behind his home. In a turn that environmentalists say yet again mirrors the mistreatment Judi Bari received in California, the FBI reportedly named Raisler Cohn the only suspect and grilled him accordingly. (An FBI agent at the Cleveland office refused to either confirm or deny that version of events.)

The "Lughnasadh 1999" issue of the *Earth First! Journal* took suspicions about the Ohio investigators one step further: "It is not known what individuals or organization(s) are behind this or other attacks. It is clear, however, that the persons involved are well-connected. There is reason to believe that the perpetrators are somehow connected to the authorities."

The authorities caught up with Raisler Cohn yet again in November 2000 when police arrested him in Georgia. He and a few thousand other activists conducted a mass trespass and banner hanging at Fort Benning, home to the School of the Americas. A federal magistrate sentenced Raisler Cohn to six months in prison for the incident.

Kleissler says that activists continually come up against ill-mannered timber thugs at public meetings. He is particularly frustrated by what he considers his opponents' juvenile tactics. Doug Carlson, for instance, a Forest County official who regularly blasts the ADP in a column that he writes for the *Forest Press*, insists on referring to the group as the "green crazies." Belitskus echoes Kleissler's complaint, especially regarding reaction to the Indiana bat. "Wipe your ass with a bat," he fumed. "You'll hear that up here. Well hey, grow up, man. It's the twenty-first century."

Kleissler and Belitskus are also furious about a bizarre confrontation that developed in 2000. They claim that the incident constituted a call to violence orchestrated by the Allegheny Hardwood Utilization Group. The alleged offense is notable largely for its ultimate source, however: a pen-wielding eighth grader named Billy.

AHUG is ostensibly an economic development organization dedicated to marketing the region's timber resources. It supports the Forest Service by intervening in lawsuits filed by the activists, but in the end, it was an essay contest that got Kleissler's goat. In early 2000, AHUG announced that it would award a $100 savings bond to the local eighth grader who could best answer the question, "What does forest stewardship mean to me and my community?" Congressman Peterson, a state senator, and a state representative cosponsored the contest.

AHUG later announced that the winning entrant was a *Star Wars* parody entitled "Leaf Wars." It chronicled the travails of a future Kane resident named Duke Sandhopper. Chagrined that anti-logging preservationists have destroyed the town's economic and ecological vigor, Sandhopper accepts the town's fate until the mysterious Kobi-Ron Denobi promises to teach him "the ways of the Forest." Here is how Billy described Sandhopper's climactic confrontation with Dark Vaper, the evil activist leader:

> Duke knew it was time to strike. He wheeled around the corner while turning on his lightsaw. Vaper immediately turned his on, too. As Duke swung his lightsaw, he heard Kobi-Ron's voice resonating through the forest saying, "Use the Forest, Duke." Duke fought Vaper very bravely while explaining to the preservationists what they had done to the people of Kane. In one decisive blow, Duke struck Vaper down. Immediately after Vaper died, the preservationists were freed from a trance. They felt a sudden guilt for what they had done.

An enraged Jim Kleissler sent an "action alert" to the Student Environmental Action Coalition's e-mail list on May 11, 2000. He charged that the contest only added to AHUG's "history of hate speech against critics of the federal timber sale program." He complained that AHUG had received $116,000 from the Pennsylvania Department of Agriculture between 1998 and 2000, and that "tax dollars should not be given to an organization to propagandize our children and then reward them for regurgitating their propaganda sprinkled with hate speech." Kleissler urged supporters to contact the state's taxpayer hotline to complain: "As we learned from Columbine High School, hate speech leads to violence."

Sue Swanson, AHUG's executive director, claims to be perplexed by that reaction. "Well, nobody was agitating for violence against anyone," she said. "This kid was just really creative in how he—and it was a parody. He wasn't from an industry family, but he knew that his friends' fathers were going out of business and that the school that he was going to was being challenged because of the loss of revenue. He was an Eagle Scout. He is an honor student. We were totally shocked that they would react in that way, to be honest. And it was—have we trained legions of little kids to go out and kill environmentalists? Absolutely not."

She sees Kleissler's reaction as a desperate attempt to draw attention away from the radical tactics he employs and the powerful forces that support him: The ADP has Heartwood, the Sierra Club, and a host of other national organizations in its corner. Groups such as the Ruckus Society have taught Kleissler how to blockade, lock down, and otherwise frustrate timber operations. And despite Kleissler's suggestions about a timber conspiracy, the Earth Liberation Front's own website indicates that the group has thrown its own destructive efforts into the mix. How can locals hope to resist such a unified environmental front? "You know, to say that someone is threatened by an eighth grade student is a stretch," Hedlund said. "That's a little different than the ELF. . . . We're talking about an eighth grader here."

What timber supporters do have is a receptive audience. Activists occasionally add to that advantage by conducting protests and other "big city" antics that some locals view with suspicion. Those fears erupted into a cautionary tale in 1998, one week after the blockade at the chipper shook Kane to its core.

Lieutenant Governor Mark Schweiker was in town to kiss some babies in an election-year blow-through. Loggers, truckers, and other concerned citizens seized the opportunity to make a political statement about surging environmental activism in the area. When Schweiker pulled into Kane, 57 log trucks, 250 timber-industry workers, and up to a thousand of their closest friends were there to greet him. They presented him with a petition highlighting their support for timber management on the Allegheny. "To stop this practice will not only place the forests in jeopardy, but thousands of people who are directly or indirectly associated with the timber industry WILL LOSE THERE [*sic*] JOBS," it read in part. "It will cause TOTAL DEVASTATION TO OUR ECONOMY!"

Schweiker stopped by the offices of the local *Kane Republican* and received a copy of the paper's annual timber edition. The paper was still in on the act the following day, proudly tossing objectivity to the wind with a lead news story that left no doubt about how editors viewed the Earth First! protest:

> Last week an organization from somewhere in Montana, likely led by the nose by local, miniscule self-interests, actually tried to stop that portion of our community from performing the responsible forest management practices they conduct on a daily basis. And have conducted for over 100 years with admirable results. Yesterday's "movement" of rubber, steel, wood and bodies was not necessarily a response

to either of those parties. It was, however, a statement to the Government of Pennsylvania.

People were fed up with "monkey-wrenching" activists. They were also fed up with Bill Belitskus. The same edition of the newspaper featured four letters to the editor deriding his efforts to close the chip mill, not to mention his congressional campaign as a Green Party candidate. It looked as if the protest at the chipper was poised to become the opening shot in the sort of timber war that had plagued the West Coast for years.

That anger is still there. It is probably even more pronounced, actually. The Allegheny's six-month bat-related shutdown was still a few months in the future when the Kane community raised its voice. The forest eventually reopened to timbering, but harvesting on the Allegheny has continued to falter. Loggers like Mike Miles and Fritz Kilhoffer have seen their worst years in the interim. Numerous mom-and-pop mills have either sold out or shut down. Given those aggravating developments, the fact that the Schweiker protest and the ELF firebombing have thus far been the exception rather than the rule on the Allegheny deserves closer attention.

Timber supporters might not want to admit it, but activists have shown some restraint. There is no evidence that anyone has ever spiked a tree on the Allegheny, and protestors have not blocked access to a business since the chipper protest. The loggers also deserve credit. They joined in the counter-protest after the chipper incident, but they have been quiet ever since. They have seen their colleagues go out of business. Some of them have lost their homes. Still, not one has reached out and popped an activist in the kisser at a public meeting.

The ELF attack on the Forest Service research lab in Irvine could conceivably shatter that uneasy peace. Jim Kleissler does not endorse eco-terror, but somebody does. There is no telling how local forces will react. Nothing has happened yet, but subsequent ELF attacks on several construction sites, a mink farm, and a car dealership near Erie have people talking.

Fritz Kilhoffer offered a good gauge of local sentiment when asked if he ever contemplated the ELF's violent threat, or if he feared that they might eventually aim their attacks at a sawmill or even his own equipment. "Myself, I'm not afraid they're going to do it," he replied. "If they do it, you just have to deal with it. It could happen, yeah. If that stuff happens and people don't get arrested or the law don't get involved, then I feel that you could have some big problems."

It remains to be seen whether those big problems will come to define the Allegheny crisis. A compromise between loggers and zero-cut activists certainly seems unlikely, but not everyone has thrown in the towel. Partisans on both sides of the debate have been exploring an intriguing middle ground on the Allegheny since 2001. Unfortunately, that middle ground can be a lonely place in the modern world of environmental conflict.

NOTES

1. United States Department of Agriculture, "Selected project litigation and effects of litigation costs to taxpayers," Warren, Pa.: United States Forest Service, n.d.

2. Judi Bari is a celebrated Earth First! activist who detailed her legal travails in a book called *Timber Wars.* In 1990, she and another activist were touring California to raise support for the cause when a bomb ripped their car apart, critically injuring both. Bari and her companion said that timber industry radicals planted the bomb, but local police and the FBI thought otherwise. They accused the two of knowingly transporting the bomb and attempted to press charges. A raucous twelve-year legal struggle ensued, pitting charges of eco-terrorism versus police misconduct and brutality. Bari died in 1997, but on June 11, 2002, a jury awarded her estate a multimillion-dollar settlement against the authorities.

Chapter Seven

Third Way or Third Rail? Zero Cut Meets Resistance from Within

It would be silliness to consider that because they are supposed to engage in timbering.

—U.S. Magistrate Judge Ila Jeanne Sensenich on May 8, 2003, responding to a lawyer who argued that the Forest Service should have considered zero cut in crafting the East Side project.

When Dave Anundson talks, people listen. His Sheffield business, Anundson and Associates, is one of the most successful forestry operations in the Allegheny region. He has managed private and corporate timberlands—including his own—for more than forty years. He organized a forest tour in May 2002 that served as my introduction to the Allegheny debate and provided eye-opening insights into the complex nature of the local activist community.

Anundson's profit-minded management techniques are anathema to activists, of course. He does not think much of the activists, either. An avid outdoorsman and lifelong area resident, he loves the woods and intends to protect them from what he views as a destructive and dishonest agenda. "Our forests are our Silicon Valley, our industry, our livelihood, a very important part of our national economy," Anundson wrote in a local paper. "Preservationists have been trying to deny you the benefits of this bonanza by any method including outright lies."[1]

The article includes his own prescription for ensuring forest diversity and economic health in the Allegheny region: "The chainsaw and the skidder will be the father of all this, uncontrolled in the past but used wisely now."

Within five minutes of arriving at Anundson's tour, I had shaken hands with Congressman John Peterson, ANF Supervisor Kevin Elliott, Bill Belitskus, and more than a dozen other interested parties. Belitskus was sitting with a strange fellow in his late teens or early twenties. The youngster had a head of straight, flat hair that ended at his shoulders in a modified bob. At ear level the color changed neatly from dark brown to bleached blond. He was wearing saggy pants that appeared to have originated in the Woodstock era, a vest of similar vintage, and a black Ramones T-shirt.

Anundson had certainly set the stage for a confrontation, but nothing prepared me for the plot twist that unfolded in the parking lot after lunch. Participants had to squeeze into a few vehicles because there was limited parking along the tour. Anundson took the lead and told me to ride in the company car bringing up the rear. I did a double take as the SUV emblazoned with the Anundson and Associates logo pulled up beside me: The activist with the two-toned hair was sitting comfortably in the driver's seat.

Meet Blair Anundson. The Allegheny College student is a devoted environmental and social activist. But that is only half the story. As Dave Anundson's son, he works summers for the family business answering phones, cruising timber, and marking trees. Blair's eclectic background has instilled him with conflicting thoughts about the Allegheny National Forest, especially the ADP's zero-cut agenda. He is not alone.

That became clear at the Allegheny Defense Project gathering in September 2002. I was scribbling a few notes when a blonde girl with a large German shepherd approached and offered her take on the whole situation. She was very excited about a series of environmental lectures she had recently attended at the University of Pittsburgh. She was struck by the rancor surrounding the issue and announced her view on zero cut before I had a chance to ask. "I really don't think it's the way to go," she said.

A while later the ADP faithful gathered around a campfire to sing songs, joke about President George W. Bush's intellectual prowess, and complain about timber companies. One of the young men—a thin, brown-haired Massachusetts native with a goatee and spaghetti-western cowboy hat—eventually started talking about the Allegheny Defense Project's efforts to stop clear-cutting, but his enthusiasm suddenly stopped short: "I don't support zero cut, though." He said his roommate, who was busy chatting up the ladies by the fire, shared that view. As he got close to the light I saw that his short, unkempt electric-blue hair framed a familiar face. It was Blair Anundson.

As a Sheffield native and the son of a prominent forester, Anundson supports the notion of a local grassroots base. In a rural area where outspoken activism and organized civil disobedience are only slightly more common than unicorns and leprechauns, he could be a powerful ally in the drive to capture hearts and minds. In fact, he should be Kleissler's Boy Wonder. And therein lies an interesting conundrum: Kleissler has been trying to generate local support for almost a decade, but somewhere along the line, he has managed to alienate an aspiring environmental superhero like Blair Anundson. There is dissension in the activist ranks, and that points to what might be the last, best hope for a compromise on the Allegheny.

Anundson agreed to an interview in February 2003. At the time, he was a junior at Allegheny College in Meadville, Pennsylvania. He was living in the Eco-House, a residential facility for a few of the school's most ardent activists. "It's going to be quite the list," he chuckled when asked to give a rundown of his activities. "I'm president of the Allegheny College chapter of the Green Party. I'm activism coordinator for our Students for Environmental Action group here on campus. . . . I'm an active member of our Amnesty International chapter and a new group on campus called Students Advocating for Reproductive Options. We're trying to expand the number of reproductive options on campus like emergency birth control, condoms, and stuff like that and fight against attempts to restrict abortion and access to abortion. I'm also loosely affiliated with the 9/11 Peace Initiative out of Erie, Pennsylvania. Some of the members there are also part of the Green Party chapter in Erie. I'm also loosely affiliated with the International A.N.S.W.E.R Coalition, which is an anti-war group."

Anundson would have been available earlier in the semester, but January was a busy month for him. First, he coordinated a bus trip to Washington, D.C., for a huge antiwar protest. Then he went to Port Alegre, Brazil, for the annual World Social Forum, an event structured as a counterbalance to the World Economic Forum in Switzerland. An Associated Press report from the conference described it as "100,000 activists venting against American-style capitalism."

Anundson's activism goes beyond the Allegheny Defense Project's official position on some issues. Kleissler, for instance, publicly denounced the Earth Liberation Front after radicals torched the Forest Service research lab in Irvine. Anundson agreed—to a point. "I don't agree with burning down the Forest Service Research Station at all," he said. "I think that was just stupid because, first of all, the Forest Service Research Station is trying to solve these problems. They are trying to learn things about the local environment."

On the other hand, Anundson gives America's most notorious eco-terror group more leeway than Kleissler ever has. "Well, this is where I'm going to get into trouble with a lot of people," he admitted. "I think that the ELF's actions really aren't that new. If you look at the Boston Tea Party, that's very similar to an ELF action, to me. There was property destruction in support of a cause where there were some serious injustices being done. I think in an area where you have a local population that opposes something, say the building of a ski resort, and big money comes in and influences the local government against public opinion and they build the ski resort anyway, I mean, what choice do you have, really? I think that sometimes those actions are appropriate."

Anundson sees no problem with spray painting SUVs, for instance, but added that he would never participate in that sort of vandalism. He also expressed reservations about how his comments about the ELF might be received when I talked to him a few months later. "I just get really fired up sometimes," he explained.

Anundson says he wants to change the system from within. His goals include law school and/or a leadership role at an activist group inside the Beltway, but first he plans to take a more hands-on approach. "It doesn't even have to be environmental," he said. "It could be like living-wage stuff, stuff like that. But right now I am actually thinking about going down to Florida . . . because there are a lot of environmental problems there. They're going to have global warming, in the Everglades, when the sea levels rise, and they already are. It's going to flood a good portion of the Everglades. And they're also having a problem there with manatees."

Anunsdon did not have such an ambitious environmental agenda when he was growing up in the Allegheny National Forest. "It's pretty much new-found for college," he said. "I mean, there isn't a whole lot of activism going on in Sheffield. . . . There's a lot of people who are active in local things. Local government and stuff. But in terms of any sort of progressive activism, there's not a whole lot of it. So I wasn't really exposed to any of it until I came here."

Still, Anundson's rural roots run deep. Unlike many of his fellow activists, he owns guns that have been passed down through his family. "I will say the one time I did have a lot of fun hunting was when I went out with my dad," he said. "He was going on an elk hunt out in Colorado. He was like, why don't you come out with me? That was pretty cool. I actually got an elk. I popped him from like three hundred yards. A big five by five."

Blair insists that his own activism rarely runs up against his father's conservatism. "Maybe to some extent, but not really," he said. "I mean, my dad is a really honest businessman and I think a lot of the stuff he does with sustainable forestry on private land is kind of light years ahead of what most people are doing. . . . There are a lot of clashes in, like, political beliefs, but we do get along on some things, too."

Blair is an activist, but he worries that the Allegheny Defense Project takes too many cues from the larger national environmental movement. "There's a difference between the Allegheny National Forest and a lot of the other national forests in the country, especially out West, in that a lot of the areas out West have never been touched by human industry before," he said.

"They've never been touched by the forest industry. There's still a lot of old-growth areas, even though they're quickly disappearing, unfortunately. And the thing with the Allegheny National Forest is, it was completely or almost completely cut over at the turn of the century."

"I think you have a different situation than a lot of areas out West," he continued, "and therefore you need a different tactic, different goals, a different style of activism. To some extent I don't know that the ADP is really changing their tactics. You know, they kind of use the same tactics that a lot of people are talking about using out West."

Anundson agrees with Kleissler on a lot of the nuts-and-bolts issues. He does not like clear-cutting, and he suspects that "even-aged management" is often a poorly disguised version of the same process. He thinks that it reduces biodiversity, especially when used extensively across the landscape. But he argues that Kleissler's zero-cut agenda reveals an inability to come to terms with local realities.

"I'm looking at it from an activist's standpoint," he said. "You have to look at the political situation in the area. And the political situation in the area, there's not a lot of environmental awareness. There's also a distrust of environmentalists, and liberals in general. It's a pretty conservative area. So, I think where the ADP makes their mistake is they come into an area like that, they expect to gain local support through preaching environmental ideals. . . . They're not only talking about zero cut, but also taking it from a completely environmental standpoint. I mean, they're great people. I love the people from the ADP. They're good people. I just think there's that divide there that separates them from the local community. So there's a lot of hostility."

Anundson fears that the group's zero-cut agenda dashes any hope of a compromise. "It's completely polarizing," he said. "The thing about that is, you take any future efforts at conservation or anything like that, they're going to be hampered by this because people are just going to see—some of them are losing their jobs, you know? McMillen Lumber Company just shut down in Tiona, which is probably like five hundred yards from my house. . . . I mean, people are losing their jobs and they see environmentalists as the root cause of losing their employment."

Anundson's qualms with the ADP go beyond the group's zero-cut agenda, however. He also has reservations about Kleissler's tactics. Anundson was at the ADP gathering the year Kleissler brought in a West Coast activist to talk about protecting California old growth through tree-sitting and other direct actions. Many locals would view such things as extremely radical, but Anundson was not taken aback. "It's not that I didn't agree with him," he said. "I just didn't agree that his tactics were necessarily appropriate here all the time."

That seems strange coming from Anundson, who rejects very few activist maneuvers out of hand. He has participated in most of them at one time or another. Naysayers might accuse him of holding back because of his family's stake in the local timber industry, but his father works on private land, not the Allegheny National Forest. Anundson says it is all about choosing the right weapon for the battle at hand. "As I started this activism thing I would sort of look at things through tactics," he explained. "It was almost like being a general, you know? You're basing your agenda on public opinion and, you know, ways you can develop public opinion on what you want to achieve."

Anundson questions the use of "street theater" like the protest at the Willamette chipper in Kane. "It can help you or it can hurt you depending on when you decide to do it in the context of your overarching campaign, which is very important," he said. "As an activist you have to have a campaign. You have to have goals. You have to have an agenda and an organized campaign to ensure that nothing just crops up. You can't just fly in there and just start tearing shit up, because then public opinion drops off the face of the planet and you get a lot of other problems."

He views the Allegheny Defense Project's numerous lawsuits in the same light. "You can take that too far," he said. "You know, when you don't make attempts to reach out to the local community and then you do all these lawsuits that people aren't going to like anyway, based on environmental ideals and stuff like that, you can really alienate people from your organization. I think to some extent the lawsuits are needed in some cases, and in some cases they aren't."

Anundson claims that even he and his associates have fallen victim to the ADP's indifference to public opinion. "Students for Environmental Action has tried to affiliate itself with ADP and tried to get them to help us do things on campus, and they really haven't been all that helpful, to be perfectly honest with you," he said.

"I don't think it's a personal thing," he continued. "I don't know if it's an organizational problem either. I honestly don't have any idea, because as an environmental group, if another environmental group, for them not to take advantage of that is kind of, to me, practically, a mistake. I mean, we wanted to have a couple of teach-ins. We wanted to do this. We wanted to do that. I even asked them for basic information from the Forest Service on increasing biodiversity and stuff like that, and they said, they told me, we'll give you these reports so you can maybe make something out of them, you know? And they never sent those either."

Anundson supports the ADP despite the standoffish tactics, but he has recently begun searching for a different way to operate. He thinks he has found it in the form of Newkirk L. Johnson and a relatively new organization called Friends of Allegheny Wilderness. "Kirk does stuff like heading out with Forest Service rangers to clear trails, et cetera," Anundson said. "The ADP does not do that. I think FAW is doing everything that ADP should be doing."

"It's just great," Anundson raved. "[Johnson] e-mailed me this huge list of volunteer opportunities where we could get involved with FAW. The only thing we've ever done with ADP has been the fall gathering. My roommate always jokes, you know, ADP is just a group that hangs out in the woods and sues the shit out of the Forest Service. Again, it's like we talked about this, we're like yeah, it keeps the Forest Service honest, but does it really get anywhere? The answer to us is like, no."

That is not an easy position to take. For a movement that professes to embrace free thinkers, the international environmental community takes a notoriously hard line on dissent. Earth First! demands loyalty in its motto: "No compromise in defense of Mother Earth." When lifelong activist and Greenpeace cofounder Patrick Moore walked away from the group after fifteen years in the trenches, former pals branded him an "eco-Judas." His decision to fight for a future that combines ecology with responsible timber harvesting prompted the Forest Action Network to declare that "Patrick Moore Is a Big Fat Liar." (You can still buy t-shirts to that effect online.) Danish statistician and Greenpeace activist Bjorn Lomborg suffered similarly for publishing *The Skeptical Environmentalist*, a book challenging the movement's more apocalyptic predictions.[2]

Efforts to compromise at the local level have also taken fire. In 1992, a group consisting of environmentalists, timber-industry leaders, and elected officials met in a Quincy, California, library to forge a middle ground in that state's contentious timber war. Activists across the country have used "the Quincy Library Group" as a slur against activists attempting to compromise ever since. The controversy migrated to Pennsylvania in early 1998 when the Heinz Foundation issued a grant to the Rocky Mountain Institute to explore a "consensus style" solution to the Allegheny's increasingly raucous environmental dispute. Bill Belitskus posted a warning on the Student Environmental Action Coalition's e-mail list after attending the first public meeting: "What better way to suppress those citizen generated 'fires' of resistance than to have Heinz hire the renowned Rocky Mountain Institute to give its 'green' stamp of approval to a U.S. Forest Service and timber-industry dominated, Quincy-consensus style, community-generated, economic development plan?" he gibed.

Attempts to find a middle ground did not end with RMI's efforts, however. One of the few that have gotten any traction leads to the Hickory Creek

Wilderness Area, 8,663 acres of congressionally designated wilderness in the Allegheny National Forest that is off-limits to logging, bicycles, roads, and all-terrain vehicles. An eleven-mile loop trail offers the only access to the interior of the reserve. Regulations are so strict that a Forest Service ranger uses hand tools instead of a chainsaw to clear broken limbs and fallen trees off the trail. Sometimes he lets them lie. It helps keep the mountain bikers out.

Kirk Johnson founded Friends of Allegheny Wilderness to push for more wilderness areas on the Allegheny. He wants to increase the set-asides from less than ten thousand acres to more than forty thousand. He promises to support intensive management and logging on other parts of the forest if his proposal goes through. Activists like Blair Anundson see it as a workable compromise, but its prospects are anything but clear.

Like Anundson, Johnson boasts local roots. He was born near Bradford, Pennsylvania, an industrial town on the northeastern extreme of the national forest. It often makes weather headlines, beating out northern outposts such as Fargo as the coldest spot in the lower forty-eight. Smokers recognize Bradford as the home of Zippo, which still manufactures its famous "wind-tested" lighters in town. The company is allied with W. R. Case and Sons Cutlery, which makes knives that are popular among hunters and collectors alike. Loyal customers insist that their lighters and knives come stamped "Bradford, PA." Combined, the two companies employ about a thousand workers. Bradford Forest, Inc., one of the biggest mills in the area, employs about two hundred.

But not everyone is staying put. Bradford was teeming with approximately eighteen thousand residents in the late 1800s, most of them there in wild pursuit of oil. There is still a refinery in Bradford that employs about two hundred,[3] but times are tough. The 2000 census listed Bradford's population at 9,175. That qualifies as a city by local standards, but it is a far cry from the boom years. Efforts to revitalize downtown businesses have met with mixed results. In 2000, Comedy Central's *The Daily Show* savaged Bradford in an extended feature on the town's new mascot, a dancing drop of oil known as Slick. ("The drop that won't stop until Bradford's on top.")

Kirk Johnson's family moved away from Bradford when he was a toddler and settled in Canandaigua, New York. They frequently returned to the Allegheny for hiking and cross-country skiing trips, however, on which Kirk first started questioning how the Forest Service conducts its timber sales. Kirk eventually enrolled at Wilkes College (now Wilkes University, in Pennsylvania), then Albion College in Michigan. In 1999, he earned his master's in environmental studies at Evergreen State College in Olympia, Washington. Despite his West Coast graduate work, Johnson continued to focus on the

Allegheny. His thesis was entitled, "A Sleeping Giant: Recreational and Ecological Potential on the Allegheny National Forest, Pennsylvania." His tenure
in Washington came in the wake of the epic environmental wars surrounding
the spotted owl, and that experience affected his outlook on the Allegheny's
potential.

Local timber supporters refer to activists as "green crazies" who have
migrated from their West Coast communes to destroy Pennsylvania's logging
communities. Kirk's M.A. from a school in Washington falls into line with
that notion, but he looks more like an accountant than a hippie. When I met
him he was wearing khaki shorts and a green-patterned golf shirt, and he had
neatly parted hair and a calm demeanor. Johnson's approach to environmental reform has not always matched his choirboy looks, however. Upon return-
ing to Pennsylvania, Johnson immediately went to work for the Allegheny
Defense Project and vigorously supported the group's aggressive zero-cut
agenda. In a post to an Internet e-mail list in July 2000, he complained bit-
terly about a Forest Service plan to harvest trees along the North Country
Trail. The Forest Service explained that the proposal would give hikers a fine
opportunity to witness good forest management in action. In the post, Johnson grumbled, "Not only is this idea patently inappropriate, it is a crock!"
The North Country Trail Association was calling for a fifteen-foot wooded
buffer along the trail, but Johnson wrote that he would not be satisfied until
that buffer extended a full mile on both sides. He argued that the Forest Service plan was a ploy to limit recreation so it would not supplant the timber
industry as the dominant political and economic force on the Allegheny.

Johnson directed even sharper rhetorical barbs at the Forest Service
through *The Hellbender*, "The Activist Journal of the Allegheny Defense
Project." In Vernal Issue 2001, Johnson levied the charge that "The Forest
Service, by intensively clearcutting for black cherry, is consciously creating
a profoundly disturbed wasteland." He even added a prescription for how the
Forest Service should proceed: "Black cherry trees should be allowed to die,
fall to the forest floor and decay—providing invaluable large woody debris
habitat for all manner of flora and fauna."

This logic infuriates locals. They angrily note that the Allegheny's black
cherry trees provide local loggers with jobs they have converted into "large
woody debris" called homes for "fauna" otherwise known as their children.
Apparently taking that criticism to heart, Johnson severed his ties with the
Allegheny Defense Project in May 2001, leaving zero cut behind. "I just
don't think it's very realistic," he told me. "It's kind of quixotic."

Johnson says that by abandoning zero cut and focusing on wilderness, he
can still talk about endangered species, watersheds, and wildflowers, but he
can do so without telling loggers that they are out of luck. "We look at taking

areas of the forest where they don't do any commercial logging and moving them into the National Wilderness Protection System," he said. "We're not taking any significant resources off the table."

Blair Anundson is not the only person convinced that Johnson's proposal amounts to an interesting middle ground. The *Warren Times Observer* and other papers in the region have repeatedly editorialized in favor of FAW's approach, but the highest-profile press has come in the *Pittsburgh Post-Gazette.* A story on August 13, 2001, allowed Johnson to distance himself from the Allegheny Defense Project: "It's not like the 'zero cut' proposal for federal forest timbering," he told the reporter. "I think a lot of different people could get behind more wilderness designation."

The *Post-Gazette* delivered an early Christmas present to Johnson when it published another story on December 24, 2001. It approvingly noted that Johnson's "low-key approach aims to build coalitions of support among the various recreational, commercial and industrial users of the forest." Three days later the paper endorsed the wilderness idea in an editorial headlined "Green vs. Green: A Sensible Path to Allegheny Forest Wilderness."

The Wilderness Act became law in 1964.[4] By the end of the twentieth century, Congress had transferred more than 105 million acres into the system. Johnson points out that more than 95 percent of that acreage is in Alaska and western portions of the lower forty-eight states. The national forest system is concentrated in those regions, but Johnson claims that the Allegheny is especially lacking. The forest's approximately nine thousand acres of designated wilderness make up less than 2 percent of the forest. That is far short of the 18 percent average that prevails across all national forests. Eastern national forests average 10 percent wilderness, five times more than the Allegheny's allotment.

Johnson's strategy involves presenting those numbers to local communities however he can. One of his first accomplishments as head of Friends of Allegheny Wilderness was establishing a historical marker near Tionesta, a tiny town on the southwestern border of the forest. The sign honors Howard Zahniser, a largely forgotten giant of the American conservation movement who was raised there. Historians credit him with writing the Wilderness Act and pushing it through Congress, although he died a few months before it became law. Johnson was instrumental in getting the state to place the marker and emceed the unveiling ceremony. Congressman Peterson, ANF Supervisor Kevin Elliott, a representative from Senator Arlen Specter's office, Zahniser's family, and a host of local citizens attended the event on August 13, 2001.

Johnson has been shaking hands and making speeches ever since. He puts a considerable amount of effort into organizing work parties and acting as an intermediary between hikers and the Forest Service. In September 2002, for instance, he helped federal officials plan events for Public Lands Day—the same day as the Allegheny Defense Project's annual gathering. Johnson was helping volunteers clean up a trail while Kleissler led his crew through the contentious Spring Creek tour (the one in which activists showed up late and Bill Belitskus charged that a federal recreation specialist was conducting secret meetings). Johnson calls that standard operating procedure for the ADP and one of the main reasons he split with the group. "I am not aware of a single congenial conversation the ADP had with the Forest Service the whole time I was there," he said. "It's all part of the shtick."

Johnson's dissatisfaction with the Allegheny Defense Project goes beyond differences in personality. He almost fell victim to activist ire when he decided to leave the group and focus on wilderness instead of zero cut. "They tried to sue me when I left," he said. "They tried to *sue* me."

Johnson says the dispute focused on a piece he wrote for an environmental quarterly called the *Natural Areas Journal*.[5] In it, Johnson laid out the case for converting the Tionesta Scenic Area, the Tionesta Research Natural Area, and surrounding land into a congressionally designated wilderness. It appeared in October 2001, approximately five months after he split with Kleissler. The article clearly mentions Johnson's former affiliation with the ADP, but a footnote lists Friends of Allegheny Wilderness as the organization to contact for more information. A note at the end of the article bolsters the FAW connection.

Kleissler charged that Johnson was using a plan conceived and funded by the ADP to promote a new splinter group. Kleissler never went through with the lawsuit, but the threat deepened the divide between the groups. He wrote an article for the Summer/Fall issue of ADP's *Hellbender Journal* claiming credit for the wilderness proposal: "Following up on an idea conceived by the Allegheny Defense Project (ADP) in 1996, Kirk Johnson wrote the paper and submitted it to the *Natural Areas Journal* last year while working for the ADP."

Johnson admits that he did substantial research for the article while working with Kleissler, but he says he was working on the wilderness issue long before joining forces with the Allegheny Defense Project. "If Jim Kleissler were a rooster he would probably take credit for the sun coming up," Johnson wrote in an e-mail. "See if you can find one mention of wilderness anywhere in ADP literature that predates when I started working there. It can't be done because they thought wilderness was 'beneath' zero cut. When I first started working there Jim thought you could force the Forest Service to designate wilderness. He had no idea that it took a federal law to designate wilderness, and when I pointed this out he disagreed with me! Now ADP would like to use wilderness to advance zero cut and to help them raise money."

Kleissler will not discuss the split on the record. He says he does not want to air "personnel issues," but stands by his claim that the proposal was already in the works when Johnson came to work for him. Johnson is more open about the dispute, in part because he has to do everything in his power to distance himself from his zero-cut past. He has struggled to separate himself from "street theater" and other aspects of the activist aesthetic that might make him look like an outsider. In fact, he says his refusal to adopt that party line hastened his departure from the Allegheny Defense Project. "It's kind of annoying," he said. "I call them the lifestyle police."

Johnson tries to bolster his case by arguing that his proposal might actually help defeat the zero-cut movement—and that it could have done so long ago. In 1975, Congress passed the Eastern Wilderness Areas Act,[6] which designated significant amounts of wilderness east of the Mississippi. It initially included about fifty thousand acres on the Allegheny, but those never made it into the final bill. "If that went through and we had 50,000 acres of wilderness since 1975, the vehement element of the ADP wouldn't have emerged like it has," Johnson said. "That might have been the beginning of it. It precipitated years later into the ADP element. If we do these wilderness designations, maybe as much as 30,000 to 40,000 acres of it, it has to water down the ADP's arguments. Maybe a few more people would roll their eyes and say, 'We just did this wilderness. Give it a break.'"

Kleissler does not sit idly by while his former colleague slams the Allegheny Defense Project, either. He told a reporter from the *Warren Times Observer* that Johnson's wilderness proposal—the same one Kleissler claims to have envisioned before Johnson was on board—does not go nearly far enough to protect the Allegheny: "It's certainly not enough if you want to talk about broad-scale conservation," he said.[7]

Many timber supporters—particularly a Forest County official named Doug Carlson—view that split as a sham. They insist that Johnson's more delicate approach is part of a devious divide-and-conquer strategy. That accusation highlights how difficult it will be for Johnson to sell his wilderness proposal to local concerns. "Kirk Johnson is the good cop," Carlson said. "Jim Kleissler is the bad cop. Whether or not they got together, it's the role they are playing."

Johnson vehemently denies that, but Kleissler offers an interesting counter-charge. "I don't care if this is confidential," he said. "I told Kirk this would happen, which is this. Let's say you put out a proposal for 50,000 acres of wilderness and we put out our Allegheny Wild proposal, which calls for forest reform. And the Forest Service and [the Allegheny Forest Alliance] are advocating that they do double logging. . . . So what do they do to look more environmentally friendly? They adopt the wilderness and try to disregard the remaining changes the forest needs to make. And that's our concern, is that it's a good cop, bad cop wedged against us, maybe unintentionally."

Or maybe not unintentionally. "I think Kirk is zero cut," Kleissler said. "But that's—I don't know that. I'm just saying. I think Doug [Carlson] is right about Kirk there, probably. But not about us. We pride ourselves on one simple thing, if nothing else, . . . that we have totally been open about what we stand for. You can't deny that we have said what we stand for. . . . We don't have a secret agenda. I guess that's one thing that I don't like about Kirk's approach, what I've seen from afar, is that I am kind of concerned about whether or not Kirk is trying to play sort of a waffling agenda, you know what I mean?"

Timber supporters do not need any convincing.

NOTES

1. Dave Anundson, "Consulting Forester Speaks Out about Preservationists." Unidentified publication located in Allegheny National Forest clip file at the Warren Public Library, Warren, Pa.

2. Bjorn Lomborg, *The Skeptical Environmentalist* (Cambridge University Press, 2001).

3. It is the oldest continuously operated refinery in the United States, according to press releases issued by ARG. See also www.amref.com/refinery/refhist.htm.

4. P.L. 88-577, 78 Stat. 890 (1964).

5. Newkirk L. Johnson, "A Proposal for Tionesta Wilderness Designation in the Allegheny National Forest, Pennsylvania, *Natural Areas Journal* 21 (2001): 338–345.

6. P.L. 93-622, 88 Stat. 2096 (1975).

7. Ben Snyder, "Wilderness Compromise Possible," *Warren Times Observer*, July 16, 2002.

Chapter Eight

The Anti-Activist: A Right-Wing Renaissance Man in the Land of Bulls, Bars, and "Dinors"

Once one does a little digging into the areas that are selected for wilderness designation, we find that the areas have little to do with what most of us consider wilderness. Oil and gas operations, scientific studies, and recreation occur in these areas at levels unacceptable for wilderness designation. More craziness. It knows no bounds, even to the point of crashing an airplane into a building full of people who have no idea what the "cause" is really about. Pathetic and crazy, all of them.

—Doug Carlson, in an editorial published in the
September 12, 2001, *Forest Press*

Forest County is a beautiful place—strange, but beautiful. It is the smallest of Pennsylvania's sixty-seven counties, at 428 square miles. The 2000 Census also revealed it to be the least populated, with just 4,946 residents—4,916 of whom were white. It has no one-light towns because there are no traffic lights in Forest County. Not a single one. There are no four-lane highways. There are no fast-food restaurants. What Forest County does have is forest, and lots of it. Approximately 119,000 acres of the 513,000-acre Allegheny National Forest are within the county's borders. According to Forest County Assessor Scott Henry, there were 1,925 permanent residences in the county compared to 6,070 "seasonal residences" in 2003. Hunters significantly outnumber locals on the first day of buck season.

It is certainly a destination for outdoorsmen of all stripes, but living in Forest County is getting harder all the time. It has been hit particularly hard by the region's economic slowdown. Annual unemployment stood at 8.2 percent in 1990, and things only got worse through the national economic explo-

sion of the following decade. By 2001, the last year prior to the recession that
ushered in the Bush era, the annual unemployment rate in Forest County
stood at 15.2 percent, compared to 4.7 percent for Pennsylvania as a whole.
Break out the numbers seasonally and things look even bleaker. The average
unemployment rate for January, February, and March 2003 was 20.2 percent.[1]

Forest County's geographic and economic isolation stands out, but so does
the quirky, independent culture it has spawned. In late summer 2002, my
cousin and I hopped into his car and maneuvered the devilish twists and turns
of Route 666. Our destination that evening was the Allegheny Mountain
Rodeo Championship at the Flying W Ranch in Kellettville. Why is there a
dude ranch in the mountains of northwestern Pennsylvania? When we saw a
flyer promising top-shelf bull riding, we dispensed with silly questions and
hit the road.

Situated on the crest of a steep hill and cleared to offer plenty of pasture,
the Flying W presented a passable facsimile of a typical Western ranch. The
parking lot was packed with hundreds of cars. The bar was full of drinkers
decked out in full rodeo regalia. Cowboy hats. Chaps. Budweiser. Marlboros.
Nobody seems to care about the unemployment rate when the bull riders
come to town.

After the rodeo, we decided to grab a nightcap down the road at Cougar
Bob's. The bar, also known as the Kellettville Tavern, is extremely popular
with hunters and motorcyclists. It sits along a snowmobile trail, so it gets
even more packed in the winter. The parking lot swells with high-powered
Polaris and Arctic Cat machines, and the inside hisses with the *swish-swish*
of expensive synthetic snowsuits. The establishment offers quality grub and
draws plenty of families and tourists, but if you weren't in the know you
might think twice before stopping. Inside, a bumper sticker behind the bar
equates the Pennsylvania Department of Environmental Protection with the
Gestapo. The pièce de resistance is a large picture off to the left that shows a
crowded scene from the very same barroom in 1985. In the middle of the
drunken tumult is a middle-aged man in a Cougar Bob's t-shirt sitting astride
an enormous white bull. Onlookers well within the range of the bull's horns
seem oblivious to the danger, whooping it up with beers raised high.

As interesting as the nightlife can be, Forest County does have other things
to offer. Tionesta, population six hundred, is large enough to serve as the
county seat. The main drag consists of two short blocks. A peculiar little res-
taurant called the All-American Dinor—people in Forest County spell diner
with an "o"—sits on a small side street. At the other end of the spectrum is
the sporting goods store. Instead of the cheap metal shelving, dim lights, and

refrigerated nightcrawlers that dominate other tackle shops in the region, the store offers high-end Orvis fly rods, glossy picture books about nature, and a line of leather bags that cost as much as $500. Forest County is a complex place, and nobody knows that better than Doug Carlson, the man environmentalists love to hate. Blind in one eye, he wears thick glasses to correct vision in the other. He was wearing jeans and a colorful golf shirt emblazoned with fishing lures when he sat for an interview in summer 2002. He grew up in northern Warren County in the 1960s, then spent eight years in Erie. "It was a miserable time," he said, recalling his urban interlude. "I wasn't going to church up there. I wasn't involved in any civic activities up there."

He made a living installing siding, selling directories door-to-door, and working retail. That changed after he moved to Forest County around 1980 to do land title research for the oil and gas industry. His catharsis came at a parade in Tionesta. "It was my third year sitting on the curb there. I realized I was sitting in America, and it was all right to wave the flag and feel good about being an American. I determined I had done nothing for my country."

Today, Carlson is Forest County's version of the Renaissance Man. His official title is Executive Director of the Forest County Conservation District and Planning Department. His office is on top of the county jail, next to the tiny courthouse. "My job encompasses an awful lot," he said. "I'm officially the recycling coordinator. I'm on the board of the Allegheny Forest Alliance, the Allegheny Hardwood Utilization Group. The Hunting and Fishing Museum of Pennsylvania, I served as chairman of that. I had done that about four years. I am the mayor of the Borough of Tionesta." He also serves as president of the local Lions Club and as a member of his church's board of trustees.

"It's what happens if you don't keep your mouth shut," he said with a grin.

Most people who know Carlson agree that silence is not one of his strong suits. Nobody enrages environmental activists more. Bill Belitskus, the outspoken Kane resident and ADP board member, said that Carlson is "a Red-baiting, McCarthy-era-spewing conservative." Rather than defending himself, upon hearing the accusation repeated, Carlson flashed a huge smile and excused himself from the room. He was back in a few seconds displaying a black baseball cap emblazoned with puffy white letters: "Member: Vast Right-Wing Conspiracy."

"I started going to church," Carslon said in a more serious tone. "Perhaps that confirms Mr. Belitskus's remarks about [my] right-wing attitude. I realized that God was more Republican than he was Democrat. At least he's conservative."

Religion is a common theme in the rhetoric Carlson aims at activists. "The culprits are those who would have us believe that only green radical activity and green spiritual philosophy will save the planet," he wrote in the Pennsylvania Landowners Association's winter 2000 newsletter. "The Green Jihad has many players, including our Mr. Gore, and for the most part, the players are bent on overturning basic Christian Theology. The New Age philosophies are full of pagan ideas and ideals and embrace the approach of a sense of sacredness of the Earth."

Carlson constantly refers to the activists as "the green crazies," or simply "the crazies." He let the phrase slip at a public meeting but added it to his permanent repertoire when he noticed how poorly they took the slight. During the interview he employed even less flattering terms: "It's our responsibility to maintain the sustainability of the forest. These dingleberries don't understand forest management."

The rhetoric went to another level in October 2001. John Street, a fine regional outdoors columnist, penned a piece about the Allegheny Defense Project's annual gathering. It accused the ADP of training its members to spike trees. His information reportedly came from a source who attended the event. Carlson immediately incorporated the information into a column he writes for a local weekly called the *Forest Press*. Unfortunately for the two scribes, ADP leaders vehemently denied the charges and threatened to sue. Jim Kleissler told Street that if tree-spiking instructions were in fact shared at the gathering—which he doubted—it was part of a sidebar conversation not officially endorsed by the group. Street published a retraction to that effect two weeks later and saved himself the hassle of litigation.

Carlson also published a correction, but he remains defiant. "My retraction was that I got my information from an article by Mr. Street," he said. "My retraction would have been—I guess they can look at it as a retraction. What would that mean? I may have mentioned tree spiking, and I didn't have any information on that. There was a mole who attended that event. Mr. Street, in order to protect the mole, retracted. . . . It was not a retraction in which I said I was sorry. I said I reported the information of another guy. It wasn't a retraction. I appreciate that they're grasping at straws, which I expected."

Carlson's deep loathing for activists comes in several guises. He expresses each with fervor and resolve. He is very well spoken, and his knowledge of the issues at hand approaches the encyclopedic. First, he rejects the notion that activists are trying to restore the forest to a condition that prevailed before European settlement. "What the crazies tell us is that they want to go back to the original forest," he said. "The hemlock-beech forest. From what I have come to understand, that forest existed from about 1550 to 1750. It has not existed for thousands of years."

Carlson believes that Native Americans had a much larger impact on the forest than previously imagined, and some experts agree. He is especially fond of an article in the March 2002 *Atlantic Monthly* arguing that currently accepted studies might substantially underestimate the number of pre-settlement natives. Carlson eagerly makes the case for western Pennsylvania. He says that "Paleoindians" settled in the area soon after the glaciers retreated, and points to evidence that these people hunted ungulates such as mastodon and woodland bison. "Woodland bison did not climb trees to eat," he said. "They ate grass."

He says natives—from these first tribes through the Seneca—made extensive use of fire to clear brush and otherwise manage the forest. In short, the woods were never "untouched," and any effort to restore them to that condition is madness. "We're not talking about the place being frigging wilderness like the crazies do," he said. "We're talking about an inhabited land."

So why did the first European settlers find so few Indians and such old trees when they finally penetrated the Allegheny highlands? Carlson theorizes that 85 percent of the natives had already died from smallpox and other European diseases. "I am strongly of the mind that once the influence of the Indians left, because they died, it did drift toward a climax forest," Carlson argued.

The facts underlying those theories are still hotly disputed. That came into focus when Bryan Black, a Kane native pursuing his Ph.D. at Penn State, gave a presentation at the Warren Public Library in December 2002. He was studying the role Seneca Indians played in creating their own environment, but he was only looking at a small window of time just prior to colonization. He concluded—as most others have before him—that Indians profoundly affected the landscape along the Allegheny River, but that impact decreased farther into the mountains.

Carlson attended the presentation and came prepared with a flurry of questions. He asked about pollen data, which can stretch back thousands of years. He suspects that studies will show that local forests were not primarily hemlock and beech until European diseases wiped out the natives. Black admitted that it is a possibility but said getting the data is difficult. The best pollen samples come from old lakes and bogs, both of which are few and far between on the Big Level. Carlson shot back with an impressive list of possible sites. A Forest Service employee on hand said that researchers have already taken samples from some of them but don't have the funding to do the analysis. Carlson politely suggested that the Forest Service find the money. And what if they do? People have a hard enough time agreeing on what is happening in the forest right now. The odds are nil that they will ever agree on what happened to it a hundred, a thousand, or ten thousand years ago—much less hash out a plan to apply that information to current management proposals.

Carlson poses sharp challenges to the activists' version of history, but he is even more incisive when he focuses on the Forest County of today. He clearly loves the place and the people who live there. He also has a powerful grasp of the culture that the juxtaposition of trees and people creates. "If there was a motto for Forest County, I think it would have to be what you saw on your report card when you were little: Doesn't play well with others," he mused. "Forest County has been on its own. The typical attitude is darned independent. We are forced to be self-reliant. Xenophobic comes to mind."

The sentiment is more pride than paranoia. The people don't have much, but they do love what is there. The culture is uniquely tied to the woods through hunting, trail riding, fishing, hiking, and logging. These people didn't just show up in these woods. Anyone as old as, say, sixty, grew up in a forest of very young trees and had a hand in creating one of the most valuable stands of hardwood in the world. They also brought the deer, bear, turkey, bald eagles, and other animals back. The woods are nice enough, in fact, that flat-landers drive all the way from Pittsburgh to buy $500 leather bags. Carlson appreciates the pride that comes along with that transformation as keenly as anyone.

Now a coalition of environmentalists is telling people that the forest is all wrong. These trees are the wrong trees. These animals are the wrong animals. Carlson feels the pain that those charges entail. "If we're doing such a bad job, why are they even fighting for it?" he fumed. "When the Feds bought it, locals called it the Allegheny Brush Heap. They're not satisfied with that."

In the end, locals like Carlson view the debate over the Allegheny as an assault on their history and very way of life—an assault that in his eyes justifies rhetorical adventures such as "green crazies." "What are they advocating?" Carlson asked. "Zero cut of trees. Not only no new roads in the ANF, get rid of the roads we have. No oil and gas activity. Less ATVs and recreation. More wilderness, which, in essence, prohibits people with disabilities, old people, and children. You tell me what they are advocating and how they should be painted."

There is also the sticky question about how local communities would survive in the zero-cut world that activists propose. "They are not going to be happy until we put on little Indian costumes and sell moccasins to these people who come in and meditate in the forest," Carlson growled. "A few of us will flip burgers. Or I guess they'll be veggie burgers. These recreation jobs they are talking about, every single one of them is at minimum wage."

Forest County suffered mightily when the Allegheny's 25 percent payment began to plummet along with the timber harvest. Townships like Howe and

Jenks were the worst hit, as almost all of the surface area belongs to the federal government. Not only were people out of work, the lucky ones who still had jobs had to bear a higher percentage of the tax burden. "This winter we had 22 percent unemployment," Carlson complained. "Where in the heck is the tax money going to come from?"

The Clinton administration tried to help by allowing similarly afflicted communities across the country to choose a fixed payment instead of the 25 percent deal. McKean, Elk, and Warren counties all refused the offer in 2000, arguing that taking the fixed payment failed to address the loss in timber jobs. Forest County, which is far more economically stressed than the other three, accepted the proposal. "We weren't convinced that the crazies weren't going to continue with the lawsuits," Carlson said. "We had to decide we couldn't sustain the hit. We needed to guarantee the income."

Carlson gets especially testy when discussing activist charges that the 25 percent system is a already form of welfare in which the federal government subsidizes the timber industry by growing trees. "Every timber sale is up for bid," he said. "The highest bidder gets the sale. The only benefit the feds provide is the money spent on roads. The benefit to society is those roads. That access. That forest fire control. [Companies] pay for the trees. It's not at cost. It's to the highest bidder. [The welfare accusation] ignores the benefit of the forest management plan that the timber sale is just a part of."

The charge that logging equals welfare is especially hard to swallow for locals in and around the Allegheny, where the timber program consistently operates in the black. Carlson suspects that the very success of the timber program is what drew activists to the area in the first place. "I think that's exactly what went on," he said. "Someone looked at a map and said there is only one national forest in the state. They started looking at it and said, 'Whoa, it's making money. We're going to have to make it more expensive to take the timber out.'"

Carlson characterizes the national environmental movement as a disease—a virus that its perpetrators knew would take unwary Pennsylvanians by surprise. "The only reason they [came to the Allegheny] is, we don't know how to combat this disease," Carlson said. "This disease came with thirty years of experience behind it. They have thirty years of experience in the environmental movement coming in from out West."

Carlson is angry that activists have brought that radical vision to Pennsylvania, where people have been practicing their own version of forest stewardship for eighty years. In his mind, the environmental movement's failure to appreciate that history—as evidenced by the Allegheny Defense Project's marriage to zero cut—amounts to the worst kind of arrogance. He is also convinced that Kirk Johnson's wilderness proposal is only more of the same.

"The horseshit about the philosophical differences?" Carlson mused when asked about the activist split. "Kirk is playing it up."

He is equally perturbed by news that Congressman John Peterson is considering the wilderness proposal as a potential middle ground. "All I want is a few acres and I'll leave you alone," Carlson said, mimicking a promise that Johnson has established as a centerpiece of his campaign. "Peterson really stepped in it thinking he's going to arrive at a compromise with the crazies. Come up for air, John."

Carlson captured the local take on the activist vision for managing the Allegheny—be it zero cut or wilderness—in a vituperative little nutshell. "This is my home," he said. "I'm not going to shit on the floor. It's kind of offensive that these people are coming in and telling us that's what we're doing."

Carlson is not alone. Many of his neighbors are equally angry about the economic hardships brought on by proposals to convert, restore, or otherwise save the Allegheny from the people who live there. Other developments in the county only exacerbate the sense of tension and fear, a reality on full display at a busy construction site where the only growth industry in Forest County is taking hold. The state recently decided to build a 2,032-bed prison on 205 acres on the outskirts of Marienville. It was scheduled to open in mid-2003 and employ approximately seven hundred. When officials started taking job applications in August 2002, they had to extend the open house to accommodate the five thousand would-be employees who came from near and far. The facility will join a large facility in the county that already houses juvenile offenders.

Make no mistake: The boom in the Forest County prison industry is largely about the jobs. The subtitle on a state press release detailing the project boasts, "Institution to emphasize public safety, bring economic benefits." It touched on security but quickly returned to the big issue: "It will also be an institution that will be a 'good neighbor' to this area—one that will provide significant long-term economic benefits for this region."[2]

It's not Microsoft, but people in Forest County will take what they can get. They might get more than they bargain for, of course. What effect will increased traffic have on roads? Where will the guards live? What will that do to property values? Where will the inmates' families stay when they come to visit? In short, do people really want a prison in their back yard? Apparently so. Every elected official from the region was vying for attention at the groundbreaking, trying to take credit for the legislative largesse.

In his glowing appraisal of the area, Carlson said that, "Forest County has been on its own. The typical attitude is darned independent. We are forced to be self-reliant." That comes through in the region's geographic isolation and its rugged beauty. It comes through in people who ride bulls into bars. It comes through in a savvy fishing-shop owner who realizes that tourists from Pittsburgh will snap up fancy gear no matter how much it costs. And it comes through in the pride that people feel when they talk about the role they played in transforming the "Allegheny Brush Heap" into the Allegheny National Forest. But exactly how self-reliant are citizens who eagerly scan the state budget for news about allocations for correctional facilities? Those who do have already gotten a harsh dose of reality. The prison is basically finished, but it is empty. The state has pushed the opening date back to at least fall 2004 because of budget shortfalls.[3]

Part of the anger that such uncertainty generates stems from the fear that, in the end, the "way of life" and economic vitality of the region will have very little to do with the final decision regarding the Allegheny National Forest. Carlson and his supporters saw what happened in the Pacific Northwest. The loggers wanted to keep cutting the old growth and claimed that a ban would wreck their communities. Whether or not that happened is an ongoing debate that reverberates throughout the Allegheny, and one that needs to be explored in full. More immediately, however, it is important to note that, for better or worse, the loggers in Washington and Oregon lost out to an owl. And they lost that battle in federal court—the same venue that has pummeled the Allegheny timber program in recent years.

The battle for judicial supremacy has yielded some of the nastiest political posturing of the whole Allegheny debate but surprisingly few definitive rulings. To this point, litigation involving the Allegheny has mirrored similar, more famous suits that defined the spotted owl crisis in the Pacific Northwest, but the Allegheny's unique place in American environmental and political history sets it apart in important ways—and again make it clear why resolving this new timber war will have such a far-reaching impact on the future of the American landscape.

NOTES

1. Numbers tabulated using the Pennsylvania Labor Market Information Database System, a service provided by the Pennsylvania Department of Labor and Industry.

2. Commonwealth of Pennsylvania, "Schweiker Administration Marks Start of Construction for New Correctional Facility in Forest County," press release issued by the Pennsylvania Department of Corrections, Harrisburg, Pa., January 25, 2002.

3. Chuck Hayes, "Opening of Prison More than Year Away," *Warren Times Observer*, August 8, 2003. The state formally dedicated the facility on September 29, 2004. It was set to start receiving prisoners by December 2004. For more information see www.cor.state.pa.us/forest/site/

Chapter Nine

Legal Eagles, Underdogs, and the Fish that (Almost) Ate Pittsburgh: Half Steps and Caveats in Federal Court

At issue is the U.S. Forest Service's management for black cherry in the Allegheny National Forest. Black cherry, according to the Allegheny Defense Project, is a naturally rare species with high commercial value. Once comprising less than one percent of the forest, black cherry now dominates 50 percent of the forest understory due to intensive management practices including clearcutting and herbicide spraying which eliminates naturally competitive species. The plaintiffs argued that other species important to wildlife, and valued for their ecological and aesthetic qualities, were being diminished in order to promote monocultures of the valuable cherry trees. The federal magistrate agreed.[1]

—*Warren Times Observer*, May 5, 2003

They do not have nearly enough money to carry on their fight. Local and national news media ignore their plight. Federal officials continually rig the system to defeat them. It is difficult to imagine how the underdogs in the struggle for control of the Allegheny National Forest survive in such a hostile environment. It is even harder to figure out who those underdogs are. Jim Kleissler insists that the timber industry's deep pockets and political power put the Allegheny Defense Project at a distinct disadvantage. Jack Hedlund from the Allegheny Forest Alliance scoffs at that notion, arguing that he cannot match Kleissler's support from national environmental groups and wealthy foundations.

Hedlund and Kleissler have a vested interest in casting themselves as underdogs, but the tremendous cultural, financial, and political firepower they have unleashed in federal court tells a different story. The bizarre catalog of muscular institutions rattled by the litigation includes the United States Forest Service, local timber companies, activist groups, the University of Pittsburgh School of Law, the Pennsylvania legislature, and one of America's most influential philanthropic juggernauts, one eventually and directly linked to presidential politics.

The upheavals came to a head in May 2001 when activists sued the Forest Service to stop a controversial management program known as the East Side project. Federal Magistrate Judge Ila Jeane Sensenich reviewed the case and issued a recommendation for the presiding judge in September 2002. It sided with the activists on almost every count. The Allegheny Defense Project greeted the news with an ecstatic press release:

> This opinion verifies that the U.S. Forest Service's use of clearcutting to perpetuate black cherry timber at the expense of wildlife, soils and old growth forest management is illegal," explained Jim Kleissler with the Allegheny Defense Project, the lead plaintiff in the case. "The magistrate agreed that the U.S. Forest Service has intentionally prioritized commercial logging over legal requirements that they manage the Allegheny National Forest for a broad range of issues including endangered species and biodiversity.[2]

The recommendation could have ended logging on the Allegheny for the foreseeable future. Dejected timber supporters began discussing a possible appeal as they settled in to await the presiding judge's ruling. They continued waiting until April 2003 when Sensenich rescinded her recommendation without explanation and summoned lawyers to District Court in Pittsburgh for another go at the case. Those proceedings began on May 8, 2003. Sensenich pointed to the immense amount of time she had spent exploring the complications involved in the suit and issued the one truly definitive statement to come out of the hearing: "This case is absolutely the most complex I have ever dealt with."

Anyone who has explored the lawsuit might sympathize with Sensenich's confusion. East Side served as her introduction to the Allegheny debate. The Earth Liberation Front torched the Forest Service research lab in Irvine less than a month before she issued her initial opinion. By that time, the Allegheny crisis had evolved into something more than a simple dispute between local loggers and their activist critics.

Filing an environmental lawsuit is an expensive proposition. The National Forest Management Act,[3] the National Environmental Policy Act,[4] and the Multiple Use–Sustained Yield Act[5] are only a few of the voluminous legislative efforts designed to protect America's federal forests. The United States Forest Service and other agencies tasked with managing public land create an even higher stack of documents to prove that they toe the line. Sifting through all those niceties requires time, which of course equals money.

So how do the activists do it? The Allegheny Defense Project has three paid employees, including Jim Kleissler. They rent an office in Clarion. They spend a good deal of money publishing newsletters and traveling extensively throughout the region. All that, and the annual budget has never topped $110,000. The activists boast an impressive grasp of environmental legislation, but they would have a hard time piecing together a complex suit like the one aimed at stopping East Side. That requires the kind of lawyer that the Allegheny Defense Project could never afford. The fact that they enjoy free representation only adds to suspicions that the zero-cut agenda is fueled by wealthy urban flatlanders who do not care a lick about rural America.

Based in Pittsburgh, the H. J. Heinz Company has been adding to its global ketchup empire since 1869, when most of the Allegheny's virgin hemlock remained intact. Howard Heinz died in 1941 and bequeathed a huge chunk of his estate to the philanthropic endowment that bears the family name. The late Vera I. Heinz added her own fortune to the mix in the 1980s, and the institutions became known collectively as Heinz Endowments. The Endowments' website speaks to their own influence: "Among the largest independent philanthropic organizations in the country, the Heinz Endowments approved over $70 million in grants to nonprofit organizations in 2002."[6]

Some of that influence began angling toward the Allegheny in the 1990s. United States Senator John Heinz (R), a dedicated free-market environmentalist who had a hand in setting aside the Allegheny's Hickory Creek Wilderness Area in 1984, died in a helicopter crash in 1991. Instead of seeking his vacant seat, his widow, Teresa Heinz, became chairwoman of the Endowments and began increasing their focus on environmental concerns—even before marrying Senator John Kerry (D-MA).

The Endowments' bankroll had swelled to an awesome $1.5 billion by 1998, which left plenty of money for a $2 million capital campaign gift to the University of Pittsburgh School of Law. Administrators used the largesse to establish a new facility called the Environmental Law Clinic. Opened in 2000, the clinic was engulfed in controversy within a year, in part because its director agreed to represent the Allegheny Defense Project for free. Republican State Senator Joseph Scarnati swooped in to defend the local timber industry from the University of Pittsburgh, an institution that receives about 20 percent of its funding from the state government. Forester Ed Kocjancic recalls the vicious melee that ensued. "When they filed an appeal and the University of Pittsburgh—the attorney—God, he took the case pro bono, which means it was free to the damn ADP," he said. "But they were getting paid by the state taxpayers. Scarnati went right after him. He damn near wrecked the damn law school."

"Law school and reality meet head-on in Legal Clinic," the University of Pittsburgh's promotional literature promises. And how. It was already quite clear where the law school was headed when the Heinz Endowments made the $2 million donation. Professor William V. Luneburg Jr., director of the university's environmental law program, represented the Allegheny Defense Project for free in its first four lawsuits against the Forest Service. Legislators from the Allegheny region threatened to sanction Pitt for that perceived transgression but never followed through. Undaunted, Luneburg served on the ADP's board of directors after stepping aside as the organization's attorney.

Then came the Heinz Endowments windfall. Flush with cash, Pitt went searching for someone to run the proposed clinic and found Tom Buchele, an Illinois attorney with an environmental worldview similar to Luneburg's. Buchele quickly raised eyebrows by signing on to represent the Allegheny Defense Project. He tweaked the system again by working with a citizens' group opposed to an expressway project in Pittsburgh. The din over his activities reached a crescendo in May 2001 when the ADP filed the East Side lawsuit. Buchele insisted that the action had nothing to do with the Environmental Law Clinic because he was representing the ADP on his own time, not as a Pitt official.

Congressman John Peterson cried foul, charging that the attorney was using the Environmental Law Clinic's address and phone number in documents related to the lawsuit. He wrote a letter to Buchele on May 29, 2001, complaining that the professor had promised not to represent anti-logging activists. Buchele balked at the allegations in an interview with Pitt's *University Times* on June 14, 2001:

> "That is simply not true, and I resent Mr. Peterson's accusations that I am a liar." Buchele also denied Peterson's allegation that he identified himself as a member of the Pitt law faculty in telephone calls related to the Allegheny National Forest litigation. "The calls in question were made prior to this lawsuit and were unrelated to it," Buchele said.

Peterson was not impressed. He warned the *University Times* that the school "should be prepared to bear its share of the responsibility for the losses suffered in jobs, by industry, people and communities." Senator Scarnati agreed. In June 2001, he attached a rider to the University of Pittsburgh appropriations bill that barred the school from using any state funds to support the clinic. Overnight, the Allegheny debate went from underdog-versus-underdog to a high-stakes power struggle involving a $100 million state educational appropriation and the region's most important law school.

Fearful that Buchele's activism would cost the university up to a fifth of its operating budget, administrators informed him in October 2001 that the clinic would have to reimburse the school for more than $62,000 in administrative and overhead costs incurred over the previous year. An October 17, 2001, article in the *Pittsburgh Post-Gazette* explained why the administration's move amounted to a death blow: "Since the clinic's annual budget is about $102,000—entirely from the Heinz Endowment grant and other private funding sources—and the university has restricted the clinic from seeking additional endowment funding until it agrees not to take on controversial cases, the assessment will cause the clinic to go bankrupt within 18 months."

The Heinz Endowments expressed concerns in the same article. "That kind of action on funding by the legislature was very troubling," said Caren Glotfelty, director of the Endowments' environmental programs. "We want the law clinic to exist and to fulfill the goals we expected when we gave the capital endowment to Pitt."

Observers from both inside and outside the university blasted Chancellor Mark Nordenberg for caving in to Scarnati. Nordenberg refused industry demands to dismiss the professors involved, but environmentalists argued that he should have defended the clinic more vigorously or shifted money from the school's endowment to cover the administrative expenses. Critics charged that Nordenberg's response (the *Post-Gazette* called it "equivocal") would lead to a serious erosion of academic freedom. The administration countered that it had no choice but reiterated that it was still committed to the clinic. In January, the *University Times* reported that the school was looking at ways to "establish its Environmental Law Clinic as a separate, non-profit entity that will be insulated from legislative retribution."

Nobody was happy with that plan. Faculty members and local papers continued slamming Nordenberg until the university finally wilted. In March 2002, administrators dropped plans to move the clinic off campus. Officials announced that they found private funds to cover administrative costs up to $75,000 a year, although they would not say where the money originated. They also promised that the faculty at the Environmental Law Clinic could continue choosing which clients to represent.

The tussle was over and the clinic prevailed, but Scarnati's brash maneuver infuriated the Allegheny Defense Project. Activists staged a rally in November 2001, in the midst of the controversy, to support the clinic's independence. Kleissler blasted the university—and re-staked his claim to sympathetic underdog status—in an interview with the *Pittsburgh Tribune-Review*. "The corporations that are cutting down our national forests have no shortage of financial resources to get legal representation," he said. "We can't do that. We depend on lawyers willing to give up their free time to defend us."

That charge raises an important question: Why can't activists afford to pay for an attorney? According to an organizational self-assessment frequently used in print, "The Allegheny Defense Project is the only grassroots forest protection organization in Pennsylvania. ADP is known throughout the U.S. as one of the premier regional forest protection organizations." Raising funds to hire a lawyer should be easy with credentials like that. It certainly impressed the Heinz Endowments, which gave the Allegheny Defense Project a direct $40,000 grant shortly after dropping $2 million to establish the Environmental Law Clinic.[7]

Bill Luneburg describes Kleissler's alleged cash crunch as "a classic free rider problem." He says that protecting the Allegheny would provide substantial benefits, but those would be diffused over a wide population. Convincing people to chip in is difficult. "It is very hard for a group like [the ADP], absent a very expensive membership campaign, to get people to contribute," he explained.

Others argue that Kleissler's inability to pay a lawyer points to a different truth: That the support he claims to have simply does not exist. Sue Swanson, executive director of the Allegheny Hardwood Utilization Group, also rejected Kleissler's contention that local timber supporters are fat with corporate cash. "A lot of money has gone into litigation," she said. "A percentage of that has come from the industry companies. But as far as the organization—I mean, the ADP hasn't had to pay anything for litigation. If you take the litigation dollars away from both our organizations, we don't have any more money than he has."

Swanson also laments that the industry was not an organized anti-activist force when the ADP began litigating in 1997. "We felt that the Forest Service would be prepared to defend their position," she said. "It wasn't really until after that that we saw there were a lot of things they were not able to present in court that we could. And so that's basically when we committed ourselves to getting the intervener status and providing as wide a range and diverse a representation as we could for the region."

And so the Allegheny Forest Alliance was born. Timber executives were not the only people concerned about activist lawsuits. School officials and township supervisors were worried that the falling harvest would lead to reductions in the Forest Service's annual 25 percent payment. There were also recreational users interested in keeping the woods open to all-terrain vehicles and hunting. "Kleissler likes to pretend that the Allegheny Forest Alliance is just a timber industry driven group," Swanson said. "The industry is a very minority position in the group. And we don't direct their activities.

It's kind of funny, because some of the people in that group are much more adamant than the timber industry."

Jack Hedlund, who heads AFA, said that all of the local school districts have given between one and five percent of their annual timber payments from the Forest Service to support the Allegheny Forest Alliance. Many of the townships have followed suit, although a few of them have refused. Hedlund said that all of the contributors cut their payments back to one percent in 2001 because of tight times, but they still remain the largest source of revenue. "Our biggest contributors by far are townships and school districts," Hedlund said. "I bet they make up 90 percent of our funding."

Kleissler sees that as a dirty bait-and-switch tactic. If local school districts are so concerned about funding, why are they spending so much of their dwindling 25 percent payment on lawyers? He also points out that Hedlund, a former high school principal in Kane, agitated against accepting guaranteed forest payments under the Secure Rural Schools and Community Self-Determination Act in 2000. Forest County abandoned the 25 percent payment in favor of a guaranteed revenue stream, and its payment stabilized. The other three counties stuck with the 25 percent payment, a move that has cost them hundreds of thousands of dollars as logging on the Allegheny continues to founder. "That to me is borderline," Kleissler said. "The way AFA has been operated, it's really borderline. I don't even really know how to say it. Certainly it is borderline conflict of interest, especially with Jack's relationship with the school district. But then to say that they are going to use that money to fight to save their school funds, and then to advocate against assurances for school funding in order to save the timber program?"

Kleissler is correct when he says rejecting guaranteed payments cost the school districts money, but Hedlund defends the decision. The Forest Service was confident that the Allegheny timber harvest was going to stabilize, and that is the information he conveyed. Communities made their own decisions. It was an unfortunate one, to be sure, and Hedlund supported efforts to switch over to the guaranteed payments when communities had the opportunity in 2003. The decision to stick with the 25 percent payments—and the subsequent process that led officials to reverse that position—speaks volumes about the region's agonizing attempts to salvage the culture and economics of logging. They deserve close attention, but first a look at the economics of litigation is in order.

Hedlund estimates that the Allegheny Forest Alliance spends approximately $55,000 on salaries, travel, rent, and other expenses every year, but he is vague about how much it has cost to intervene in litigation. "When I'm talking significant, I'm talking more than $100,000," he said regarding East

Side. "And I'm just talking about this litigation, not the previous ones. This latest round . . . that we're involved in is in excess of one hundred grand. Far in excess, and that's just this round. . . . We're purchasing the Cadillac version of legal teams, and the Cadillac of legal teams can range from $350 to $500 an hour. I'm sure Kleissler can call Buchele and get those things for free."

That is true, so it is difficult to compare how many resources the opposing sides have been able to bring to bear in federal court. Does the ADP's free representation approach "Cadillac" quality? Pitt professor Luneburg provided some guidance. "I think if you look at a typical rate of a firm downtown, I think $250 an hour would not be an excessive hourly rate for an attorney," he said.

So how many hours have the activists' attorneys logged? Luneburg was the ADP's attorney in the Mortality II case, which served as the precursor to East Side. He recalls that even though it was a relatively simple lawsuit, he probably spent between 150 and 200 hours preparing and executing it. He estimates that the far more complex East Side suit has required even more attention. "I know the East Side sale, I haven't talked to Tom [Buchele] about this, but I'm sure it's far in excess of 200 hours," Luneburg said. "If someone told me it was 500 hours I wouldn't bat an eye."

By Luneburg's estimate, Kleissler's free legal services in the East Side case have a market value approaching $125,000. As for the Allegheny Forest Alliance, Hedlund distributed documents at the organization's annual meeting in 2004 revealing that the American Forest and Paper Association, co-interveners in the East Side litigation, had contributed upwards of $40,000 to the AFA's legal defense fund. All claims of poverty aside, both sides in the Allegheny dispute have managed to secure robust legal representation. It is less clear that the lawsuits in question have made any headway in clarifying the best way to manage the Allegheny.

The primary argument in the East Side lawsuit stands years of environmental debate on its head. One of the strongest complaints that national activists have leveled against the Forest Service involves "below cost timber sales." Timber programs typically operate in the red because building roads and administering the sales exceed the amount companies pay for the trees. But the Allegheny is different. Its black cherry is so valuable that the Allegheny is one of the few national forests that turn a profit on its timber sales.[8] The Allegheny Defense Project has responded by breaking from the national pattern and arguing that the Forest Service should abandon even-aged management on the Allegheny *because the program is designed to turn a profit.*

Timber supporters argue that radical activists are opposed to logging on ideological, even spiritual grounds. Unable to change the Forest Service through legislation, those activists file suits and create an administrative quagmire commonly derided as "analysis paralysis." Many people think that

East Side proves the point: Activists have been complaining about below-cost timber sales for decades. Confronted with a national forest that operates in the black, they suddenly decide that timber sales aimed at turning a profit pose the greater danger.

Suspicions about motivation are nothing new. Environmentalists were trying to save the Pacific Northwest's remaining old growth long before the spotted owl became the movement's cause célèbre. Angry loggers insisted that the owl gave activists an opportunity to leverage the Endangered Species Act and stop logging through a disingenuous back-door attack based on birds rather than timber. Environmental reporter William Dietrich explored that notion in *The Final Forest*, detailing remarks that Andrew Stahl, a prominent activist working for the Sierra Club Legal Defense Fund, made at a conference in Eugene, Oregon, in 1988:

> There were no laws protecting old-growth ecosystems, Stahl explained. There were, however, laws protecting wildlife. "It's quite biologically sensible to hypothesize that one or more species of wildlife would, in fact, be unique to old-growth forests because such forests for millennia were the dominant forest type in the Pacific Northwest," he said. "In addition, wildlife are measurable and you can count them . . . and thanks to the work of Walt Disney with Bambi . . . wildlife enjoys substantial, substantive statutory protection."

> "Well, the northern spotted owl is the wildlife species of choice to act as a surrogate for old-growth protection," Stahl went on, "and I've often thought that thank goodness the spotted owl evolved in the Northwest, for if it hadn't, we'd have to genetically engineer it."[9]

People involved in Allegheny logging say that Kleissler has pulled a similar switcheroo with regard to even-aged management. The ADP's pro bono legal team argues that logging has to stop because even-aged management abandons ecological integrity in favor of profit, but keep in mind that Kleissler's goal is not to shift to a different harvesting system. The ADP is a zero-cut organization, not "less-cut" or "better-cut." Any commercial logging, no matter how limited and well designed—profitable or unprofitable—offends that agenda.

"The bottom line is that there are groups of people who genuinely, fundamentally, have a different value system about how our national forests should be managed," said Kevin Elliott, supervisor of the Allegheny National Forest since 2001. "It's not about economics. It's about cutting timber on national forests. . . . Even if we weren't doing even-aged management, even if we had a preponderance of uneven-aged management, I would suspect that we would still have the same amount of appeals and litigation on the Allegheny National Forest. It's not whether or not we're doing even-aged management or uneven-aged management. That happens to be a vehicle to try to drive the challenge."

It comes as no surprise that Forest Service officials and communities that rely on federal timber disagree with Kleissler about the legality of even-aged management, but one of the Allegheny Defense Project's critical allies in litigation is also questioning the group's agenda. Caren Glotfelty, the director of environmental programs at the Heinz Endowments, defended the University of Pittsburgh's Environmental Law Clinic in 2001. In May 2003, she sang a different tune as the keynote speaker at the Allegheny Hardwood Utilization Group's annual dinner. There were approximately seventy-five people on hand, all of them were still furious with the Endowments for funding the law clinic and shuffling at least $40,000 directly to the ADP. "I know that there are those of you in the room and others in the region who have had some questions and maybe a little bit of concern about a few grantees of the Heinz Endowments over the years," she began. "I think that it is important that we have this opportunity to talk about those concerns."

Glotfelty revealed that she operates a sheep farm and has sold timber off her own land. She also stressed that the Heinz Endowments have supported "sustainable forestry," the certification concept aimed at striking a balance between timber harvesting and environmental concerns. Timber companies undergo strict audits to earn approval from one of several certifying organizations. Once graced with that seal of approval, the companies try to market the wood to ecoconscious customers willing to pay a premium. Glotfelty impressed the crowd by revealing that her kitchen is made of certified black cherry produced by Kane Hardwood. She also detailed how much money the Endowments gave to have the entire Pennsylvania State Forest system certified.

More importantly, Glotfelty distanced the Endowments from the Environmental Law Clinic. "The Environmental Law Clinic was started at the University of Pittsburgh through part of a capital campaign gift that was made to Pitt in 1998, a couple years before I got there," she said. "It was an endowment, which means from a grant-maker's standpoint that money is put to create a program, and then we don't manage or have continued involvement in that program after the endowment gift is made. . . . So you could say that we supported the creation of the Environmental Law Clinic, but we don't have an active role . . . with respect to who they hire and the cases they take on."

Distance turned into outward hostility when Glotfelty discussed the Allegheny Defense Project. "My predecessor did make a couple of grants to the Allegheny Defense Project," she said. "He did that because there was a strong concern that the wilderness that had been made possible through Senator Heinz's advocacy might be threatened by some very specific timber sales. When I came to the Endowments, there was a grant request [from the ADP] pending before me, and I looked at what was being proposed. I looked at the grant-making that the Endowments had done around sustainable forestry, working to promote certification of the state forest system, working to support industry approaches to sustainable forestry, and I said these two things aren't compatible with one another: You can't be supporting an industry that's trying to do better, . . . and at the same time be supporting a destructive organization. So I said no to that."

People attending the dinner applauded the Heinz Endowments' reported change of heart, but they also realized that it had little bearing on the current controversy. Glotfelty can say whatever she wants about "destructive organizations," zero cut, and sustainable forestry. That does nothing to stop the litigation that the Heinz Endowments helped launch in the late 1990s.

Kleissler's critics—which now apparently include Glotfelty—continue to blast the Allegheny Defense Project's agenda. But if it is such a radical organization and its demands are so outrageous, why do federal judges keep ruling in its favor? Kleissler offers a simple answer. "The problem is, the laws allow for logging on the national forests if you follow the laws," he said. "The problem here is, they haven't followed the laws."

Nothing is ever that simple, of course.

Successive waves of droughts, diseases, and invasive species began ravaging western Pennsylvania forests in the late 1980s. Foresters eventually noticed a disturbing number of dead and dying trees across ninety thousand acres of the Allegheny. They designed two successive projects to remedy the situation and, in a public-relations blunder, dubbed their own proposals Mortality I and Mortality II. The combined projects called for treating eleven thousand of the hardest-hit acres almost exclusively through even-aged management. Mortality I got underway without a hitch in 1995, but the Allegheny Defense Project introduced Pennsylvania loggers to environmental litigation when Mortality II came up for consideration.

The Forest Service performed an analysis called an "environmental assessment" to justify the second phase of treatments in early 1997. The executive summary informed readers that there would be only three acres of clearcutting but cautioned that "It is true that some of the treated areas will look like a clearcut when the overstory is removed. Some large openings greater than 40 acres already exist because of the mortality situation. These openings will occur naturally by the trees dying whether we harvest them or not."[10]

Activists insisted that the affected areas would look like clearcuts because they were going to be clearcuts, complaining that the Forest Service was proposing to save the Allegheny's trees by cutting them down. Convinced that Mortality II flew in the face of common sense and good science—and buttressed by free legal representation—a coalition including Susan Curry, Jim

Kleissler, and their supporters at Heartwood sued to stop the project. United States District Court Judge William L. Standish issued his decision on October 15, 1997, an action that still resonates loudly through the hills and valleys of the Allegheny. Exploring the decision requires wading through an alphabet soup of legal acronyms, but it is important to realize what the activists won, what they lost, and why.

Standish ruled that activist claims regarding the Migratory Bird Treaty Act[11] (MBTA) were "meritless." He was less kind to the Forest Service when it came to the National Environmental Policy Act (NEPA). NEPA requires an environmental impact statement (EIS) for all major federal actions "significantly affecting the quality of the human environment." EIS documentation is far more complicated and costly than the environmental assessment (EA) that the Forest Service completed. In fact, the EA is typically used to determine whether or not the more extensive EIS is required. The Allegheny's Forest Supervisor reviewed the EA in Mortality II and decided that no further analysis was necessary. He was wrong.

Standish wrote that there were several "intensity" factors such as old growth and endangered species that argued for an environmental impact statement. He also wrote that the sheer size of the project and the predominant use of even-aged management required further analysis. He chastised the Forest Service for failing to figure that out. After all, an appendix to the Mortality II environmental assessment dealing with public comments weighed in at 155 pages. "Based on a review of this appendix, it cannot seriously be disputed that the Mortality II Project is a highly controversial project," Standish decided.

All of those factors made the case clear in the judge's mind: "Therefore, the failure of the Forest Service to prepare an EIS for the Mortality II Project violated its NEPA obligations, and the decision of the Forest Service to approve the project was arbitrary and capricious."

It got worse. Regulations require federal officials to consider "a broad range of reasonable alternatives" when designing a project. The Mortality II environmental assessment considered exactly two alternatives: No action at all and the 5,000-acre even-aged harvest that the Forest Service eventually adopted. That did not please Judge Standish: "In the court's extensive research in connection with plaintiffs' claims under the [National Forest Management Act] and NEPA," he wrote, "the court did not find one case in which the Forest Service had considered so few alternatives. . . . Under the circumstances, the failure of the Forest Service to consider more than two alternatives in connection with the Mortality II project was arbitrary and capricious."

The decision was a rude awakening for the Pennsylvania timber industry.

The Forest Service had been managing Allegheny timber sales unchallenged for the better part of a century, and a brash coalition of activists managed to dismantle those efforts overnight. The Allegheny was supposed to be a success story—a miraculous environmental recovery accompanied by decent jobs and lucrative hardwoods forever. What happened? Luneburg thinks he knows. In June 2003, six years after he filed the Mortality II case, he was still shocked that anyone was complacent enough to believe that the brief environmental assessment and two alternatives were enough to justify a contentious 5,000-acre timber sale. "I wouldn't even give that case to first-year law students on an exam," he said in detailing its open-and-shut nature.

Judge Standish's decision to stop Mortality II and demand a rigorous EIS delayed what activists considered an egregiously irresponsible management project. The Forest Service even had to compensate the plaintiffs' lawyers for $30,000 in expenses. But the decision was perhaps even more important because of what it failed to do—a failure that left the environmentalists' most basic complaint on shaky ground.

Federal regulations limit clear-cutting to areas where that technique is considered "optimal," and they restrict other even-aged techniques to where they are "appropriate." Activists argued that the failure to apply those strict standards in Mortality II violated the National Forest Management Act. They also charged that the project violated NFMA by using even-aged management without conducting a rigorous stand-by-stand analysis and allowing those techniques on stands larger than 40 acres. The arguments' radical implications were crystal clear: Significant portions of the Mortality II lawsuit aimed to wreck even-aged management, the very philosophy that had guided Allegheny National Forest management for decades.

Standish ruled against the activists on all of those counts. His statement regarding even-aged management on stands larger than 40 acres was particularly telling. He said that planners erred by failing to consider other options but added that the ultimate decision was up to the Forest Service, not the court. "Accordingly, the Forest Service's determination to use even-aged management on various areas of Management Area 3 that exceed the 40-acre limit did not violate its own regulations and was not arbitrary and capricious," he wrote. "When the Forest Service prepares an EIS and considers more alternatives in connection with the Mortality II Project, it may again conclude that it is necessary to exceed the 40-acre limit."

In short, the Forest Service can only use even-aged management when it is necessary, but it is up to the Forest Service to decide when those conditions exist. Standish issued a similar opinion regarding a complex computer program known as SILVAH. Foresters use SILVAH (short for Silviculture of

Allegheny Hardwoods) to decide—among other things—when even-aged
management is appropriate. Activists charged that SILVAH breaches requirements to analyze each stand of trees separately. Standish rejected that argument, agreeing with the defendant's contention that SILVAH was only one
tool among many used to determine appropriate management techniques.
Again, the court argued that the Forest Service must consider more options
but the left the power to decide among those options to the agency's discretion.

That position is important because it strikes at the heart of the Allegheny
Defense Project's agenda. Jim Kleissler insists that Forest Service officials
illegally operate the national forest as a black cherry tree farm. Standish
decided that they can manage it however they see fit as long as they jump
through procedural hoops required by federal law. Mortality II's plan for
extensive even-aged management would have been fine if the Forest Service
had completed an EIS, considered a slew of alternatives, and rejected them
one by one. The failure to follow that procedure, not an argument about hard
science, doomed Mortality II.

The litigation that erupted after researchers discovered an endangered Indiana bat on the Allegheny National Forest in 1998 resulted in a similarly
mixed decision.[12] With visions of the northern spotted owl swirling in their
minds, environmentalists and timber supporters began another mad scramble
for control. The Forest Service adjusted existing timber sales to take the bat
into account, while consulting with the United States Fish and Wildlife Service to find a permanent solution. Activists charged that those temporary
measures were insufficient and asked a federal judge to intervene. They
hoped that an injunction would force the Forest Service to engage in a radical
redesign of the 1986 forest plan.

The *Pittsburgh Post-Gazette* reported on the results of that argument on
January 22, 1999:

> A federal judge has clipped the wings of forest activists who had asked for a halt
> to all logging in the Allegheny National Forest to preserve habitat for the endangered
> Indiana bat. U.S. District Judge Donetta Ambrose yesterday denied the request of
> Heartwood Inc. and its state branch [*sic*], the Allegheny Defense Project, to stop 44
> logging projects, saying the U.S. Forest Service acted in a reasonable manner in
> allowing tree cutting to continue.

That hardly amounted to a timber triumph. The Forest Service had already
stopped approving new projects because of the bat. Officials also agreed to
"voluntarily" stop all harvesting for six months, beginning in April, while
they brought management into compliance with the Endangered Species Act.
And that's exactly what they did. The new guidelines required loggers to

leave a number of live, dying, and dead trees—even in clearcuts—to serve as roosting areas for the endangered bat. The consultation also resulted in new measures to protect four other endangered species either known or thought to exist on the forest. Logging resumed six months after the moratorium began.

That progression stands in stark contrast to Endangered Species litigation in the Pacific Northwest. There, the federal courts ultimately ruled that the spotted owl's survival required huge swaths of old-growth forest. So far, researchers have found only two Indiana bats on the Allegheny. The forest is on the far reaches of the bats' range, and far more substantial populations exist elsewhere. Moreover, it is not clear that the bat requires old growth to survive.[13] John Palmer, the Allegheny's forest supervisor at the time of the bat litigation, issued a "Record of Decision" detailing new bat-friendly measures in July 2000. The document described eight (eight!) alternative plans that the Forest Service considered before making its ultimate decision. One of the rejected alternatives was zero cut. The Record of Decision also explained why the chosen alternative did not require revising the entire 1986 forest plan: "The long term relationship between the outputs of multiple-use goods and services originally projected will not be substantially altered, as documented in the effects analysis of the [Final Environmental Impact Statement]."[14]

The Allegheny Defense Project's primary purpose is to profoundly alter that output of goods and services, of course. In particular, activists want to eliminate commercial logging. The northern spotted owl brought environmentalists tantalizingly close to that goal in the Pacific Northwest, but the Indiana bat was a less effective surrogate for zero cut. It did halt logging for a few months, but federal officials—armed with wide discretionary power—successfully meshed the critter into the existing management plan. Kleissler managed to bend the Allegheny timber program, but he failed to break it.

The mixed impact of environmental litigation on the Allegheny allows every interest group to claim vilification. Kleissler said Mortality II was illegal, and the federal court agreed. On the other hand, even the activists' biggest victories came loaded with caveats, leaving the ultimate decision about an appropriate management plan up to the Forest Service. The Allegheny's current forest supervisor, Kevin Elliott, offered his own take on the score after looking back at the first four lawsuits. "What was the outcome?" he pondered in a March 2003 interview.

> Well, Mortality II was filed in June of 1997. Judge Standish didn't rule on the merits of whether or not the forest was doing the right thing on the ground, if you will. What the judge did rule was that, relative to NEPA, the judge felt that, yes, the forest should have done an EIS instead of an EA. Again, NEPA is a procedural act. Then relative to the National Forest Management Act, one aspect of that is that when you

propose to do clearcutting, when you propose to use even-aged management, you need to make a determination that it is an optimal and appropriate treatment. The judge in Mortality II thought that the [F]orest [Service] should go back home and beef that section up. So again, not really a ruling on whether or not timber harvesting should occur. But again, procedurally, there were a couple of procedural issues that the forest should shore up. And then basically on all the other counts [the judge] basically ruled in favor of the forest.

The next suit was the South Branch, Willow Creek and Minister [Project] filed in December 1997. And that one, the same judge basically dismissed the plaintiffs' claims for lack of following the administrative appeals process. [He] also dismissed the plaintiffs' claims that the Forest Service should have prepared an EIS in order to implement a landscape corridor approach that had been developed. The third suit was an Endangered Species Act lawsuit. Again, that was dismissed. The next suit was Shingle Mill, and there again the judge in that case, Judge Ambrose, basically ruled against the plaintiffs.

So I am trying—how many have we won and how many have we lost? I'll let you answer that.

Any such assessment would have been wildly premature at that point because of an even more far-reaching debate over the East Side Project—the son of Mortality II. Forest Service officials went back to the drawing board after reviewing the court's Mortality II decision. Now known as East Side, the project's environmental impact statement considered five alternatives instead of two. Officials released their final decision in December 2000, revealing that the 5,000 acres of even-aged management originally proposed in Mortality II would not fix the forest. Trees kept dying while the Forest Service jumped through the required procedural hoops, so officials decided that East Side needed to treat 8,000 acres, the most severely affected tracts across a 140,000-acre swath. Almost all of the proposed treatments amounted to even-aged management.

The scientific justification for that treatment had not changed—and neither had the activists' resistance to it. The protesting began in 1998 when Forest Service officials released a document detailing where they were headed with East Side. The May 1998 sit-in at ANF headquarters in Warren was a direct response to that preliminary analysis. An excerpt from an Earth First! press release reveals the extent of the protesters' fury. The author was one James Hansen, at one time the Allegheny Defense Project's New York City contact:

Myths of replanting and forest "regeneration" are a flimsy excuse for turning the Allegheny into a Black Cherry tree farm. . . . This reliance on single species planta-tions ma[k]es the "forest" much more susceptible to disease or insects, decreasing economic stability. The US Forest Service has only one use planned for the Alle-gheny National Forest: selling it to the highest bidder!

A Scandal by Any Name, The "East Side Project" is Mortality, Too!

> After a Federal judge halted the Mortality II timber sale in October of 1997, forcing
> the Forest Service to examine the environmental impacts of clearcutting several
> thousand acres, many thought the Allegheny was on the road to recovery. Instead,
> Mortality is back with a vengeance. East Side doubles the logging planned for Mor-
> tality, threatening entire ecosystems including protected old-growth areas. Of 8,206
> acres of cutting, over 7,000 acres are to be clearcut or prepared for clearcutting. . . .
> The Allegheny National Forest is closer to large U.S. populations than any other
> National Forest. People depend on the Allegheny not only for recreation (and the
> recreation industry) but also for clean water and air, for food and shelter and for life.
> Instead, the Forest Service offers dirty business and politics, starvation and exposure
> for endangered species, and death for local ecosystems and economies.

Zero-cut activists were still aiming their rhetorical barbs at even-aged management. They still do today, despite repeated judicial decisions indicating
that the Forest Service has a huge amount of leeway in making management
decisions. That is not to say that the case is closed, however. To the contrary:
The lawsuit designed to stop East Side is a direct attempt to whittle away at
that discretion—and a whole lot more.

Tom Buchele, director of the Environmental Law Clinic at the University
of Pittsburgh, set out to devise a judicial tour de force to halt East Side. The
lawsuit, filed in May 2001, involved ten separate claims against the Forest
Service. One argued that new protections for the Indiana bat were insufficient, but the highest-profile charge was the one accusing the Forest Service
of using even-aged management to reap illegal profits from the lucrative
black cherry.

The National Forest Management Act prohibits the Forest Service from
selecting a logging method "primarily because it will give the greatest dollar
return or the greatest unit output of timber." Activists insist the Forest Service
designed East Side to do just that. If a federal judge agrees, the court could
stop all logging and force the Forest Service to revamp its entire Allegheny
management strategy, a process that could take years. That would mean zero
cut—and victory for Jim Kleissler—in the meantime.

The Forest Service insists that the Allegheny's unique history and current
conditions demand a carefully balanced management plan that features even-
aged management. East Side is not an 8,000-acre clearcut in this view: It is a
sincere effort to grow trees on a landscape where they are currently dying.
Yes, the Forest Plan is designed to provide local loggers and mills with quality hardwood timber, but that is only one of many considerations.

Ultimately, the East Side decision might rest on how a federal judge in
Pittsburgh defines the word "primarily." All those Ph.D.s among all those

foresters and environmentalists, and the struggle for the Allegheny comes down to semantics.

The import of the final ruling has not escaped the litigants—or Federal Magistrate Ila Jeane Sensinich. Her initial recommendation agreed with the Allegheny Defense Project on almost every count, setting the stage for a stunning activist victory. Subsequent developments in the case have rocked the Allegheny region and highlighted how important the final decision will be: It could effectively turn one of the federal government's most profitable forests into a zero-cut proving ground.

However it turns out, one of the most intractable problems facing communities is that litigation takes time. Efforts to counteract tree mortality on the Allegheny have been tied up in court for the better part of a decade. During that decade, the region's economy has slipped further into the tank. East Side might eventually provide a defining moment for American environmentalism, but that does not make it any easier for the people stuck in the middle.

NOTES

1. Ellen Kranick, "Logging project targeted," *Warren Times* Observer, September 10, 2002.

2. Allegheny Defense Project, press release issued 9 September, 2002, www.alle ghenydefense.org/press/release_020909.shtml [accessed April 12, 2004].

3. P.L. 94-588, 90 Stat. 2949.

4. P.L. 91-190, 83 Stat. 852.

5. P.L. 86-517, 74 Stat. 215.

6. www.heinz.org, June 12, 2003.

7. "Report 2000: What Sort of Community Do We Want to Create?" The Heinz Endowments, 1999 annual report, 97. Available online at www.heinz.org/index.asp in the Library section.

8. Activists do not accept the Allegheny's profitability as a given. Jim Kleissler told me that even in its best years, "The Allegheny did not make money for taxpayers. In fact, it cost taxpayers money. Because although we use funds out of the general treasury to operate the timber sale program, we don't take any of the revenue and put it back in the general treasury. It goes into the timber sale slush funds, the salvage sale fund, and there's a different set of them. So we don't make money."

Randal O'Toole is less sure. Currently working for the Thoreau Institute, O'Toole's work regarding the Forest Service's inadequate accounting practices over the past two decades helped fuel opposition to below-cost timber sales. In short, he is no friend of government bureaucracy or shady environmental bookkeeping. "You are right to be suspicious of both sides," O'Toole wrote in an e-mail to me on June 10, 2003. "TSPIRS is not the right source for data. TSPIRS is a [wacko] accounting system that foreshadowed many of the accounting offenses of WorldCom and Enron. For example, it amortizes about half of all road costs over eternity—which means that it zeroes them out." O'Toole was not particularly enthusiastic about Kleissler's charge that the Allegheny never made money, however. "It wasn't true in 1997 or any of the ten years before that for which I have records," he wrote on June 12, 2003.

9. William Dietrich, *The Final Forest* (New York: Penguin Books, 1992), 84–85.

10. United States Department of Agriculture, "Mortality II Environmental Assessment" (Warren, Pa.: United States Forest Service, 1997), executive summary.

11. P.L. 65-186; 65 Cong. Ch. 128; 40 Stat. 755.

12. For more on the identifying characteristics of the Indiana bat (*myotis sodalis*) and its preferred habitat, the reasons for its being endangered, and the relevant management programs, see the Pennsylvania Department of Conservation and Natural Resources website at http://www.dcnr.state.pa.us/wrcf/inbat.htm.

13. Allegheny National Forest Supervisor Kevin Elliott informed me that a radio collar placed on one of the captured bats indicated that it was feeding on a golf course near Bradford.

14. United States Department of Agriculture, "Record of Decision for the Environmental Impact Statement for Threatened and Endangered Species on the Allegheny National Forest" (Warren, Pa.: United States Forest Service, 2000), 2.

Chapter Ten

Wilderness Revisited: What Is Pretty? And Why It Matters

The ideal towards which the Forest Service works is the presence throughout the Forest of as many permanent communities and settlers as the region and resources will satisfactorily support. It is never desirable to depopulate the Forest. Men are needed to aid in the protection and development of the area and to work up the material grown. Resident labor is much the more satisfactory.

> —L. L. Bishop, the Allegheny's first forest supervisor, in a 1925 essay, "The Allegheny National Forest—Pa. Why, What and Where"

Note that Bishop considered "protection and development" complementary rather than conflicting goals. His optimistic essay detailed a future in which timber production would encourage rather than deter camping, hiking, and watershed protection. Many local residents insist that the Allegheny has already achieved that happy symbiosis and view efforts to abandon logging as a betrayal of Bishop's vision.

Kane activist Bill Belitskus has a different take. He says that intensive even-aged management is destroying the ecosystem and, in turn, preventing people from enjoying the forest. His bible in that regard is a little orange book called *Woodland Ecology: Environmental Forestry for the Small Owner*, by the late Leon S. Minckler. Belitskus's endorsement rests in part on the book's call for a more reserved approach to harvesting. "The points of conflict between timber on the one hand and wildlife, recreation, and aesthetics on the other are not critical," Minckler wrote, but added:

They can be blunted or eliminated by proper use of silviculture and some adjustments of values received. Forest diversity and timber production can exist side by side if a group selection system of silviculture is used. . . . Clearcutting large areas

135

is simply not compatible with optimum diversified wildlife production and is a disaster for recreation and aesthetics.[1]

People opposed to Belitskus point out that Minckler did not call for zero cut. If Belitskus really believed in the book, they say, he would argue for more limited logging instead of an outright ban. Still, it is worth exploring Minckler's larger environmental vision. Chapter 12 of *Woodland Ecology* is called "Forests of the Future." Minckler argued that the American environment was at a crossroads: "One future world would be one where Man has reached a harmony with Nature and evolved a life style where materialism is only incidental to the good life. The other world of the future would be a logical and accelerated extension of the industrial revolution."[2]

Minkler admitted that the end result would probably split the two predicted outcomes, but his optimistic "Man with Nature" scenario offers an intriguing look into his mindset. Note what he thought the forests of the future might look like when he imagined them thirty years ago:

> But people pressure on the forested areas is light. The pollution disasters of the 1980s finally convinced the country that pollution control was an imperative and vitally serious business. The three-day war in 1994 decimated the population to about half of its former size. The disasters from pollution and war made 'believers' of the American people. They adopted a new life style, using technology and population control to achieve human and spiritual values rather than former materialistic goals for an ever-increasing population.[3]

Minckler's *rosy* scenario rests on depopulation by half, and people opposed to zero cut believe he is right. They argue that converting the Allegheny into a landscape that the Green movement deems acceptable would require a shift to "spiritual values" and a large-scale human exodus. But locals are not interested in leaving the forest or profoundly changing how they enjoy it. Maybe Belitskus thinks hiking on the Allegheny National Forest would be more serene if the black cherry disappeared, but why should he get to decide? On the other hand, why should local timber interests get to choose which trees are better? Unfortunately, the only compromise proffered so far involves "wilderness," a term so loaded with spiritual and political baggage that it serves as fitting proxy for discussions about what the Allegheny should be.

The Wilderness Act of 1964 defined wilderness as "an area of undeveloped Federal land retaining its primeval character and influence, without permanent improvements or human habitation, which is protected and managed so as to preserve its natural conditions and which (1) generally appears to have been affected primarily by the forces of nature, with the imprint of man's work substantially unnoticeable."[4]

That would appear to eliminate almost every acre of the Allegheny National Forest. Activists constantly gripe about the black cherry as an unnatural intrusion. They blast oil and gas companies for the wells operating everywhere on the forest. And unless paved roads can be categorized as something other than an "imprint of man's work," it is hard to see much room for wilderness on the Big Level.

Activists do, however, and that makes residents who resist them incredibly angry. Just look at the activities permitted in federally designated wilderness areas: Hiking and backwoods camping, which happen to be activities environmentalists enjoy. But no logging. No ATVs or snowmobiles. No mountain bikes. No RV camping. Those happen to be activities that many local residents pursue. You can fish and hunt, but access is limited because roads are forbidden.

Kirk Johnson says that the federal definition of "wilderness" has changed since 1964 and currently allows more areas to be considered. According to wilderness ranger Eric Flood, loggers clear-cut much of the land that makes up the Hickory Creek Wilderness Area not once but twice prior to its federal designation. At one point, part of it was an artillery range. If that kind of human impact does not disqualify a given tract of forest, what does? Johnson promises that only fifty thousand acres of the Allegheny meet the current requirements for wilderness designation, but will that be true tomorrow? Twenty years from now? Anti-wilderness forces fear that environmental activists are bent on seizing the Allegheny and turning it into the kind of forest they like: Namely, a forest without pesky locals trying to eke out a living.

Kleissler insists that his vision has nothing to do with depopulating local communities. "We're not doing that," he said. "That's such a stupid analogy because we're not going into Sheffield and saying you have to get the hell out of Sheffield. We're going into a national forest, which is already public land, which is already in public ownership, which is already supposed to be for watershed protection, not for private timber interests, no matter how well meaning they are. It is not theirs."

Kleissler envisions a zero-cut forest dedicated to other uses, and he does not deny that a few of them appeal to him. "What we want to see is a high quality of life in the region," he said. "A healthy economy. Of course, a healthy forest. And of course for selfish reasons such as hiking."

Sifting through the "selfish" aspects of the Allegheny debate is a monumental task, especially considering how hard it is to get a grip on the basic facts and figures. Exactly how many acres do activists want to restore? Their responses have not been consistent. Take Johnson's master's thesis, submitted in 1999. On page 46, Johnson suggested making a wilderness out of the

Tionesta Research Natural and Scenic Areas and the second-growth forest that surrounds them. He estimated that the total area would be between 10,000 and 15,000 acres. But on the same page, he argued that the ideal set-aside would be much larger. Johnson had settled on that larger area by the time he wrote the Allegheny Defense Project's Tionesta Wilderness Area proposal a few years later. It appeared in the October 2001 Natural Area's Journal and suggested approximately 32,000 acres.

A glossy flyer Johnson produced after his contentious split from the ADP was less specific about the Tionesta Wilderness Area, but it mentioned four additional areas totaling about 27,000 acres. He wrote a letter to the *Warren Times Observer*, published April 23, 2001, in which he stated that "As much as 50,000 acres of additional wilderness is not unreasonable to ask for." His summer 2002 article in *Wild Earth* argued that "An additional 30,000 or more acres of Wilderness in the Allegheny would . . . help ensure the well-being of native Allegheny Plateau flora and fauna." In September of the same year, he wrote an op-ed for the *Centre Daily Times* that argued, "As much as 40,000 additional acres would be appropriate." In March 2003, Johnson told the *Warren Times Observer* that he was shooting for 11 percent of the Allegheny—56,000 acres.

In November 2002, the Allegheny Forest Alliance hosted an evening with Tennessee forester Matt Bennett at the Kane High School. Bennett runs Treekeepers.org, an organization vehemently opposed to additional wilderness designation. He warned that a national organization called the Wildlands Project—and local organizations like Friends of Allegheny Wilderness—will not rest until at least half of the United States is cordoned off from humanity. Johnson read about the presentation in the paper the following day and called me to address Bennett's allegations. "This idea that it's like a conspiracy theory, that it's part of a broader social engineering plan to kick people out and take away property rights, is being overblown," he said.

Johnson added that he was putting his plan together, which he said might include proposals for as many as twelve separate wilderness areas. He was especially optimistic about Tionesta. "This is something where Congressman Peterson's office is still interested," he said. "We're going to talk to them and a few timber industry people. We're coming in with a proposal [for the Tionesta tract] that's probably over ten thousand acres."

Johnson admitted that his own vacillation with regard to total acreage might be fueling suspicion, but called it a function of continued research and poor communication. "The idea, it was real conceptual," he explained regarding the initial plan. "I don't think we're going to propose thirty thousand acres. Originally, when I started thinking about this when I was in grad school writing my thesis, I proposed an area closer to ten to fifteen thousand acres. In the *Natural Areas Journal* I expanded on it. I guess I need to do a better job of communicating that. It's not like we're shooting for a certain acreage."

That position mirrors the one taken by the Wildlands Project. The organization distributes a fact sheet addressing the question: "How much land is needed for a continental wildlands network?" The document's 433 words fail to answer it, instead offering an official hedge: "The conservation goals of the Wildlands Project are not based on the protection of a pre-determined number of acres. . . . According to Wildland Project's southwestern representative Kim Vacariu, there is no way to estimate in advance the amount of land needed for a wildlands network design."

Unfortunately for Johnson, the whole premise of his pitch is that he will support logging on the rest of the Allegheny if he gets more wilderness. Well, how much does he want? "When he started I really thought he was talking about five thousand acres," AHUG's Sue Swanson said. "Then it was thirty thousand. Now all of a sudden it's fifty thousand. How can you trust anyone who does that?"

Others doubt Johnson will stop agitating for more wilderness no matter how much he gets. "Bullshit," Doug Carlson said when asked if he believed Johnson would be satisfied with fifty thousand acres. "Fifty today, a hundred tomorrow. He's never going to be happy."

Would Johnson be satisfied with twenty thousand acres? What if the final plan amounted to forty thousand additional acres? Would he support logging on the rest of the forest if he got that much? "That's something we'll really have to talk about when we get at it," Johnson said.

That's the rub: People want to know what is going to happen before they agree to "get at it." And that might the least of Johnson's problems. The Allegheny Defense Project is not bound by any of the promises he makes. Moreover, by proposing to convert huge swaths of the Allegheny to something approaching pre-settlement conditions, activists are demanding that locals accept their vision of a "better" forest. Part of that demand rests on their sincere belief that a hemlock-beech forest would be an environmental improvement, but it is also based on a few far more subjective considerations. That came through on a hike in May 2003. Kleissler was doing a bit of "ground truthing" to make sure that prevailing forest conditions would support a trail he wants the Forest Service to build outside of Marienville. After walking for about a half-mile on a gated road, he spied some hemlock in a gully off to the right. "Let's walk through the hemlock," he said. "I guess I just have an affinity for hemlock."

It was a passing remark, but it explains a substantial portion of the animosity surrounding the Allegheny debate, especially when cast against people who do not feel such a strong sense of affection for the stately hemlock. Ed Kocjancic was born in a lumber camp outside of Sheffield in 1932, and few people can match his passion for the dual form and function of an Allegheny hardwood forest. His parents ran the camp, tending to the needs of woodsmen at the tail end of the railroad-logging era. His father, a Yugoslavian immigrant, died in a car wreck when Ed was five, but his mother continued running the camp to provide for the family. "My mother was clever," Kocjancic recalled. "She raised us in the wood camp."

Kocjancic began working in the woods when he was twelve, cutting small trees for the remaining chemical wood plants. He moved on to pulpwood and, eventually, a stint in the army. He and his family managed to squirrel enough away for college, however, and he received a forestry degree from Penn State in 1954. He worked as a logger for almost a decade but eventually got into the lucrative business of managing timber for individual and corporate landowners. Today he is considered one of the most influential foresters in the state. His brother Joe was head sawyer at a local mill. Rudy and John were both loggers. Two of Ed's sons currently work for the family's forestry business. Another has his own trucking company. "We have one male member of the family tree who has made a living outside of the forest, and he's an ER doctor in Erie," Kocjancic chuckled. "We still haven't fully accepted it yet."

Kocjancic's financial ties to the forest tell only part of the story. He and his brother were mainstays at a regional lumberjack competition for decades. The basement at his business still contains a mountain of trophies, pictures, and competitive gear. "These guys would come in with their world championships and we'd beat them," Kocjancic said. "I started when I was eighteen. When I quit competing I was fifty. John was fifty-two. We could still pull a pretty good saw."

Kocjancic has witnessed the region's transformation from a brush patch to a hardwood forest up close, and he has developed strong feelings about what constitutes natural beauty. "What is aesthetic for me in a forest is between one and a hundred years old," he said. "It's a beautiful thing for me to view."

The debate over what kind of forest looks nicer might appear to be a sideshow in light of larger political and environmental concerns, but it's not. A piece of land that activists needed to complete the Tionesta Wilderness proposal published in the October 2001 *Natural Areas Journal* belongs to Ed Kocjancic. Kirk Johnson was working on several purchase plans and land swaps he thought might spark some interest, but so far nothing has. "Our family owns over four hundred acres up there," Kocjancic said. "I'll take a line from Charlton Heston: You'll get the deed to that property out of my cold dead hands. What if I don't want to sell them? What if I'm as strong on owning timberland as they are on wilderness? Maybe I like areas that are managed."

The Tionesta proposal is such a touchy issue because it would wrest control of the disputed land from people who have an intimate connection with it. The conjoined Tionesta Research Natural and Scenic Areas are just five miles west of downtown Kane. At approximately 4,100 acres, they amount to the largest tract of virgin old growth between the Adirondacks and the Smoky Mountains. Logging is forbidden on both, but there is still oil and gas development on the Scenic Area.

That industrial pressure has not stopped recreational pursuits. On any given weekend, there are dozens of pop-up campers, tents, and trucks nestled along the roads. Some people bed down directly in the shadow of pumping wells. Hunters park off to the side and walk into areas their families have been enjoying for generations. A snowmobile trail runs through that section of the forest. People who enjoy hiking in the old growth can access its outer boundary via Forest Route 133E. Activists bristle at the notion of chainsaws, roads, and wells spoiling their outdoor adventures, but locals do not seem to mind. Maybe they prefer that sort of landscape, or maybe they have simply come to terms with it. Whatever their reason, the activist manifesto published in the *Natural Areas Journal* informed them that it wasn't good enough anymore. The article contained a map with a black line detailing the border of the proposed wilderness. It flirted with the borders of Kane, Ludlow, Russell City, and Sheffield. Johnson noted that the plan would "benefit hikers and campers by providing greater opportunity for solitude and primitive recreation, as well as additional designated wilderness along the [North Country Trail]."

People who prefer a different sort of recreational experience altogether appeared to be out of luck. "In concert with the designation of the proposed Tionesta Wilderness Area," Johnson wrote, "the closure and obliteration of all or substantial portions of Forest Roads 126, 133, 148, 149, 195, 198, 443, 446, 469 . . . and others would eventually be necessary."

Those are roads that people use. Slating Forest Road 133 for obliteration was especially controversial. Locals use it for access to the forest for hunting, fishing and camping. It also serves as an alternate route between Ludlow and Kane. The Forest Service did a roads analysis in 2003 that declared maintaining it number seven on its list of transportation and access priorities. Local forester Ken Kane reacted accordingly when asked what would happen if 133 ceased to be. "Oh boy," he said. "It's probably one of the most heavily used roads in the system. . . . You'd have a social revolt."

Activists knew that. They simply thought that they had discovered a higher use. The article argued that "Given time, the complete Tionesta Wilderness Area, as described above, would come to resemble its native old-growth forest core." It did not take into account that some people might not view that as an improvement.

In compiling his master's thesis, which is in many ways a longer version of the *Natural Areas Journal* article, Johnson offered his opinion of local attitudes toward nature. "There is a tradition of timber cutting in the region," he wrote. "There are those in the Allegheny region, and throughout the country, who do not accept the idea of deliberately living a lifestyle that accommodates nature's processes. To treat the natural environment with sincere respect is a subversive notion to these people."

His observation reveals his unwillingness to take local concerns into account, but wilderness advocates are not the only ones who can adopt a hard line. Doug Carlson believes that the Seneca Indians and tribes before them had a profound impact on the forest. Part of that belief rests on the notion that the natives once hunted large ungulates such as elk and woodland bison. As those animals tend to eat grass, Carlson reasons that the Indians must have used fire and other means to create a thinned forest with plenty of appropriate vegetation. "I'd like to see the re-introduction of the woodland bison," he said when asked about reverting to pre-settlement conditions. "We're going to pull the rug out from underneath the crazies. In the process of restoration we're going to have to clear-cut. We're going to have to thin [the forest]."

In Carlson's mind, true restoration entails harvesting, not walking away and hoping that the forest will revert to a hemlock-beech cathedral of "old growth." That means actually decreasing or eliminating the acres already set aside as wilderness areas. Few timber supporters have publicly embraced that proposal, but several have already come out against any increase in the Allegheny's wilderness allotment. Jack Hedlund cites forest health and the local timber economy as reasons, but his views on wilderness also rely heavily on his belief that local residents have no interest in the remote experiences that wilderness provides. In fact, he says that hardly anybody likes to do those things.

"Recreationalists don't want wilderness," Hedlund said. "They don't seek wilderness. They don't seek it nationwide. So why would they seek it here? If less than one percent of the people nationwide seek wilderness as a means of recreation, why would they seek it more here? The national statistics for wilderness nationwide is that one percent of people recreate in a wilderness. In the Allegheny National Forest it's less than one-tenth of one percent. There are very, very, very few people who are actually looking for the complete solitude that Kirk Johnson is talking about."

On the national level, Hedlund cites a 1998 report released by the Chicago-based Heartland Institute called "Whither Wilderness? How Much Is Enough?" It states that more federal wilderness "will best suit the purists, people seeking 'remote reaches traditionally inhabited only by bears, black flies, and backpackers of an esthetic sensibility so refined that their wilderness experience could be irrevocably impaired by the sight of a discarded tea bag.' Far greater numbers of people with lesser esthetic sensibility will seek more readily accessible areas, perceived as wild but likely to have at least some developed facilities."[5]

Locally, Hedlund points to the Allegheny National Forest 2001 annual report. It indicates that the Allegheny's wilderness resources have generated forty-five thousand "recreational visitor days" since 1986. Motorized activities such as ATV and snowmobile use generated 10 million recreational visitor days over the same period. Other "roaded natural" activities in dispersed recreation facilities were three hundred times more popular than wilderness. Hedlund reads that and asks why anyone would want to add more. He voiced that interpretation in the *Warren Times Observer* on November 15, 2002: "Certainly, we're not saying cut [it] all," he said. "I don't have a problem with the wilderness (that's already been designated on the ANF). What we have already is satisfying the need for wilderness . . . and [it] holds no benefit in any way shape or form to have more than we need."

The Allegheny Defense Project's Ryan Talbott blasted Hedlund's comments in a letter to the editor that appeared in the paper five days later. "Of course, you cannot accurately interpret statistics if you do not consider all the data," he wrote. "What Mr. Hedlund left out of his letter is that less than two percent of the Allegheny exists as wilderness. When viewed in light of this important factor, the results do not suggest that wilderness is unpopular to visitors, as Mr. Hedlund wants you to believe, but rather that the seemingly low recreational use of wilderness is directly related to the fact that there is so little wilderness to recreate in. I am sure that if there is more wilderness, these figures would increase."

Officials in charge of Pennylvania's 2.1-million-acre state forest system seem to agree. On May 31, 2003, the *Pittsburgh Post-Gazette* kicked off an article about the state's forest planning process in dramatic fashion: "The buzz over recreational activities like hunting, fishing, hiking and cross-country skiing in Pennsylvania's forests has finally gotten loud enough to be heard over the timber cutters' chainsaws."

State officials believe that the demand for outdoor recreation is increasing. A proposed plan could add as much as twenty thousand acres to the state's Natural and Wild Areas, set-asides similar to federal wilderness. People opposed to additional wilderness point out that wild and natural areas provide substantial recreational access, even roads, that federal wilderness does not. Seeing that the whole promise of economic vitality through wilderness rests on increased usage and spending, doesn't it seem suspicious that people agitating for more wilderness on the Allegheny have not made any of those compromises? That argument went out the window in May 2003.

The Allegheny Defense Project finally went public with its detailed plan for the Allegheny National Forest by posting its Allegheny Wild! proposal online. The main body is sixty-six pages long. An attachment called "The Citizen's Alternative" divides the forest into zones designed to address needs such as restoration, old growth, trail buffers, and watershed protection. Not surprisingly, none of those reported needs includes timber, oil or gas extraction. The proposal for the Tionesta Wilderness Area offers a clear departure from the one published in the *Natural Areas Journal*, however. Part of it would become a more accessible "national recreation area" instead of a federally designated wilderness, an adjustment that allows for the continued use of a popular snowmobile trail that would have been obliterated under the initial proposal.

"Yeah, yeah, yeah," Kleissler wrote in response to a request for clarification. "The Snowmobile Trail was a major reason for the change from Wilderness to [national recreation area] for the northeastern piece. . . . We haven't actually gotten into specifics yet on what roads need to be removed, although identification of Wilderness and other special area boundaries took this largely into account. For example, roads that we thought ought not be removed for one reason or another often ended up as boundaries. . . . [T]he change from the [*Natural Areas Journal*] article to the final proposal is significant—the difference [between] an idealistic goal and a realistic one I guess."

"Realistic" is a matter of opinion, of course. The Allegheny Wild! proposal calls for obliterating approximately a thousand miles of road across the national forest. The revised Tionesta Wilderness Area proposal still calls for more than 17,000 acres of wilderness on heavily used land west of Kane. Despite surging demand for more snowmobile trails, the proposed national recreation area would only maintain what is already there. There is even less consideration for all-terrain vehicle riders, one of the fastest-growing user groups on the forest. Allegheny Wild! calls for a moratorium on the construction of new ATV trails, although it does allow for the continued use of ones that already exist. If that position amounts to a concession, so does Jack Hedlund's: He supports moving forward with the wilderness areas that already exist, but he wants a moratorium on designating any more.

Timber supporters could conceivably separate logging concerns from the rest of Allegheny Wild! and consider proposed wilderness and recreation areas on their individual merits, but Kleissler did not submit his demands as such. Allegheny Wild! offers an integrated approach to forest management, and zero cut is the undeniable centerpiece of that approach. His proposal carefully carves up the Allegheny and dedicates it to what he considers better, more environmentally conscious uses. It does not leave room—not a single acre—for logging. People with a stake in the industry view that as further proof of Kleissler's radical agenda. Ed Kocjancic recalls that in the late 1980s and early 1990s, the Forest Service warned timber companies that they would eventually have to compromise with activists, but he thinks developments since then have been incredibly one-sided. "They didn't meet in the middle," he fumed. "It got to be a bitter hatred."

That hatred might justify the timber industry's wholesale rejection of Kleissler's proposal, but it cannot explain why so many people are just as angry with Kirk Johnson. He backed away from zero cut years ago. Maybe his past allegiance to the ADP suggests caution, but proposals to actually decrease the amount of wilderness on the Allegheny are no more conciliatory than Kleissler's zero-cut demands. Unfortunately for Johnson, his efforts to gain credibility with local timber supporters suffered a serious blow on April 26, 2003. The *Warren Times Observer* had previously written editorials supporting more wilderness, but someone tipped editors off to Johnson's hidden history with one of the activist movement's most controversial tactics. They gave it serious play in a front-page article that included a huge color picture of Johnson looking off into the forest:

> In a post made on July 29, 1996, Johnson apparently advocates the practice of tree-spiking to halt timbering. Johnson wrote: *Believe me, a couple of well-placed spikes will not hurt a tree—the tree will be happy for the protection!*
>
> Johnson mentioned the book *Ecodefense: A Field Guide to Monkeywrenching* as a resource for various tree spiking techniques. He went on to say it could be purchased through the *Earth First! Journal.*
>
> Johnson signed the post, "spike on."

A reporter interviewed Johnson for the story, allowing him to point out that he made a subsequent post insisting that activists never undertake the practice for the purpose of hurting anyone. He also stressed that the posts were rather long in the tooth and that his views had changed. He denied ever spiking a tree and said, "Show me a post where I'm saying "spike on" in 2003. You can't do it. I just tried to cut out all the crap, all the radical stuff. All the provocative rhetoric."

Johnson was clearly angry with whoever dug up the posts, and he blasted them for it during his interview:

> "What did I ever do to these people?" he said. "I understand that I've taken on a public persona and people are going to attack you. But any rational person who

looks at these [posts], sees the dates and had any familiarity with what I am doing would realize it's not relevant. I've found a niche with the Friends of Allegheny Wilderness. I'd never do anything to jeopardize that. . . . I'm mad at the people who would do this kind of research, who would try to dredge up something to discredit me. But I'm also mad at radical groups that try to indoctrinate young, impressionable people. When you're young and impressionable, you want to do things to make a difference. . . . I believe that's what happened to me. It was not responsible to make these [posts]. These groups take advantage of the idealistic."

He was still fuming when I spoke to him a week later. "My attitude is, it's over with, and I'm going to continue doing what I have been doing all along," he said. "Nothing changes as far as I'm concerned. . . . I shouldn't have to talk about this. It's a stupid post on a news group. It was a dumb post, but so what? I'm not going to go around apologizing for it."

Whether he has to remains an open question. "He's painting himself as a moderate," Jack Hedlund said, "but the information on the web obviously doesn't paint him as a moderate."

Still, Hedlund said he believes Johnson is sincere. "I obviously believe he's grown out of that mentality," Hedlund said. "I think he's transcended that. He can still use that as part of his defense, as far as I'm concerned."

Sue Swanson was more aggressive. She was especially critical about Johnson's insistence that his youth at the time of the posts made them irrelevant. "Well, he was twenty-seven or twenty-eight at the time," she said. "That just didn't ring true to me. . . . I don't know how people can look at it and not be affected by that level of dishonesty. Not that he lied about it, but he portrayed himself as the middle ground."

Swanson's criticisms are particularly important. Hedlund, Carlson, and other timber advocates have come down squarely against any additional wilderness designations. She has not. As one of the region's most important economic development organizations, the Allegheny Hardwood Utilization Group's endorsement would be a huge feather in Johnson's cap. "I think what Kirk is asking for is too much," she said. "But if he is willing to use that as a starting point and accept less, we'd be willing to talk. . . . A lot of people are really willing to consider it. . . . I could agree to wilderness if they would agree to back off the litigation."

A coalition including AHUG and Friends of Allegheny Wilderness would certainly be a powerful voice for compromise, but Swanson doubts that enough people will accept Johnson as an intermediary between loggers and zero-cut activists. "Personally, I think it might have to be someone else unless there is a way Kirk can come up and establish himself with some level of trust," she said. "But I think that will be hard."

The scuffle over wilderness highlights how a few seemingly minor issues such as aesthetics and recreation can infuse the debate with new levels of rancor. Despite that explosive potential, however, it is only one aspect of a much larger battle for control of the Allegheny.

NOTES

1. Leon S. Minckler, *Woodland Ecology: Environmental Forestry for the Small Owner* (Syracuse, N.Y.: Syracuse University Press, 1975), 128–129.

2. Minckler, *Woodland Ecology*, 165.

3. Minckler, *Woodland Ecology*, 172–173.

4. 78 Stat. 890 (1964).

5. James H. Patrick and Raymond L. Harbin, "Whither Wilderness? How Much Is Enough," Heartland Policy Study No. 89 (Chicago: The Heartland Institute, 1998), 14. Internal quote from Jerry Adler and Daniel Glick, "No Room, No Rest," *Newsweek*, August 1, 1994, 47–52.

Chapter Eleven

Old Growth, New Economy, and the Tourism Promise: If You Build It, Who Will Come?

Like you, I have enjoyed this forest since I was under 12, shot my first buck
as a kid, south of Hermit Springs, along the Minister; there wasn't any snow
and I didn't have a rope, so I had to drag him with my belt, back to Hermit
Springs. Like you, I have a million memories and the tree huggers make me
mad, too. They think they know everything and they can come in here and
take our jobs and ruin our lives. I don't think they care one whit about us or
our forest. I think they are paid by foundations such as Heinz to come up here
and get us out of here. Their lawyers and judges don't give a hoot about us,
either.

—Letter to the Editor, *Warren Times Observer*, June 20, 2003

Ridgway, Pennsylvania, is the center of the chainsaw-carving universe. It is
a strange distinction, but one that speaks volumes about efforts to revitalize
struggling communities in and around the Allegheny National Forest.

The town identifies so strongly with its logging heritage that even its most
prominent contribution to the art world, an annual event called The Ridgway
Chainsaw Carving Rendezvous, entails screeching chain saws and flying
dust. Thirty-nine carvers participated in 2000, the first year it was open to the
public. In 2003, 150 artists from thirty-one states and nine countries came to
showcase their talents. The community has seized on the event, declaring
itself "The Chainsaw Carving Rendezvous Capital of the World." The Pittsburgh airport is three hours away, so volunteers drive there to collect many
of the carvers and bring them to town. Local families house participants when
necessary. "We tell people, if you can get to Ridgway, we'll take care of
you," said Liz Boni, organizer Rick Boni's wife. "Yeah," he chimed in with
a chuckle. "It's almost like a New Age type of a happening."

Rick Boni, fifty-three, has been a full-time carver for the past fifteen years. A Ridgway native, he earned a degree in commercial art from the Art Institute of Pittsburgh. "Americans, I mean—just like if you were going to study oil painting, you'd go to Europe," he said. "And that's why they come here. I mean, if you want to study carving, go to the U.S. because this is where it began, and we're way advanced of all the other countries."

But is it art? Besides plenty of traditional "arts-and-crafts" subjects such as animals and Indians, there was a fine rendition of Edvard Munch's iconic nineteenth-century painting "The Scream" in white pine. If the proof is in the purse strings, chainsaw art can give ritzy SoHo galleries a run for their money. Several of the pieces carved at the 2003 Rendezvous brought well over $1,000 at the auction held at the end of the event. (All proceeds go to the Make-A-Wish Foundation and the Ridgway YMCA.) The market beyond the Rendezvous is even stronger. Participant Steve Backus, a veritable mountain of a man from Washington State, has sold pieces for as much as $15,000. Boni has seen his go for up to $8,000.

So does Ridgway's economic future rest on events such as the Chainsaw Carving Rendezvous? Probably not. It happens once a year, and even then there are not enough hotels and restaurants in the area to fully capture the tourism windfall. That does not point to any deficiency in the event itself. It has been a fabulous addition to the local culture and a growing source of civic pride. Expecting it to become the basis for the local economy would be a stretch, and nobody appears to be doing that. Instead, people are trying to mesh it together with larger attempts to redefine their community.

Those efforts, in Ridgway and other towns throughout the Allegheny region, encapsulate the confrontation between activists and the locals who oppose them. Take Kane, which proudly declares itself "The Black Cherry Capital of the World." Zero-cut activists want the black cherry to go away. There are many scientific and economic arguments for and against that proposal, but none of them addresses an even stickier issue: Part of the Kane's cultural identity is wrapped up in those trees, and replacing that hard-won identity might be even tougher than salvaging the local economy.

If history is any guide, changing the heart of local communities is not impossible. Towns in the Allegheny region have proven incredibly resilient, both culturally and economically. Bradford still has substantial oil interests. In fact, the banner topping the *Bradford Era* still trumpets the town as "The High-Grade Oil Metropolis of the World." But Zippo has arisen to compete with oil as the town's touchstone industry. Ridgway has seen successive waves of industries pack up and leave, but (for now at least) black cherry and powdered metals remain.

Forward-looking residents are attempting build on what they have, and they recognize that the Allegheny National Forest is a valuable resource. They know that tourists will come and spend money if the right amenities are in place, so they are trying to strike a balance between the past, the present, and the future. Chainsaw carving, eco-tourism, hunting, fishing, gas, logging, and oil will sometimes compete with each other for limited resources, but the Allegheny is a "multiple-use" forest, after all. People hope that they can make room for everyone.

Some activists see no future in that balancing act, arguing that ecological and aesthetic degradation associated with logging alienates tourists who would otherwise come to the Allegheny. Kirk Johnson's master's thesis, written while he was still toeing the zero-cut line, cites numbers arguing that timber, oil, and gas extraction sustained 1,920 jobs and added approximately $78 million a year to the Allegheny's economy. It contrasted those with far more impressive recreation statistics: 2,700 jobs and $91 million. "Whether or not the above data are strictly accurate," Johnson concluded, "it can be seen that there are two formidable conflicting interests in the ANF—resource extraction, and recreation."

His former employer agrees with that assessment. "The Allegheny, if you look at it in a lot of ways economically, we're suppressing our strongest economic base," Jim Kleissler said in a January 2003 interview. "You know, if you look at the numbers up here, the economy up here is really recreation and tourism. So why do we only have two backpacking trails on the forest? We went skiing by my house the other day. You know, [forest managers on the Allegheny] clear-cut along cross-country ski trails. So what's wrong with that? Who cares about the aesthetics—what's wrong with that? When you expose sun to snow, it melts. So what happens on the trail? Well, it ends up that the snow doesn't last as long, so it's harder to get a good day on the snow trails. Also it becomes softer, which is not as good for skiing. Then you add the aesthetics to it. Why would I go out of my way to ski the Brush Hollow ski trail, which otherwise would be a great trail? Yeah, recreation is the leading industry, and look at how poorly the forest is managed. Look, if we had eight good backpacking loop trails in the Allegheny and this area, look at what kind of businesses we could run."

There are, in fact, more than "two backpacking trails on the forest." Kleissler concedes that but uses it to illustrate what he sees as a fundamental failure to provide what dedicated hikers really want. The North Country Scenic Trail runs approximately ninety miles through the forest, but it is not a loop trail that allows people to walk into the woods, sleep under the stars, and return to their cars along a different route. By failing to provide such amenities, Kleissler says, the Forest Service is ignoring a potential economic bonanza. "We have to realize that we're in the twenty-first century," he said, "that we live in a world where we have urban and suburban and rural populations all living on the fast track now. They need places to go to get away from that. And they don't need to go skiing and run into clearcuts and stuff like that. We have an opportunity to provide a public service that really, at this point and stage in America, benefits everyone."

But can't those amenities coexist with logging, however limited, which might support more traditional aspects of the local economy? Kleissler countered that an economic study performed in Warren County proves that those industries have already abandoned local communities. "You know, we had economists come in," he said. "Not our economists, their stinking economists came in and said there won't be an impact [from zero cut]. That economic study said that [the wood products industry] was, and I think this is really true, in Warren County it was only like 2 percent of the economy."

The economists in question compiled a report in 2001 titled "The Role of the Allegheny National Forest in the Warren County Economy."[1] Their data showed that jobs related to recreation outnumbered timber jobs in the county 440 to 380. Even more surprising to many people was an extrapolation that indicated what zero cut might do to the Warren County economy, assuming private timber made up for all the logs that would otherwise come off the Allegheny: The study said the change could *add* eight jobs and more than $170,000 in wages.

The study supposedly confirms what activists have been saying all along: That the Allegheny region's industrial economy is suffering, and communities looking to stop the bleeding should turn to recreation and tourism for a boost. Locals who focus on economic development have responded to that revelation in several revealing ways. The first amounts to a resounding, "No kidding."

Residents are not blindly sacrificing their precious natural resources to the all-powerful god of Big Timber. They recognize the area's natural, historical, and cultural bounty, and they are trying to capitalize on it. The Ridgway Chainsaw Carving Rendezvous is a case in point. It started out as a quaint regional affair, but word of mouth, Internet postings, and community action have pushed it to a critical tipping point. Officials hope—and are trying to make sure—that spendthrift tourists continue following the carvers into town.

Hunting is another huge attraction, and people are trying to capitalize on its popularity. The Forest Service has joined with the Sand County Foundation, the Bradford Water Authority, and several corporate landowners to initiate the 73,250-acre Kinzua Quality Deer Cooperative, an attempt to reduce the deer herd in northwestern McKean County. Hunters who take game in the project area and report the circumstances of the kill receive an invitation to an impressive annual awards dinner. The real incentive, however, is the hope that fewer deer will mean bigger deer. The Allegheny National Forest Vacation Bureau plays to the hunters' desire to improve forest health while simultaneously stoking their interest in bagging the Big One at a website detailing the possibilities.[2]

The list goes on. The Zippo/Case Visitors Center in Bradford opened in 1997 and continues to attract hordes of eager collectors. The facility hosts "swap meets" that draw thousands of Zippo aficionados from all over the world. The company claims that it is the "most popular museum in northern Pennsylvania."[3]

The Pennsylvania elk herd, located south and east of the Allegheny in a series of state forests, was just a few hundred strong when I graduated from high school in 1991. It currently stands at more than seven hundred, and 2001 ushered in the state's first legal elk hunt since the 1930s. More than seventy thousand people come to see the majestic animals every year. Eager to develop the resource as a premier tourism attraction, the North Central Pennsylvania Regional Planning and Development Commission (NCPRPDC) and several other agencies released a 164-page study in August 2002. Titled "Plan for Elk Watching and Nature Tourism in North Central Pennsylvania," it is a filled with maps, tables, and charts detailing the possibilities.[4]

An even more ambitious effort to market the area as a state-designated "heritage region" has been under way since 1995. Project coordinator Bob Imhof, a NCPRPDC employee, said the plan came to fruition in September 2001 when the state government declared all or part of fifteen counties— including the four that make up the Allegheny National Forest—as the Pennsylvania Lumber Heritage Region. According to the Pennsylvania DCNR, "the region will be developed, managed and marketed to attract visitors, create new jobs and offer an understanding of the dynamics of the early lumbering industry and its relationship to the development of the region's economic base."

Residents clearly understand that tourism and recreation can bolster their ailing economy. Rather than providing a rare piece of common ground on which environmental activists and local development officials can operate, however, competing definitions of "tourism," "recreation," and "wilderness" have driven them even further apart. That discussion begins with contentious decisions about economic potential. It ends with far more difficult questions about community self-determination and cultural identity.

Kleissler's economic plan includes "good backpacking loop trails," which he theorizes would induce eco-tourists to spend their money in the Allegheny region. The problem with that analysis, according to critics, is that taking those acres out of timber production would cost far more jobs than the tourism would create. Take a 20,000-acre tract. You could arguably log two hundred acres every year for a hundred years. In year 101, loggers could move back to the first plot and start all over. Throw in periodic thinning on all of those tracts, and it amounts to a substantial amount of work for local loggers and the mills they supply. Moreover, it is not as if those managed lands would not attract ecoconscious travelers. Most of the areas where Kleissler camps today are forests less than a hundred years old.

So how many outdoor equipment stores would it take to supply a heavily used loop trail through twenty-thousand acres? Enough to hire all the displaced loggers? If so, would those jobs pay as much? "The service economy doesn't pay as well per hour," Kleissler admitted. "There's no doubt about that. However, if you want to use examples, number one, you would have more service jobs. There is more employment, which is key, because there is high unemployment up here, so we need more overall employment. Then what you end up doing is you add manufacturing employment because you add—businesses come here because of what we have to offer. That's what happened in the Northwest. People want to complain about it, but actually the economy in the Pacific Northwest has improved since the spotted owl, average salary included. Income has increased."

Kleissler's take on the Pacific Northwest's economic transformation is still open to debate a decade after the spotted owl drama unfolded. He pointed me to several studies, one of which was "The Sky Did *Not* Fall: The Pacific Northwest's Response to Logging Reductions." The Earthlife Canada Foundation and Sierra Club of British Columbia had the report prepared by ECO-Northwest, a company that bills itself as "the Northwest's largest and most respected economic consulting firm." According to the report, which was issued in 1999:

> The reduction in logging triggered widespread fear of economic catastrophe. Some predicted as many as 150,000 workers would lose their timber-related jobs, hundreds of communities would become economic wastelands, and the region as a whole would fall into a depression that would take years, if not decades, to reverse.
>
> These dire predictions, however, did not materialize. Instead of collapsing, the region's economy expanded. The PNW weathered virtually unscathed the national economic recession that occured at about the same time as [the federal court's spotted owl decision], and both Oregon and Washington have consistently outperformed the national economy throughout the 1990s.

The study argued that the timber industry had been overcutting for years and a reduction was imminent no matter what the federal court decided. The study also found that decreased logging led to improvements in the region's quality of life, which drew tourists, families, and companies with good jobs to the area. That conclusion supports Kleissler's version of events, but a more recent study conducted by Oregon State University and the Oregon Employment Department offers a far gloomier assessment. Issued in April 2003, it is called "Employment Transitions in Oregon's Wood Products Sector during the 1990s." The *Oregonian* newspaper previewed the study's findings on January 7, 2003:

> One of the great unknowns following the collapse of Northwest timber cutting through the 1990s was what happened to thousands of loggers, sawmill workers and others who lost their jobs.
>
> Researchers mining a decade's worth of obscure state employment records have unearthed an answer, and it's not pretty:
>
> More than half the 60,000 workers who held jobs in the wood products industry at the start of the 1990s had left it by 1998. And almost half of those who left disappeared from work rolls altogether—probably moving to another state, retiring or going unemployed.
>
> Roughly 18,000 of the workers who left the field found a job in Oregon. But of them, nearly half took jobs in service and retail businesses—such as restaurants and department stores—ending up with lower wages, on average, than they had earned almost 10 years before.
>
> Viewing job shifts by region, researchers found that about a third of those who lost jobs in rural Southwest and Eastern Oregon did find work at higher wages—but only after moving to the urban northwest part of the state.

The seemingly disparate findings in these two studies cannot be attributed to their source. The lead author of the 2003 report was Ted L. Helvoigt. He is currently an economist with ECONorthwest, the same company that compiled the 1999 study. Instead, they point to the difficulty in analyzing something as complex as a regional economy over the course of a decade. Applying that data to the Allegheny—ten years later and three thousand miles away—would yield questionable results at best. That is not to say either side has stopped trying, or that using examples generated closer to home is any more productive.

Jim Kleissler offered a particularly interesting response when asked about the veracity of seemingly unrelated rumors indicating that he is an anarchist. "I've flirted with it sometimes," he admitted. "But, you know, I think the problem with anarchy—and I've had an argument with people, with professors and stuff before, when I was in school—the problem with anarchy is that it's really good on critique and really bad on a solution."

Kleissler's critics charge that the same problem applies to his promises regarding the region's economic future. In a January 2003 interview, he expressed concerns about jobs at the Johnsonburg paper mill. "How long do you think that Willamette mill is going to be open?" he asked, continuing,

> It will be done in twenty or thirty years. I guarantee it. The fact of the matter is, the workers at the mill in Johnsonburg will tell you the same thing. The reason is

because Willamette has absolutely zero stake—now it's Weyerhaeuser, and Weyerhaeuser is even worse—in giving a damn about what I care about or what [workers]
care about. . . . At least I give a rat's ass. Maybe I don't have the time to go out there
or the money to go out there and create alternative jobs automatically, but you know
what? A lot of times these things happen as a result of changes that occur. You could
say you need to organize these alternative businesses first. Well, based on what? No,
you need to create the place where alternative businesses can come in, OK?

That certainly is OK—for an economist writing a textbook on economic
development. Kleissler is asking residents to take a huge leap of faith. He
expects them to believe studies that say loggers in the Pacific Northwest did
just fine. He wants them to ignore reports arguing that the opposite is true.
Kleissler tries to focus on the positive by pointing out the Allegheny's prox-
imity to large urban markets to support his case for recreation and tourism.

Where in the Northeast is a similar type of urban/suburban base that the Allegheny
has within its reach, an area that's been given strong protection, where they designed
a world-class or a state-class trail system, and promoted it? Come on, have you ever
seen an Allegheny brochure for a hiking trail? They're the worst things I've ever
seen in the entire world. I know little dinky agencies that do better brochures. We
thought about publishing our own because in a week I could do better brochures on
just about every hiking trail. The bottom line is, if you do those things, and if you
look at the examples, whether it's the Adirondacks or the Catskills, they all thrive.
Even the Monongahela [National Forest in West Virginia] thrives in comparison to
the Allegheny.

In what sense? Jobs? Income? Tax base? He had trouble answering. "Well,
I'm speaking in general because I don't know the specifics of the Monongahela," he said. "But you can just tell by being there. This is just anecdotal. If
you go down there it's a much healthier business climate."

Kleissler might be right when he claims that he has neither the time nor
the money to establish a detailed alternative economic plan, but he might consider something more substantial than "If you build it, they will come." As
it stands, that is basically what he has to offer. When asked how many ski
rental shops it would take to replace Kane Hardwood, which employs over a
hundred people, he discussed multiplier effects—and the prospect of much
bigger things to come. "The thing with recreation and tourism is it brings in
money that didn't originate in the community into the community," he said.
"When you have locally operated places like ski rental places, more of that
money stays within the community. . . . And so the wealth here will increase,
actually. And as the wealth increases, opportunity increases and so forth.
Also, you have to recognize that it's not like Kane's just going to close down
and no one else is going to recognize the opportunity. You know, one of the

big things is that electronics companies really want to locate in these kinds of areas."

Is there a booming market in electronics? Is that market centered in the Mid-Atlantic? If so, would he support that kind of manufacturing base so close to the Allegheny? Kleissler's failure to get specific makes him a target for people already opposed to his agenda. "Bullshit," Jack Hedlund said upon hearing Kleissler's vague but glowing assessment of the Adirondacks region. "He's crazy. I was just up to Glens Falls [New York], and the place is a dying community. I mean I was just up there in the past six months and I'm telling you, it's a distressed area. The houses are falling apart and everything else, and Glens Falls is right on the border of the Adirondacks. I don't know what he's seeing that I'm not seeing. People aren't moving there. They just aren't moving there. The communities, at least as I saw it driving up through there, are dying communities. They're not thriving. He's nuts."

Glens Falls is on the southeast border of New York's enormous Adirondack Park. Population fell by about 4.4 percent during the 1990s, but the city's website indicates that the drop was due to emigration into outlying areas. The larger metropolitan area has actually grown in recent years. Then again, four of the top thirty employers listed on the county's website are involved in pulp and paper manufacturing, contributing more than eighteen hundred jobs to the economy. So is Glens Falls thriving or dying, and what would that mean either way?

If it is thriving, is that because the paper mills are still running or because tourists use it as a starting point for adventures in the park? If it is dying, does that indicate that pulp and paper are dead industries that should be abandoned, or that vast outdoor playgrounds like Adirondack Park do not draw the alternative industries environmentalists keep talking about? Kleissler and Hedlund can look at the same issue—economic vigor in the Adirondacks—and see completely opposite realities.

Comparing Adirondack Park with the Allegheny is problematic anyway. The former is a state park rather than a national forest, and public portions of it are already operating under a de facto zero-cut system. It is also twelve times larger than the Allegheny. Warren County, New York, where Glens Falls is located, is 200 miles from New York City, 220 miles from Boston. Montreal is approximately seventy miles from the park's northern border. Ridgway, Pennsylvania, is 120 miles from Pittsburgh and Buffalo, much smaller cities already facing their own population exodus. A more appropriate model for the Allegheny's eco-tourism potential might be found a lot closer to home, and Jack Hedlund is even more concerned about the evidence he sees there.

The Quehanna Wild Area, about thirty miles southeast of Ridgway, contains 48,186 acres of protected forestland on the Elk and Moshannon state forests. That amounts to more than three times the surface area of Manhattan. Snowmobiles, off-road vehicles, and vehicular campers are prohibited, but it is not the same as a federally designated wilderness. There are a few roads through the area. Limited commercial logging is theoretically allowed, but there is a moratorium in place as officials reconsider the state's long-term forest plan. State "natural areas," where roads and logging are forbidden, are managed more like federal wilderness areas. There are two natural areas totaling more than two thousand acres either in or adjacent to Quehanna.

It would seem to have many of the elements associated with Kleissler's economic dream world. The main Quehanna Trail, which weaves in and out of the wild area, is nearly seventy-five miles long. Cross sections, which allow hikers to do shorter loops, bring the total closer to a hundred miles of trail. It offers 9,790 feet of vertical rise. There are more than sixty miles of cross-country ski trails in the wild area. That whole length can also be hiked. People interested in water sports can take advantage of a twenty-acre lake at Parker Dam State Park a few miles to the east. The bulk of Pennsylvania's remaining state forestland rests directly to the north and east. To top it all off, the state's growing elk herd, a popular tourist draw, roams over a huge portion of Quehanna's range.

All of those resources are even more accessible than the Allegheny because Quehanna is just a few miles off Interstate 80's Penfield exit. It is farther away from Pittsburgh, but it is probably a quicker drive because of the highway. Compared to the Allegheny, Quehanna is closer by roughly half to Altoona, Johnstown, and State College. Any eco-tourists who would purportedly flock to a restored Allegheny National Forest from Baltimore, Boston, New York City, and Philadelphia would drive right past Quehanna on the way.

With all that going for the area, Jack Hedlund wonders what happened to the electronics companies Kleissler says are attracted to environmental destinations. "Why hasn't Bill Gates moved to Quehanna or even considered moving there?" he asked. "Why haven't people considered moving to Quehanna since it's been essentially designated as a wild and natural area for a long period of time? Why hasn't there been a big influx of people moving there? Has anybody asked him that?"

He has a point. Clearfield, population 6,600, is approximately twenty miles away from Quehanna's outdoor splendor. It even has its own exit on Interstate 80, an incredibly attractive economic feature that communities on the Allegheny cannot match. It seems strange, then, that companies are fleeing Clearfield rather than beating a path to its door. FCI Electronics—that is correct, an electronics company—closed its Clearfield plant and canned its last 360 workers in October 2002. At one point it employed as many as 750. Desperate for work, employees decided to market Clearfield to potential employers instead of looking for jobs individually. They unveiled a website called clearfieldworks.com in June 2002, five months before the plant closed. They paid for part of the marketing effort with money from vending machines at the plant. That innovative approach led to an Associated Press story later that summer:

> [T]he local economy has struggled in recent years. Its coal mines have closed. So have the brickyards that once manufactured firebricks for steel mills. A textile industry that thrived decades ago has shriveled to almost nothing.
>
> Now, workers read news about plant closings as they would an obituary page. Global competition is often blamed for the shutdowns of former competitors and partners alike.
>
> The telecommunications industry had a banner year in 2000 but then slumped badly, and Paris-based FCI began laying off workers.
>
> At the Clearfield plant, which has been in operation since 1966 under three different owners, word came in April that remaining employees would be laid off. They were not offered jobs at FCI's two other Pennsylvania plants because future demand appears weak, company spokeswoman Sheila Himes said.
>
> The company is wishing its workers the best in whatever it takes for them to find jobs, Himes said.
>
> Workers at FCI are out of places to work in the region—even retail jobs have been hurt with the closing of local Ames and Kmart stores, said Don McClincy, executive director of the Clearfield Foundation, a non-profit group that fosters economic growth in the region.[5]

Clearfieldworks.com promotes local outdoor attractions like Quehanna, but organizers realize it can hardly be the whole pitch. Microsoft did move to Bellevue, Washington, in 1979, but the fact that Bill Gates was raised in Seattle might have had something to do with it. The corporate behemoth shifted to Redmond, Washington, in 1986. The region's scenery might have affected that decision, but Gates did not choose the Pacific Northwest because his workers were begging for an opportunity to live near protected spotted owls. The old growth was still falling when Microsoft came to town.

People behind Clearfield's marketing effort also tout the community's low rent, highway access, and available workforce. NBC *Nightly News* weighed in on the effort on April 21, 2003, with a story entitled "Town for Hire." Correspondent Ann Thompson swooped into Clearfield and did a two-and-a-half-minute feature on the workers' attempt to court another electronics firm, which to date remains unsuccessful. Many workers have started making plans to move their families elsewhere.

That is not to say that the Quehanna Wild Area is a failure. Like the Ridgway Chainsaw Carving Rendezvous, it performs its intended functions admi-

rably. Locals hunt, fish, and hike there. A few guide services have sprung up
to lead tourists on rigorous hikes, take them skiing, and show them where the
elk roam. Several backwoods bars and restaurants cater to the crowds. Yet as
wonderful as those amenities can be, they do not provide nearly enough jobs
for all of FCI's 360 displaced families. And even if they did, they would not
provide wages high enough to support them.

Jim Kleissler's proposal deals with a different piece of land, of course.
Many of the changes he envisions for the Allegheny afford more stringent
land-use restrictions than Quehanna does. He has also crafted what he considers a unique system of trails, overlooks, visitor centers, and other recreational
amenities designed to draw the kind of development he discussed. Many people are still dubious, however. The Allegheny already has almost ten thousand acres of federally designated wilderness centered around Hickory
Creek. There is no electronics company anywhere near it. The Forest Service
maintains it with a single wilderness ranger, and there is no cadre of guides
getting rich off hordes of tourists.

But maybe Kleissler is right—about everything. Assume that the pre-settlement forest looked like the one he wants, and that restoring it to something
approaching that condition makes good environmental sense. Assume that his
plan will bring that forest about despite nagging problems such as acid rain,
deer overpopulation, tree diseases, and insect infestations. Finally, assume
that the ecosystem so restored will provide the recreation opportunities people want and attract high-tech electronics companies eager to relocate near
such amenities. Kleissler has studies backing him at every turn, after all, so
it is worth considering what the future would look like if his experts are correct and his opponents are wrong.

At first glance it looks like a vision that everyone would support: The
world's next Bill Gates invents the next great gizmo and opens a factory in,
say, Kane. Workers from the Johnsonburg paper mill and the refineries in
Bradford and Warren, joined by loggers who used to cut on the Allegheny,
go to work there and earn world-class wages. The forest recovers, the tax base
increases, schools improve, and everyone is happy. Or maybe not. Some
locals fear that any such progress would do more damage to local communities than any benefits it might bring.

"People will only move here [if] they have the amenities that they're used
to having, and those amenities are going to cause whatever just happened
down on the Route 99 corridor going through Huntington," Jack Hedlund
said. "What did they do? They sold off this huge chunk of land so they could
build this four-lane highway right on through the woods. The environmentalists have to be going nuts. But the fact of the matter is, that's what happens
in urban areas, and if you're going to have an influx of people in here that

want the urban amenities in a rural area, you're going to have four-lane highways in here. You're going to have a lot different types of stuff, which is
exactly what happened in the [Pacific] Northwest."

The difficulty in assessing exactly what happened in the Pacific Northwest
has already been discussed, but Hedlund has a point about the larger problems associated with high-tech or any other kind of development. Anyone
who has tried to buy a house in Silicon Valley in recent years can attest to
the astronomical real estate prices. Long-time residents of Northern Virginia
can also go on at length about what the influx of Internet corporations has
done to local traffic patterns.

Kleissler probably has more limited development in mind, but his agenda
entails ending all commercial timber, gas, and oil production on the Allegheny. His alternative industries would have to employ all the newcomers in
addition to the displaced locals. The Weyerhaeuser paper mill—one of Kleissler's least favorite relics of the old economic order—currently employs four
hundred. Another, American Refining Group in Bradford, employs two hundred more. More than a hundred work for Temple Inland's medium-density
fiberboard plant in Mount Jewett. Kleissler says that zero cut would not put
them all out of business completely, but he would clearly like to see them go.
Throw in loggers, oil field workers, and any support staff who might suffer
in the transition to a tourism economy, and the total number of jobs involved
becomes substantial.

So how many jobs would Kleissler's new economy have to create to
replace those lost? A figure like 1,707 is either way too high or terribly low,
depending on whom you ask, but it offers an easy comparison to Coudersport's recent flirtation with the Information Age. Coudersport is on Route 6,
approximately fifty miles east of the Allegheny National Forest. Equally rural
and connected to a similarly strong timber heritage, the scenic hamlet
boomed in the 1990s. Its population surged, largely because the nation's fifth-
largest cable company decided to establish its glittering headquarters there.

The move proved an economic bonanza. Corporate heavies began infusing
the town with money, eventually constructing parking garages to handle the
related influx of workers. The company employed 1,707 by early 2002,
according to an Associated Press report. Many were highly paid professionals
who put relentless upward pressure on the housing market. Some locals
profited handsomely by selling their homes to the wealthy newcomers, and
others did just as well by going to work for the cable giant. On the other hand,
some people who lived in the area during the boom were forced out when
rent payments soared higher than anyone had ever seen them. Some had to
move and commute from outlying towns.

That is the price of progress, of course. It would be interesting to see how long-time residents fare in the new system, but observers might not get the chance. The cable company in question was Adelphia, the brainchild of local-hero-turned-suspected-robber-baron John Rigas. On July 24, 2002, federal officials arrested Rigas, two of his sons and two other high-ranking Adelphia executives in a massive corporate scandal. By early 2003 the executives who replaced them were hinting that they might move corporate headquarters to Colorado. Only about two hundred high-level officials have relocated so far, but people are wary.

With all the financial shenanigans going on, perhaps it is understandable that residents closer to the Allegheny National Forest cast a skeptical eye on Kleissler's prosperity promise. First, many refuse to believe that creating a pristine wilderness would draw such companies. Second, just look at what happens when those companies do set up shop in town.

Zero-cut advocates do not base all their economic promises on new companies moving in, however. The economic study Kleissler cited showed that the timber industry made up only 2 percent of Warren County's economy. Moreover, it found that zero cut might actually lead to a slight increase in jobs. Kleissler admits that those jobs might pay low wages, but in the end that is not what residents fear most.

The study assumed that private land would make up for all of the Allegheny timber lost to zero cut, but it also discussed the possibility that such substitution might not be viable in the long term. Moreover, the Warren County study was just that—an economic analysis of one county out of four that contain the Allegheny. The study results are hard to extrapolate over the other three because Warren County is home to so few of the timber industry's secondary processing plants, such as sawmills. Zero cut would likely be far more painful where those facilities are concentrated, namely in Elk and McKean counties.

Kleissler was quick to respond when I asked him to reassess the strength of the regional timber industry.

"Have you ever been to Tidioute?" he asked. "It's a tourist town. All that's there is a tourist town. There hasn't been a sawmill there as long as I've been here. Tionesta? How many sawmills does Tionesta have? They have the Allegheny River. They don't have a sawmill. Marienville, the only reason Northeast Hardwoods mill is so big is because they expanded so much in the mid to late 1990s. We don't live in a timber economy, especially in Forest County. McKean County is the closest thing you can get."

That is true, but what has that tourist economy wrought? Twenty-two percent seasonal unemployment in Forest County, where Tionesta is located. Warren County recently decided—amid howls of protest—to close Tidioute's high school and bus its dwindling student population to Youngsville more than thirty miles away. Tionesta and Tidioute are fine little towns, but Kane and Ridgway residents understandably wince at the thought of using them as models of economic vigor.

The greatest fear is not low-wage jobs. The aching belief is that zero cut would bring no jobs at all. "I would say our declining school population and population in general would continue to decline more drastically than it has," Jack Hedlund predicted when asked what Kleissler's plan would do to local communities. "And I'm not just talking Kane. I'm talking Ridgway and Johnsonburg. Who knows? I feel quite certain that you would see a drop in population because people have to move where they can work. That's just the long and short of it. I don't know how it could be any other way."

It is not a completely unfounded fear. Recreation-based economies in the American West have been struggling with the same issue for decades. From Aspen, Colorado, to Jackson, Wyoming, long-time residents have seen their traditional employment opportunities disappear. Many move away as wealthy urbanites sweep through and build one preposterously large chalet after another. People who provided essential services such as fire and police protection are forced to commute from more affordable communities up to seventy miles away. The toilet scrubbers and burger flippers face an even grimmer economic reality.

Teton County and Jackson, Wyoming, commissioned the Urban Land Institute to conduct a study on the contentious issue. The 2000 report, entitled "Strategies for Addressing Future Growth," details a loathsome caste system that some people on the Allegheny view as an inevitable consequence of Kleissler's proposal:

> In Jackson and a few other places uniquely blessed by Mother Nature, and uniquely constrained by geography and public lands, market dislocations have risen to extreme levels that threaten the very social fabric of the community by pricing out of the market whole cohorts of the population. The average wage in Teton County is $21,000 per year. In 1999, the average single-family home sold for $775,000. The least expensive single-family lot on the market today is approximately $200,000. Although progress is being made in providing employee housing, the demographics of Jackson could soon resemble the demographics of the third world—the very rich, the heavily subsidized poor, and the transient including both visitors and workers. The middle class, the young families, and the community service personnel who want ownership housing or who desire single-family homes will be gone, and the community will be permanently changed because of it.

Studies indicate that many loggers in rural Oregon displaced by the spotted owl had to move to urban areas to find work. There are places where that did not happen, but the threat is certainly real. Worse, where would people displaced from the Allegheny go? At least loggers in the Pacific Northwest lived in a region humming with Internet boomtowns like Seattle. Western Pennsylvania has Pittsburgh, which is having a hard time retaining the people already living there. Whatever the future holds, it is clear that some people suffer when outside forces disrupt traditional industries. And whatever benefits it might bring, zero cut certainly qualifies as disruptive. The national electorate might view that suffering as necessary in the long run, but denying that it exists does not make it so.

At this stage the argument veers away from economics and charges headlong into a far more explosive debate about control of the Allegheny's cultural identity. Many people suspect that the economic demise they associate with zero cut is not based on any sort of interpretive lapse on Kleissler's part: They think that their financial ruin is an integral part of his plan to control the forest and discard anyone who gets in his way. In this view the potential class war in Jackson, Wyoming, is not an unfortunate economic byproduct of zero cut: it is exactly what the flatlanders have been after all along.

Residents betrayed that suspicion at a dismal community meeting in Ridgway on March 18, 2003. Township supervisors, school board members, and educators from throughout Elk County met with Forest Service officials to discuss the future of the Allegheny's timber industry. They were deciding whether to continue operating under the 25 percent payment system—in which the Forest Service redirects a quarter of all receipts to local communities for use in maintaining roads and schools—or switch to guaranteed payments as described in the Secure Rural Schools and Community Self-Determination Act of 2000.[6] Elk County opted for the 25 percent payment in 2001, a decision encouraged by the Allegheny Forest Alliance and everyone else who thought the situation was going to improve. It didn't, and the county's funding from the Forest Service ended up being hundreds of thousands of dollars less than it would have been had they accepted the guaranteed payment.

Forest Service officials at the 2003 meeting told local authorities that there was no way the annual timber harvest would ever get back to the 94.5 million board feet predicted in the 1986 forest plan. In fact, they told them it would never even reach the 53.2 million board feet determined as the allowable sales quantity in 1995. The headline in the next day's *Kane Republican* captured the tone of the meeting: "ANF Timber Harvesting Past Its Prime."

Local officials decided to abandon the 25 percent payment and opt for the guaranteed funds. There was no disagreement on that count, but consensus did nothing to cut through the harsh sense of surrender in the room. Dr. Francis Grandinetti, superintendent of the Ridgway School District, summed up his fears and suspicions about the decision late in the session. He noted that by decoupling school funding from timber harvesting, the district might lose its ability to intervene in lawsuits filed against the Forest Service. He also predicted that Congress would hang the community out to dry by refusing to fund the Secure Rural Schools Act when it comes up for review in 2006.

"To me it's a perfect plan," Grandinetti told the crowd. "You buy off the townships and the school districts. I'm not casting aspersions because I agree to [the guaranteed payment]. But you buy us off so we can't litigate. We're paid off for three years. At the end of those three years, don't refund it. We're down to a minimum amount of money that will come to the school districts and to the townships. We won't be able to do a thing about it and basically, as Jack [Hedlund] said, we go into a wilderness area for all of our economics. . . . If you start looking at your charts and you see the management activity [on the Allegheny], you start looking at the loss of that [timber] asset, you start looking at the loss of the economics, you start looking at the preservationists' motivation and the preservationists' mission, and you say, shut off the Rural Schools and Community Act in 2006, and mission accomplished. . . . There has always been the undercurrent that the preservationists mission and goal is to turn the area into a noneconomically productive wilderness area."

Grandinetti does not see a future in that wilderness, and he does not believe that Kleissler honestly does either. He thinks accepting the guaranteed payments is the first step toward the kind of economic servitude certain tourist towns in the West have been experiencing for years. "I don't want . . . one superintendent sitting here suggesting that I think what we're doing is right," he said. "Because in the long term, I think we're all going to pay for this decision."

Doug Carlson's assertion that environmentalists "are not going to be happy until we put on little Indian costumes and sell moccasins to these people who come in and meditate in the forest" captures the essence of Grandinetti's anger quite nicely. For Carlson, Kleissler is merely a proxy for thousands of arrogant, privileged urbanites who lack the knowledge to manage a forest responsibly but are willing to destroy isolated communities if it means they will have a nice place to showcase their expensive camping gear once or twice a year. It is not about economics. It is about control.

Carlson vented his consternation at the Allegheny Hardwood Utilization Group's annual dinner in 2003. He was sitting with Joe Arnold, an experienced local forester who frequently lambastes the Allegheny Defense Project in letters to the editor. Carlson compared the activist vision to ethnic hatred, in terms of both strategy and tenacity, as "rural cleansing."

"It's a function of the Wildlands Project," he said, referring to the national organization that has acted as a fiscal sponsor for both the Allegheny Defense Project and Friends of Allegheny Wilderness. He captivated Arnold with stories about the organization's plan to convert huge tracts of land into inaccessible old-growth forests connected by wilderness corridors teeming with reintroduced predators. In Carlson's telling, there is no room for human beings in that plan. "We're in the way," he said.

The activists' plan, according to Carlson, goes something like this: First, they stymie active management on the national forest through litigation. Find any angle—whether it is an endangered species like the Indiana bat or a technical violation of an environmental statute—and tie up everything as long as possible. (They learned this from the spotted owl case, of course.) Next, wait for the communities that depend on the forest to whither and die. And just who will be there to snap up all the abandoned homesteads in the rurally cleansed landscape?, Carlson asked. Arnold's son gave a telling response through his teeth: "Ted Turner."

Ted Turner, indeed. In the late 1980s the media mogul purchased a gargantuan ranch near Bozeman, Montana, a transaction that still has some locals pining for simpler times. On November 26, 1996, an irked columnist from the *High Country News* quipped, "Thanks to a land swap, Montana commoners will no longer be able to hunt, fish or hike on state lands nestled deep within the private kingdom of media mogul Ted Turner and his wife, Jane Fonda." Many people have been impressed with Turner's efforts to cultivate a herd of buffalo, but others cannot overcome their sense of rural prejudice. A backpacker who hiked through the area captured the sentiment for *Outdoor Bozeman*:

> Much of the first part [of the hike] crossed over Ted Turner's infamous Flying D Ranch, a fact hard not to notice given the many signs warning us of the consequences of leaving the trail. We snickered at the graffiti (and worse) that had tarnished most of these signs. There's nothing like the evidence of a good redneck shotgun blast at a "No Trespassing" sign to renew your faith in Montanans.[7]

Carlson cringes at the notion of stepping lightly around no-trespassing signs erected by interlopers, and he obviously has no interest in seeing his neighbors reduced to selling them moccasins or any other sort of cheap souvenirs. That is not to say that he is some kind of standoffish yokel opposed to any sort of change. On the contrary, he has spent years spearheading an effort to establish the Pennsylvania Hunting and Fishing Museum in Tionesta. Plans call for a 27,000-square-foot interactive facility that would cost more than $9 million. Governor Edward G. Rendell's (D) administration recently came through with a promise of matching funds, bringing the museum that much closer to reality. For all the rhetorical barbs Carlson aims at the zero-cut vision of a tourist economy, Carlson's efforts to establish the Hunting and Fishing Museum might eventually bring more visitors to the area than all the hiking trails in the world ever could.

Carlson's recreation vision differs from Kleissler's in a fundamental way. So do most of the projects that locals have proposed or implemented. They include tourism, but they tend to do so in a way that celebrates the region's history and heritage. The Chainsaw Carving Rendezvous speaks to logging and the surprisingly creative nature of the men who have pursued it. Elk viewing offers a testament to the resiliency of the forest, the majesty of the animals, and the foresight of the people who decided to reintroduce them so long ago. The elk hunt speaks to the success of that effort. The Zippo Museum documents the region's continued ability to create products with international appeal. The Lumber Heritage Region speaks for itself.

Contrast these with what some residents see as the zero-cut take on tourism. To them, it says that for people to visit the area, the Forest Service must first erase as much of that history as possible. The animals, trails, trees, and vistas currently on display are insufficient. Take the Allegheny back to what it looked like before humanity crashed the party, and maybe folks will come from afar and distribute some money. Do all that and maybe, just maybe, a new industry will move in to replace all the terrible ones that short-sighted locals still endorse. There are elements of truth to that assessment. Activists certainly think that pre-settlement conditions are preferable to current ones, and they celebrate the virtues of eco-tourism over extractive industries that have employed many workers in the Allegheny region for over a century.

Kleissler readily admitted his disdain for the area's history when I asked if it might make the Allegheny a poor choice for zero cut. "That was the problem," he said as he launched into a passionate indictment of industrialization. "That's why we created the Allegheny National Forest, because of what the timber industry and the oil industry did to it. That's the whole idea of history. You're supposed to learn from history, not repeat history. People just want to repeat history over and over again. You know, we never learn anything in this world. It drives me crazy. The bottom line is, this is a national forest. You can point out to me another 500,000 acres in Pennsylvania but it won't be national forest. Are you suggesting that we should only preserve and conserve land in other states? That doesn't make any sense, you know? And, where else can we preserve this ecosystem? You can't preserve this ecosystem somewhere else. You can't preserve the biodiversity that is supposed to be here somewhere else. Nor can you provide a place that provides the resources it does to Buffalo, Cleveland, Pittsburgh, and other surrounding communities that the Allegheny does. You can only do it here, and that's where we are."

The Allegheny certainly is where they are, and they clearly intend to stay as long as it takes to end 150 years of industrial extraction. The problem rests in the fact that many of the people who already live on the Allegheny have different ideas about what the forest should be. They point out that they were there first, and that they have already gone a long way toward saving the Allegheny from the brush heap that history bequeathed them. That might not make a difference to the power brokers who will eventually plot a course for the Allegheny, but it means the world to people who have spent their lives on the forest.

NOTES

1. Martin Shields, Timothy W. Kelsey, Allen Brady, and Adam Downing, "The Role of the Allegheny National Forest in the Warren County Economy," Community Impact Model–Penn State University, compiled from three public meetings held in Warren County in February and March 2001. http://cimpsu.aers.psu.edu.

2. www.allegheny-vacation.com/kqdc.php3 (accessed April 13, 2004).

3. www.zippo.com.

4. The study, commissioned by the NCPRPDC, the Pennsylvania Game Commission, the Pennsylvania Department of Conservation and Natural Resources and the Pennsylvania Lumber Heritage Region, was conducted by Fermata, Inc, a firm based in Austin, Texas. As of April 2004, it was available online at www.fermatainc.com/pennelk/reports.html.

5. Charles Sheehan, "Employers Encouraged to Apply," Associated Press, June 20, 2002.

6. P.L. 106-393, 114 Stat. 1607 (2000).

7. www.outsidebozeman.com/

Chapter Twelve

Epilogue: The Great Green Pendulum

Decision Could Pave Way for Logging Plan on ANF, but May Be Too Late Say
Loggers

—Headline in the *Kane Republican*, February 25, 2004

Federal Magistrate Judge Ila Jeane Sensenich dealt a serious blow to the
American zero-cut movement on Christmas Eve, 2003. She had issued a recommendation in the landmark East Side case fifteen months earlier siding
with activists on seven of ten counts. If accepted by the presiding judge, it
could have effectively ended even-aged management on the Allegheny
National Forest. That never came to pass. Sensenich's revised recommendation urged the presiding judge to reject nine of the Allegheny Defense Project's ten complaints. Timber supporters greeted her reversal as "a worthy
Christmas gift."[1]

The 126-page Magistrate's Report is a testament to the vagaries of modern
environmental law. Sensenich paid particular attention to the activists' charge
that the Forest Service chose even-aged management in the East Side project
primarily because it offered the greatest dollar return, a direct violation of
the National Forest Management Act. "Unfortunately," Sensenich wrote, "it
appears that neither congress nor any other court has ever defined what was
meant by the use of the term 'primarily.'"[2]

Sensenich went on to discuss the wide range of complications facing timber management on the Allegheny and issued her decision accordingly:

Considering that: (1) Congress did not define the meaning of "primarily" in the
NFMA; (2) no court has held that the Secretary of Agriculture has acted arbitrarily
and capriciously in violation of the Administrative Procedure Act and the NFMA by
selecting even-aged management as the harvesting system primarily because it
would give the greatest output of timber; (3) when the ANF was established in 1923

it had already been substantially clear-cut, resulting in stands of conifers and white pines being replaced by stands dominated by hardwoods such as black cherry, red maple, sugar maple and white ash, which were excellent for sawtimber; (4) the Forest Service is required to consider the costs and benefits of its management practices; (5) in developing the East [Side] Decision the Forest Service included in its purposes, in addition to providing a sustained yield of high quality Allegheny hardwood, the provision of a variety of age or size class habitat diversity as well as diversity of wildlife; (6) health problems existing in the ANF; and (7) management of the ANF is a complex matter; this court cannot find that in the East Side decision Defendants arbitrarily and capriciously selected their harvesting system primarily because it would give the greatest dollar return or the greatest unit output of timber in violation of the NFMA.[3]

Sensenich expressed sympathy with charges that the Forest Service should have adopted a "Landscape Corridor Proposal" that could have added additional old growth to the Allegheny but ultimately decided that the agency has wide discretion to manage the forest for other purposes. "Plaintiff's enthusiasm for the Landscape Corridor Proposal is understandable," she wrote. "But they have not shown that Defendants did not consider the concepts upon which it was based. The fact that it would have been a better alternative for wildlife than the actions developed in the East Side Decision does not render the refusal to implement it arbitrary and capricious."[4]

The activists' sole victory came regarding complaints about a plan to use even-aged management on four hundred acres of poorly drained soils. That was a hollow victory, to be sure. When the Allegheny Defense Project filed its lawsuit against the Mortality II project in 1997, it was trying to fundamentally alter forest management. Timber supporters have spent hundreds of thousands of dollars resisting that effort. The Forest Service has dedicated countless man-hours and other resources to reconsidering Mortality II and recasting it as East Side. All that, and it looks as if the only thing the litigation will actually change might be management plans for a few hundred acres— less than one-tenth of 1 percent of the entire Allegheny National Forest. District Judge William L. Standish accepted Sensenich's radically revised recommendation in a brief opinion issued March 23, 2004.

Perhaps the most frustrating aspect of the Allegheny experience is that the litigation fails to address one of the most critical aspects of the current environmental debate. Sensenich's report complained that "The battle between environmentalists who favor uneven-aged management and the Forest Service which extensively uses even-aged management . . . has raged in the federal courts since the 1970s."[5] Actually, those battle lines no longer apply. The divide separating timber supporters from the increasingly ardent activist community is much deeper and wider than it has ever been.

This book does not propose any legislative or judicial elixirs that will magically bring those forces together. Anyone who claims to have such a surefire solution is either a charlatan or a fool. Instead, it attempts to explore the Allegheny's singular importance in this great, growing American timber war, and use it to accomplish the one thing that only the most important political crises manage to achieve: Change the tone and direction of the debate.

Consider the spotted owl's mixed legacy. The unassuming little bird became a media darling, animating and amplifying a simmering debate and thrusting it into the national spotlight. In the end, the complex policy questions involved came down to a vague but critical formulation: Is it possible that, in certain instances, ecological concerns outweigh timber economics?

For many, the answer was a resounding "yes," a response that established an important limit on the American logging industry—but only with regard to very specific pieces of federal land. In the end, it "solved" little if anything. Outrage surrounding plans to extract oil and timber from the Arctic National Wildlife Refuge and the Tongass National Forest in Alaska prove that the debate rages on. Part of that fury stems from the fact that a lot of people already know and care about old growth, wilderness, and other versions of the ideal "pristine landscape." The spotted owl provided activists with much of that public support and, perhaps even more critically, political momentum.

Rolling Stone captured the extent to which activists have run with that momentum in a December 2002 feature. It detailed unsuccessful efforts to capture suspected eco-terrorist Michael Scarpitti, also known as Tre Arrow, and the proposed national forest timber sale in Oregon that reportedly sent him over the edge in 2001:

> It had been clear for at least a couple of years that the success or failure of the forces aligned against one another at Eagle Creek would define the struggle for Northwest forests. The Cascadia Forest Alliance agreed with the U.S. Forest Service that Eagle Creek was probably as well planned as any timber sale in the agency's history. No old-growth timber was targeted; trees would be thinned rather than clear-cut; little, if any, road building would be required; and the endangered species with the highest profile, the spotted owl, would not be affected. "It probably is the best they can do," conceded Cascadia [Forest Alliance] spokesman Donald Fontenot. "But guess what? That's not good enough. . . . Nothing short of ending logging on public lands is good enough."[6]

That sentiment is not isolated on the margins of radical environmental discourse: It is the Sierra Club's official position. What started out as a movement to improve federal timber programs or forbid them in particularly sensitive areas has morphed into something far more ambitious. And it is defining the struggle for forests well outside "the Northwest." The Allegheny Defense Project, like the Cascadia Forest Alliance, is going to resist logging projects on Pennsylvania's only national forest no matter how limited or well designed. East Side and Eagle Creek are part of the same national struggle. That is important because it eliminates one of the Green movement's central conceits—that they are agitating to protect "ancient forests" because of their unique age or environmental attributes. Timber supporters always suspected that there was something more driving the activist passion. The fact that zero cut has spread to Allegheny's industrial landscape proves the point.

Unfortunately, zero cut is not the only thing that has spread. The *Rolling Stone* article also named Tre Arrow as a suspect in the Earth Liberation Front's August 2002 attack on the Forest Service research laboratory in Irvine. The magazine characterized it as "far more aggressive" than other bombings because of its accompanying threat of physical violence.[7] The article also argued that the incident might serve as a watershed moment for radical activists:

> The argument is no longer just about crossing the line from civil disobedience into criminal mischief but about transforming a campaign of protest and sabotage into an armed rebellion. The communiqué issued by ELF after the August fire in Pennsylvania "is definitely upping the ante," [activist/convicted arsonist Rodney] Coronado says.[8]

That armed rebellion suffered a setback on March 13, 2004, when authorities in British Columbia arrested Tre Arrow for allegedly shoplifting a pair of bolt cutters from a home improvement store. Whether investigators ultimately link him to the fire in Irvine remains to be seen. Either way, simply discussing that possibility might finally focus long-overdue attention on the Allegheny and drive the national debate beyond the inadequate "old growth versus industry" formulation.

A violent windstorm hit northwestern Pennsylvania in July 2003, uprooting and shattering trees across ten thousand acres of the national forest. That timber, much of it lucrative black cherry, might be worth between $50 million and $100 million.[9] Armed with controversial new "streamlined process tools" enacted by the Bush administration, the Forest Service quickly issued contracts allowing operators to retrieve the timber before it rotted and lost its value. Local industries had salvaged more than 900,000 board feet of timber with a total contract value of more than $600,000 by March 2004.[10] Congressman John Peterson, still dissatisfied, invited Forest Service Chief Dale Bosworth to visit the Allegheny and discuss ways to further expedite salvage operations.[11]

Activist Ryan Talbott e-mailed a warning to ADP supporters on February

18, 2004. "The Forest Service and politicians have been hard at work scaring the public into thinking that trees on the ground is a horrible thing that cannot be tolerated," he wrote. "Local papers have claimed if these trees aren't removed, the Allegheny National Forest itself might become an endangered species. Of course, this is ridiculous."

Jim Kleissler issued another e-mail alert on March 19. "The Forest Service is attempting to turn a natural forest event into an opportunity to sidestep environmental laws," he wrote. "The loophole involves the use of a new 'category' of logging activities, created by the Bush administration, which can go forward without detailed environmental review."

The controversy is similar to the one surrounding fire-suppression efforts in the American West. There, the Bush administration has proposed expedited "thinning" projects in areas threatened by the incredible infernos that have plagued the region in recent years. The arguments are the same: Activists insist that the Forest Service is frightening the public in order to gain approval for controversial timber sales that would never pass environmental muster otherwise. Timber supporters counter that activists are using labyrinthine process rules to block essential management projects.

The main difference? On April 15, 2004, the *New York Times* ran a thousand words of on-the-spot coverage about Forest Service plans to do fire-related salvage logging in southern Oregon and Northern California. The article pushed all the right buttons, warning that "environmentalists also see the salvage proposal as a test of how the protections for old growth forests set 10 years ago in the Northwest Forest Plan . . . extend to burned forests."[12] Unfortunately, the paper has never mentioned wind throw on the Allegheny or the resolution of the East Side case.

Perhaps all the factors involved in the Allegheny debate make it too complicated for a thousand-word story. Consider its oil and gas rights, more than 90 percent of which are still in private hands. The Allegheny Defense Project is calling on the federal government to eventually buy all of those rights and end commercial extraction. I asked Jim Kleissler how much that would cost in May 2003. He could not offer a specific figure but estimated that it would approach hundreds of millions of dollars. I also asked him where people would turn for those resources, specifically natural gas. "There's no shortage of supply," he replied. "There's an overcapacity."

Six days later the *Kane Republican* ran an Associated Press story headlined, "Concern about Inadequate Natural Gas Supply Rises." In June, the Energy Department held a "natural gas summit" in Washington, D.C., detailing a looming crisis. *Time* magazine ran a story on July 13 titled "Why America Is Running Out of Gas." On August 6, the *Kane Republican* reported that "House Speaker Dennis Hastert's Task Force for Affordable

Natural Gas will hold its first public field meeting" in State College, Pennsylvania.

So much for an overcapacity. To achieve their environmental vision for the Allegheny, activists need to convince a cash-strapped Congress to allocate untold hundreds of millions to buy oil and gas rights, then take those resources off the table at a time when the public is increasingly anxious about their price and availability. And that is not the only thing that sets the Allegheny apart. Its timber program turns a profit. While failing to approach the eco-utopia that some activists demand, environmental indicators such as wildlife diversity and water quality are undeniably better than they were when the Forest Service took over in 1923. Culturally speaking, the people who live there have an even stronger claim to a logging heritage than the Pacific Northwest timber communities that gave observers pause in the early 1990s.[13]

The great, green pendulum of American environmentalism has been swinging toward a harder line for at least a decade. Demanding real protection for endangered species no matter what the cost was an important development along that arc. Demanding zero cut in the federal government's remaining old growth was another. Zero cut on all public lands is next. Or at least it could be.

The Allegheny offers a critical opportunity to pause and consider whether current environmental trends are leading toward a fair, rational, sustainable and economically viable future. It is the same sort of defining moment that the spotted owl presented so long ago, only now the choice is different. That crisis asked Americans to decide if proposals to continue logging in sensitive virgin forests were going too far. This one asks if the pendulum has swung too far in the other direction.

Sensenich's revised recommendation and the Bush administration's expedited process regulations could indicate that things might be tipping in the loggers' favor, but the mood on the Allegheny is still apoplectic. The Allegheny Forest Alliance held its annual meeting at the Kane High School on January 14, 2004. Jack Hedlund claimed that, in recent discussions, Allegheny National Forest Supervisor Kevin Elliott told him that the Forest Service would probably offer 22 million board feet of timber in the coming year, 14.2 million the following year, and just 11.3 million in 2006. Those numbers come nowhere near the 53.2 million board feet offered as an annual harvest estimate in the 1995 "Harvest Program Capability Report," much less the 94.5 million presented in the 1986 forest plan. Hedlund blamed the anemic estimates on a host of factors, including bureaucratic foot dragging, lack of manpower, and institutional paralysis brought on by litigation.

Whatever the case, he argued that zero-cut activists were losing battles like

East Side but, ultimately, winning the war. Kevin Elliott explained his frustration to the *Pittsburgh Post-Gazette*:

> "Some of the timber, because the lawsuit took three years and the origin of the project is seven or eight years back, has deteriorated," Elliott said. "That means that some of the treatments we were proposing, even though we've got the green light now, may need to be changed."
>
> Even though the case has been tied up in court, timbering has continued on eight sale areas containing approximately 6 million board feet of wood—mostly valuable woods like black cherry, oak and red maple.
>
> But 19 tracts containing 23 million board feet of wood valued at $7.5 million have been held up by the lawsuit. If the cutting plans for those tracts are changed significantly, they would be subject to new appeals and litigation, Elliott said.
>
> "We don't know yet, but if we do something different, if we have to make new decisions, all of that would be subject to litigation all over again," he said. "So it's not over yet."[14]

Allegheny Forest Alliance board member Dale Anderson, who also serves as executive director of the Pennsylvania Forest Industry Association, presented a seemingly radical solution to the judicial bottleneck in the AFA's winter newsletter. It speaks to the polarized nature of the environmental debate on the Allegheny and beyond:

> The United States Forest Service and especially the Allegheny National Forest was once a proud organization, a good neighbor and a positive contributor to the rural way of life.
>
> National forest lands were purchased from county tax sales and from the private sector. They were a considerable asset to the area and were by and large managed by very competent staff. The current National Forest system, however, is broken. It does not work as it was intended by the founders of the system. In fact, it has been corrupted through politics to fail. I suggest it may be time to sell the ANF and other forests like it to someone, anyone with the where-with-all to return these lands to their righteous role in our rural economy.
>
> . . . Surely, in the last 10 years at least, we have seen this valuable asset turn into a complete liability. The ANF has become a lousy neighbor, an unreliable supplier of wood, and a case study in the art of government boondoggle. The net result is a forest in very poor health and a governing agency that has become virtually impotent.

Anderson did not invent the notion of privatization. Libertarians have been advocating federal divestiture for years.[15] From the economic perspective, at least, the Allegheny is probably one of the finest candidates in the federal system. National forests, according to historian Paul W. Hirt, "began, in general, with marginally productive or largely inaccessible forest lands that states, private industries, and settlers had passed over. . . . [T]he national forests, with a few regional exceptions, remain on the margins of commercial viability."[16]

The Allegheny is one of those exceptions. The most heavily exploited land in the region—that which was most accessible to the railroad-logging tycoons—was the some of the easiest for the federal government to capture when it established the forest. Most foresters working in the area today report that the most commercially viable timberland is on the national forest.

While many might view selling a national forest to timber interests as an environmental calamity, the Allegheny might deserve another look. The Kane Hardwood Division of Collins Pine, one of the major corporate players in the region, owns and manages approximately 125,000 acres. All of it meets or exceeds the sustainability standards established by the Forest Stewardship Council, widely considered the world's most stringent certification organization. The land is open to public camping, hiking, hunting, and other recreational pursuits other than all-terrain vehicles. While the company obviously violates the central tenets of zero cut, Collins Pine has clearly found a way to please at least some environmentalists. Moreover, activists do not necessarily reject the notion of private stewardship out of hand. The Nature Conservancy owns and manages an immense land base for ecological rather than industrial purposes. Presumably, its money would be welcome at the auction, too. Privatizing the entire system might seem politically far-fetched, but no more so than spending hundreds of millions of public dollars to buy the oil and gas rights.

These disparate forces are angling for control of the Allegheny at a critical juncture in the forest's history, a fact that only increases the need for a full and open discussion about its place in the national debate. The Forest Service is currently in the midst of revising the Allegheny's hugely controversial 1986 management plan—a process that should have been completed in 2001. Fully aware of the explosive potential, officials have called on three academic experts in the field of "collaborative learning" to guide a series of public workshops. The first one unfolded in May 2003. That and subsequent meetings have been relatively civil, but they have also shown how difficult it is to get anything done in the highly polarized world of federal forestry.

The most heated discussions have focused on process and politics rather than the critical issues at hand. The Forest Service intends to complete the revision by mid-2006. That might seem like a long time to spend creating a document that is supposed to be revised again in fifteen years, but the current timetable sets a scorching pace compared to national forests that have spent up to ten years revising their forest plans. Allegheny officials plan to streamline the process by whittling the discussion down to three or four critical issues such as wilderness, recreation, vegetation management, etc. Planners would then develop a few alternatives to address those issues, conduct a detailed analysis, and make a final decision after another round of public meetings.[17]

Activists smell a rat. They claim that for years, the Forest Service has claimed to be powerless to implement certain environmental proposals not included in the 1986 plan. "That's a forest plan issue," activists report being told. "It will have to wait until the revision." Now that the revision is here, activists charge that the Forest Service is limiting discussion to make sure no one challenges the fundamental philosophy underlying management on the Allegheny. The Forest Service counters that the revision is supposed to be just that—a revision of a long-range management plan—not a wholesale rewrite. "They might just end up getting sued," Bill Belitskus fumed at one of the revision workshops in Warren.

They almost certainly will, although it is not quite certain which features of the forest plan will ultimately meet with judicial action. Activists have used litigation as their primary weapon in the battle for zero cut for years, and there is no reason to think they are going to stop now. Initially taken aback by Sensenich's reversal on East Side, the ADP and its allies announced on May 20, 2004, that they would appeal Standish's ruling to the Third Circuit Court of Appeals. They did not reveal the basis for their appeal—besides repeating familiar diatribes against the alleged "black cherry tree farm."[18] At this stage, it appears that the only thing the Forest Service can do to preclude a lawsuit is develop and implement a forest plan that embraces zero cut, and that seems highly unlikely.

Efforts to reach a compromise outside the official planning process have been more productive. Congressman John Peterson, cautiously optimistic that setting more of the Allegheny aside as federal wilderness might provide a middle ground, formed an "unofficial working group" to consider the possibilities. It included, among others, representatives from the timber, gas and oil industries and environmentalists from the Wilderness Society and the Sierra Club. Kirk Johnson, who founded Friends of Allegheny Wilderness, also participated. In March 2004 Johnson was sanguine enough to predict that Peterson—one of the most vocal timber supporters in Congress—would submit a bill by the end of the year seeking to add as much as forty thousand acres to the Allegheny's wilderness allotment.

The zero-cut response to those developments has been mixed. Jim Kleissler wrote a letter to the *Warren Times Observer*, published October 10, 2003, reiterating his contention that the wilderness solution does not go nearly far enough because it fails to address management issues on the rest of the forest. On the other hand, he was conciliatory toward his former zero-cut compatriot. "First I would like to commend FAW for coming forward with a vision for wilderness in the Allegheny National Forest," he wrote. "The truth is that ADP and FAW's wilderness proposals are quite compatible."

Someone obviously forgot to forward those talking points to Belitskus. At one of the forest plan workshops he roundly criticized Peterson's working group for conducting "secret meetings." He also shared his suspicions with the *Warren Times Observer*. "The Congressman's closed process violates federal law and the Forest Service's stated intention of a 'public' forest plan revision process." Belitskus wrote. He expressed suspicion about what the congressman offered in exchange for support from "token environmental groups" like the Sierra Club, and went on to complain that the Forest Service was forced to spend public money to provide material and maps requested by the people invited to "Peterson's private ANF management meetings."[19]

The newspaper's editors were not impressed, and responded with a scathing editorial:

> Excuse us, but hasn't it been the ADP which has been trying to circumvent, undermine and generally sabotage forest planning on the ANF for the past several years through a strategy of lawsuits and legal challenges? ADP's strategy for trying to create its own private version of a national forest has involved virtually no public involvement; instead it is a vision shared by virtually no one except the relatively small active membership of the group. While Belitskus excoriates Peterson for having ANF personnel supply digitalized maps for his meetings at public expense, the ADP activist completely ignores the enormous cost his group's lawsuits have imposed on the public.
>
> We suspect, when all is said and done, that the ADP's ire springs from the fact that it is not included in the talks. It's little wonder. Over the course of its history, ADP has adopted an all-or-nothing strategy in its vision for the ANF. That unwillingness to compromise has marginalized the group to the point where it's difficult to take it or its complaints seriously.[20]

The *Times Observer* is not alone. Kirk Johnson abandoned zero cut and has taken activists like Blair Anundson with him. Former supporters at the Heinz Endowments walked away from the Allegheny Defense Project over similar concerns. Apart from Kleissler, his wife, Rachael, and Belitskus, Talbott, and Sheffield native Janis Trubic, I have found little support for the group's larger agenda at the local level. The vast majority of observers on the Allegheny have looked at zero cut and decided that the environmental pendulum set in motion by the spotted owl has finally swung too far.

That is not to say that the idea is doomed. As the activists point out, the Allegheny is a national forest, and its management is a national issue. In the end, that reality is what makes the Allegheny crisis so important. No other forest poses the economic, environmental, and cultural questions about zero cut in such stark and compelling terms. As the Allegheny goes, so goes the entire national forest system. Or, in the words of an activist arrested there in 1998: "If we can stop logging there, we can stop it everywhere."

NOTES

1. Allegheny Forest Alliance, Winter 2004 Newsletter, 2.
2. Ila Jeane Sensenich, "East Side Litigation December 2003 Magistrate's Report," 53–54.
3. Sensenich, 57–58.
4. Sensenich, 105–106. The magistrate cited *Robertson v. Methow Valley Citizens Council*, 490 U.S. 332 (1989), which ruled: "It is now well settled that NEPA itself does not mandate particular results, but simply prescribes the necessary process. . . . If the adverse environmental effects of the proposed actions are adequately identified, the agency is not constrained by NEPA from deciding that other values outweigh the environmental costs."
5. Sensenich, 54.
6. Randall Sullivan, "The True Flight of Tre Arrow," *Rolling Stone*, December 12, 2002, 52.
7. Sullivan, "True Flight," 54.
8. Sullivan, "True Flight," 56.
9. Ted Lutz, "Fallen Trees Litter Forest," *Kane Republican*, January 24, 2004.
10. United States Forest Service, "Allegheny Brambles: An informational article about the Allegheny National Forest," March 19, 2004, Warren, Pennsylvania.
11. "Bosworth Will Visit ANF, Work to Address Blowdown," *Kane Republican*, March 4, 2004.
12. Matthew Preusch, "Amid a Forest's Ashes, a Debate over Logging Profits is Burning," *New York Times*, April 15, 2004.
13. Forks, Washington, a central setting in the West Coast's recent drama, did not become a real timber boomtown until well after World War II. The population doubled in the 1970s as loggers hacked away at the old growth. They were still working on it when the spotted owl finally stopped them. Society, increasingly interested in ecological integrity and wilderness recreation, chose an ancient forest over an economy that had been in place for three decades. Forks undoubtedly suffered the consequences of the shift in environmental ethics, but communities on the Allegheny have industry roots that run four times as deep—in many cases within the same family line. For a discussion of Forks's history, see William Dietrich, *The Final Forest* (New York: Penguin Books, 1992), 66–71, 86–96, 246.
14. Don Hopey, "Judge OKs Timbering in Allegheny Forest," *Pittsburgh Post-Gazette*, Thursday, April 1, 2004.
15. Terry L. Anderson, Vernon L. Smith, and Emily Simmons, "How and Why to Privatize Federal Lands," *Cato Institute Policy Analysis*, no. 363, November 9, 1999. Note that this is not a new position. For an interesting take on earlier privatization efforts, see Paul W. Hirt, *A Conspiracy of Optimism* (Lincoln: University of Nebraska Press, 1994), 121–125.

16. Hirt, *Conspiracy of Optimism*, xviii.

17. *Chuck Hayes*, "Forest Planning Takes Too Much Time," *Warren Times Observer*, January 23, 2003.

18. http://www.alleghenydefense.org/press/release_040520.shtml.

19. Beltiskus shared his accusations with the newspaper through a letter. Editors assigned a reporter to write a story concerning those allegations, which included portions of the letter. It appeared in the August 22, 2003, edition. The paper published the initial letter in full ten days later, at Belitskus's request.

20. "Our Opinion: ADP Complaint Marginal," *Warren Times Observer*, August 27, 2003.

Index

Adelphia Communications Corporation,
161–62
Adirondack Mountains, 156–57
ADP. *See* Allegheny Defense Project
AHUG, 85–87, 107, 165–66. *See also*
Allegheny Hardwood Utilization Group
Allegheny Forest Alliance, 62, 71–72, 102,
107, 120, 138, 164, 175, 179n1. *See
also* Jack Hedlund
Allegheny Defense Project, 20n1, 22–32,
63, 67, 118n18, 122, 128, 132n2, 139,
177–78, 180n18; Allegheny Wild! proposal, 144; annual fall gathering of, 26–
32, 79–82, 92, 101, 108; local views on,
51–54, 57, 88, 108, 111–12, 123, 164–
65, 178; membership of, 27–29, 79;
other activists on, 95–97, 99, 100–103,
124–25; tactics of, 78, 94–97; zero-cut
evolution of, 24–25, 172. *See also*
Buchele, Tom; Environmental Law
Clinic; Kleissler, Jim; lawsuits
Allegheny hardwood forest type, 3, 16
Allegheny Hardwood Utilization Group,
25, 42, 56, 85–86, 124, 146. *See also*
Swanson, Sue
Allegheny Mountain Rodeo Championship, 106
Allegheny National Forest: history of, 3,
9–17, 29–30, 94–95, 108–9, 20n34;
health of, 62–72, 125, 130–32, 153,

160, 169, 174, 20n33; profitability of,
5–6, 63, 111, 122, 132n7, 168n1, 174;
project tour of, 79–82
all-terrain vehicles, 80, 110, 120, 144
American Forest and Paper Association,
122
American hemlock, 13–15, 17, 65, 139–40
American Refining Group. *See* oil and gas
Anderson, Dale, 175
Anundson, Blair, 92–98, 178
Anundson, Dave, 91–92
ANWR. *See* Arctic National Wildlife
Refuge
Arctic National Wildlife Refuge, 2, 171
Arnold, Joe, 165
Arrow, Tre. *See* Scarpitti, Michael
Asel, Norm, 76, 78
Aspen, Colorado, 163
Association of Forest Service Employees
for Environmental Ethics, 69

Backus, Steve, 150
Bari, Judi, 83, 85, 89n2
Belitskus, Bill, 24, 29, 57, 63, 69, 76–81,
84, 88, 91, 97, 107, 135–36, 177–78,
180n19
Bennett, Matt, 138
Bishop, L. L., 30–31, 32n9, 135
Black, Bryan, 109
black cherry, 5, 55, 116, 122, 130–31, 136;

About the Author

Sam MacDonald was born and raised in Ridgway, Pennsylvania, a rural community on the southeastern border of the Allegheny National Forest. He returned to the region as a Phillips Foundation Journalism Fellow in 2002 to research and write *The Agony of an American Wilderness.* His mother, father, three sisters, and fifteen nieces and nephews still live in Ridgway. MacDonald currently lives in Silver Spring, Maryland, with his wife, Michelle.

MacDonald was previously Washington editor of *Reason* magazine and a reporter for the *Laurel Leader*, a community newspaper in Laurel, Maryland. His work has also appeared in the *Pittsburgh Post-Gazette*, the *Pittsburgh City Paper*, *Preservation*, *Insight on the News*, and other publications. He graduated from Yale University in 1995.